HORSHAM

(*Overleaf*). **Frontispiece:** Carfax (right) and the western part of Horsham in 1970. The distributor road now runs across the upper part of the picture.

By courtesy of Aerofilms Ltd.

HORSHAM

An Historical Survey

by

ANTHONY WINDRUM

PHILLIMORE

1978

Published by
PHILLIMORE & CO., LTD.,
London and Chichester

Head Office: Shopwyke Hall,
Chichester, Sussex, England

© Anthony Windrum, 1978

ISBN 0 85033 284 2

Printed in Great Britain by
UNWIN BROTHERS LIMITED
at The Gresham Press, Old Woking, Surrey

and bound by
NEWDIGATE PRESS LIMITED
Book House, Dorking, Surrey

CONTENTS

		Page
	Foreword	ix
	Acknowledgements	xi
	Introduction	1
I	The Church	12
II	Parliamentary and Local Government	41
III	Crime and Punishment	69
IV	Health	91
V	Military	100
VI	Industries and Trade	113
VII	Social Life	135
VIII	Education	150
IX	Information	166
X	Communications	177
	Bibliography	198
	Index	201

*Dedicated
to those who love Horsham*

LIST OF PLATES

Aerial view of Horsham in 1970 (*frontispiece*)
between pages 84 and 85

1 Interior of the Parish Church in 1862
2 The *Normandy*, about 1870
3 The 11th Duke of Norfolk
4 The whipping post
5 Horsham Hospital's first building
6 Royal Sussex Volunteers, 1888
7 The Arms Depot
8 The Albery collection of horse bits
9 The Town Mill
10 Making bricks by hand
11) The old and the new cricket fields
12)
13 The Borough Silver Band in 1937
14 The 1840 Collyer's School
15 Elegant horse-drawn transport
16 West Street a century ago
17 The first railway engine between Horsham and London

LIST OF FIGURES

		Page
1	Effigy of Thomas Clerke (1411)	15
2	Borough independence at the 1841 election	52
3	A furtive meeting arranged	55
4	Assize Sermon, 1712	73
5	The Gaol in Queen Street	86
6	The first mains water	96
7	A Call to Arms!	110
8	The first book printed in Horsham	133
9	Employment for the unemployed poor	145
10	Magazine of the British School	156
11	A lecture at the Mechanics' Institution	160
12	Horsham's first newspaper	168
13	Spreading information by poster	170
14	Railway development	192

FOREWORD

This book is not a definitive history of Horsham, still less is it an authoritative essay on the several subjects which make up the chapter headings. It is an attempt to consider the main features of that stream of life which has made our community in times past, up to about a generation or two ago.

The current malaise which makes it such a difficult matter for many people to gain and retain support for communal activities is no new thing. Horsham has always had a remarkable faculty for losing out to other places, from the days when it was one of the most important towns in Sussex, the seat of assizes and of the County Council, the centre of large marketing operations, to the present day when Crawley is nibbling away at the outskirts to the extent of nearly getting hold of our Registrar of Births but recently! Henry Michell knew of this difficulty in stirring Horsham to bother about things when he wrote in his diary a little over 100 years ago 'I am fully convinced of Horsham it may be said that if you wish to do anything to benefit the people, you must find some way of doing it in spite of themselves'.

Yet it is not all debit, and there are times when the town can be stirred even now, such as the occasion when it looked possible that the hospital might go. A lot has already gone, a lot remains, and we will get the town we deserve.

In 1822 Cobbett said, 'This is a very nice, solid, country town'. How can we describe it today?

Horsham, May 1977   Anthony Windrum

ACKNOWLEDGEMENTS

For permission to quote from quarter sessions records I am indebted to the County Archivists of East and West Sussex, and to the latter also for the quotations from the churchwardens' accounts, to the Public Record Office for assize records, and to the Sussex Archaeological Society for the servant's reference in Chapter Six.

I would also like to thank Mr. George Coomber for information on windmills, Major J. F. Ainsworth of the Royal Sussex Regimental Association for letting me see his draft history of the 4th Battalion, and Mr. Stephen Freeth of the County Record Office at Chichester for help and advice.

Thanks are also due to my wife, who not only had to live with the book for a long time, but also typed the final draft, and sketched the chapter headings.

The correction of errors of fact would be appreciated by the author who largely perpetrated them on the 5.28 from Victoria.

INTRODUCTION

HISTORY, according to Tolstoy, would be a very good thing if only it were true. But what, in the context of our history, is truth? People even argue about the 'truth' of history which is being made in their own time, with all the facilities of mass media, photography and mechanical recordings, so what chance have we of giving any 'true' account of Horsham over several thousand years? Direct evidence is very slight, and that has to be interpreted, and interpretations can vary.

To approach the subject of Horsham, by whatever path, the seeker at once is confronted by the paradox that there is so much and yet so little upon which to go. Although man has almost certainly been in the vicinity for half a million continuous years or more, and therefore must have left ample traces of himself, those who have made investigation frequently comment that there is so little. Mark Anthony Lower, one of Sussex's great antiquaries, said in 1870, 'Little is known of this town and parish'; Elwes thought in 1876 that 'the annals of Horsham are devoid of much interest'; and even our own historian, William Albery, wrote in 1947, 'Its records are few and thin'. This last comes from a man who collected a mass of information over many years and to whose book *A Millenium of facts in the history of Horsham* every student is indebted. But 'England is an old house packed with memories' (P. Vansittart), so it must be possible to do a little unpacking provided that too much is not looked for at once.

For the purposes of this book it has been assumed that Horsham means a little more than the original borough, and less than the original parish, in fact, approximately the old Urban District. However, as boundaries are artificial it is perhaps not necessary to define too closely the scope of what we call our town.

The Very Beginning

Something like 100 million years ago south-eastern England was a fresh-water lake; this is known from fossils such as Paludina, a kind of fresh-water snail. Rivers poured in great quantities of sand and clay from the weathering of rocks elsewhere, and reptiles such as the iguanodon lived in this warm, wet environment. The iguanodon is of particular interest to us because its fossilised bones have been found not far from Horsham, in Tilgate Forest, and Southwater, and Horsham Museum has specimens. S. E. Winbolt suggested that the legend of the dragon in St. Leonard's Forest may be a folk-tale with the basis of truth that so many of them have, in this case the iguanodon. Gideon Mantell was born at Lewes in 1790 and was a doctor who became famous for his hobby of collecting fossils, which he left to the British Museum. He knew Sussex well and was convinced from his geological studies that large reptile remains should be sought where he eventually found them—in Tilgate Forest sandstone which we can see today marked with the ripples of the shallow lake described earlier. Visit Horsham churchyard to see these ripples, or other places where local stone is used as paving.

The land was by now sinking, and the sand was many feet thick, and overlaid by an even thicker deposit of clay. Next, the sea flooded everything, and countless marine animals died and bequeathed their shells and skeletons of chalk and silica to the bottom of the ocean. More millions of years, and a bed of chalk formed which can be shown to be continuous under the present English Channel through to France. The silica was most important in our story because nodules of it were the raw material for primitive man to make his tools which survive until today, although, of course, even earlier tools of wood would have perished without trace.

Originally the continent of Europe had been all one land mass with Britain, but during the ages when the vast ice sheet had alternately grown and shrunk with the changing climate, Britain was re-connected and separated from the rest of Europe several times, finally becoming isolated by the formation of the English Channel about 20,000 B.C. During the time that a land bridge existed, early man had migrated

Introduction

from France to Britain, but of the earliest (Palaeolithic) man we have no traces in our locality, although Slindon has produced some fine stone axes from this period; our local human story therefore begins about 7,000 B.C. Evidence for the migration has been obtained from Mesolithic (Middle Stone Age) fish spears brought up from the bottom of the North Sea. When the bypass was being constructed on the south-west of Horsham, excavation brought to light about 2,000 flints, both flakes and worked tools. Study of these identified them as Mesolithic, and they were very similar to ones found earlier this century at Pilfolds Farm, near Christ's Hospital and not far away. The latter are in the Barbican Museum at Lewes, and others have been found at Rusper and Warnham. Here, then, was Horsham's first industry.

Mesolithic Ancestors

We do not have enough local material to draw much of a picture of the first known inhabitants of Horsham, so we must look elsewhere for detailed evidence, notably in Yorkshire and in France. Peat beds have the quality of preserving organic material, most fortunately for the archaeologist, and near Scarborough a large quantity was found which contained flint flakes very similar to ours, and also tools made of elk antlers, bone scrapers and fish spears. What sort of people were our first inhabitants? They were of the culture called Maglemosian, from Maglemose in Denmark. The climate was warmer than it is now, and this encouraged thick forest growth, which brought about the replacement of reindeer by roe deer, red deer, and wild pig. These changes in the environment not only made changes in the way of life of Mesolithic man, but also helped to provide evidence of the way in which his culture developed. A conventional picture of our ancestors at this time might suggest that they were rude and brutish, but it is only fair to mention that their art-forms would sell today as contemporary art with no trouble at all. Pebbles have been found (but not here) painted with red ochre, the designs being now interpreted as possibly, conventionalised human forms, and if these had any religious significance they may have played a part in ancestor-worship. Bead necklaces were made of animal teeth and snail shells, and the things they made were remarkably sophisticated for 10 thousand years ago. As hunters and fishers the dog was their only domesticated animal. The stone axe felled trees, which suggests a life less nomadic than that of their ancestors. They used bows and arrows, the latter tipped with microlith barbs, and they hunted the cave-lion, the hyena and wild pig. Fishing was practised with hooks and nets, and they used boats with paddles. A red deer antler made a good harpoon when barbed on both edges and given a hole for the line. They were keen fishermen in those days, especially for pike, using in summer spears tipped with barbed bone and in winter live-baiting with bone hooks. For smaller fish, they used dragnets with floats made of pine bark and stone sinkers. Rolls of birch-bark were sewn into boxes for holding hazelnuts and water lily seeds.

These descriptions are not speculation and guesswork, but the result of the most careful analysis of actual finds. Settlements were on low ground near to marshland, and our Horsham bypass site fits this description although the water levels have changed a lot in 10 millennia.

Microliths

One aspect of stone culture used to puzzle archaeologists very much. Very small worked flints were found, and these microliths were too numerous to be idle toy-making. Some even thought they were the implements of a race of pygmies, but their true purpose has now been established many times. They were used as sharp points for arrows or for insertion in some kind of tool-holder of reindeer antler or bone, much as the harpoon mentioned above. In Yorkshire, birch resin was found adhering to one flint which was secured to the shaft of an arrow. When mounted, these small flakes could make excellent saw-teeth. The bow was used not only for propelling arrows, but also for drilling, and a small flint point would be just the thing for making holes in shells of

Introduction 5

pebbles for stringing on a necklace before the discovery of metal. Jewellers today use bow-drills in exactly the same way.

Not one microlith has been found on the chalk downs, which is significant when we consider the probable movements of these peoples. Incidentally, no Mesolithic pottery is known in Britain, which is in accordance with the Maglemosians' known preference for dry sandy soils rather than sticky clays. The most important tool of early man was the axe, which might be described as an implement of some weight with a cutting edge. With it he could fell trees for his shelter and to make his traps. He could then kill the animal he had trapped, dismember it with his axe and crack the marrow-bones for his feast. The axe plays a prominent part in the history of our forebears right up to medieval times. In the Mesolithic period we are now describing, the axe was made by selecting a suitable flint nodule and knocking off chips with a harder stone until it was shaped with an edge either for hand use or for mounting on a wooden handle. The edge was very efficient and was kept sharp by knocking off more flakes when required.

Our Maglemosians later mingled with another wave of immigrants from the Continent, no doubt as a result of another land-shift which joined up the land masses once again. These newcomers were of the same original stock and have been called Tardenoisians, from Tardenois in Northern France, and they are distinguished by the different way in which they manufactured their flints. We have no hut sites known near Horsham, but who knows what may yet be found? Elsewhere considerable remains have been excavated. Forked poles were put into the ground and a crosspiece rested on them, while branches and grass, and perhaps animal skins kept out the weather, in the fashion that woodland huts are still made today. Some cooking was done, in spite of the absence of pottery: this may have been roasting and grilling, and also heating water in animal skins by dropping in hot stones.

Among archaeologists, Horsham has given a name to a particular kind of microlith, having a concave base made by chipping away small flakes. We have to put a lot of emphasis on flint evidence because the sandy soils which these people liked are acid, and thus vegetable and bone remains are destroyed. The size of the implement is a good indication of which culture it belongs to—a Mesolithic microlith is under two inches long and usually has the opposite end to the business one blunted by tiny flaking. The piece of flint left after flakes have been struck from it is known as a core, and these cores have sometimes been re-used. There was a lucky find on the bypass site which consisted of a core and a flake which fitted perfectly together.

The Beginning of Farming

The later Neolithic people preferred chalk hills to live on, so they were able to exist side-by-side with the earlier tribes, but there is some evidence of their mingling. An axe found at Thakeham was originally made by a Mesolithic man and then re-worked by his Neolithic cousin to make a better job of it. The new arrivals brought with them the idea of farming, in all its aspects—cereal crops and animal husbandry. As they knew nothing of manuring or letting land lie fallow, they had to make frequent moves to fresh ground, which eventually brought them here, or at least near here. A Neolithic axe head has been found on Hernbrook Hill, and others in sites not far from Horsham, but no extensive settlements are known, which is not surprising when one recalls that these people liked chalk hills, of which Horsham has none. One downland feature was attractive to the Neolithic tribes —the absence of woodland compared with the thick forest of the Weald, which contained wild beasts as well as enemy tribes. Also, farmers always appreciate not having to clear thick woods for crops and animals, even with modern machinery, and when one recalls that Stone-Age man used a hand axe and nothing else it is incredible how much he achieved. Once the ground was cleared, and to do this he undoubtedly called on fire to his aid, it was comparatively easy to keep it clear as his animals would eat the seedlings of trees and shrubs.

Introduction

The various cultures merged from one to another without abrupt change, and while flint mining continued when the Bronze Age began, there is not much evidence of this period here, although in 1933 S. E. Winbolt recovered from deep sewer trenches between the cricket field and the River Arun a fragment of skull which has been identified as early Bronze Age. There is no evidence of Iron Age occupation near Horsham.

The Romans Arrive

So far we have been dealing with pre-history, but now there are written records to help with our story. When writing of the conquest of Gaul, Caesar mentions trade with Britain, and the tribes which fled before the Romans to these shores are well described by the Latin authors. No Roman invader set foot in our area, but after settling down they built Stane Street from Chichester to London, which passes by at Alfoldean, only three miles away, so a patrol might at least have paid a visit here, and the recently-discovered Roman iron workings at Broadfield might have been connected by road with Stane Street. Timbers from the Roman bridge at Alfoldean may be seen in the Horsham Museum, and Winbolt issued a warning to those who discover Roman material at Farthing's Bridge—it was dumped there from Alfoldean.

Saxon Settlement

When the Romans withdrew from Britain and left us to the Saxon hordes, Sussex (the country of the South Saxons) became a settlement area, leaving considerable traces in many parts. The present century has seen a great advance in place-name research, which has been most valuable in tracing the progress of the Saxon settlement. Names which end in -ham can be shown to be those of minor settlements often found near Roman roads, which might indicate that the Saxons used Stane Street for penetrating this part of Sussex, as -ham names were used at the very beginning of colonisation in the fifth or sixth centuries. Horsham, which until a generation ago was always pronounced and frequently spelt 'Horsam', almost certainly means a settlement or enclosure for horses. Our first record of the name is very early, in two Saxon charters of 947 and 963 A.D. which describe us as a denne (swine pasture) belonging to the manor of Washington. We shall probably never know whether there has been continuous human occupation up to this point, but from this time on there certainly has. It is undetermined whether the reference to Soreham in Domesday Book is to Horsham: the entry occurs next to that for Ifield, and Norman-French clerks had considerable difficulty in understanding and transcribing names given them when they arrived in a rural locality to make the great record, so perhaps we are enrolled, perhaps not.

Chesworth and the Normans

The focus for Norman development was undoubtedly Chesworth, as this manor together with over 40 others in Sussex, was given to William de Braose by William the Conqueror as part of the spoils with which the chief Normans were rewarded. Until recently Chesworth was always pronounced and frequently spelt 'Cheeseworth', which is more correct as it originates from 'Ceoldred's worth' (meaning Ceoldred's farm). Here the de Braose family lived for some 250 years until John de Mowbray married a de Braose heiress in 1298 and inherited the property. The arms of Horsham are derived from these two families. Chesworth has had a sad history. A century later Thomas de Mowbray was created Duke of Norfolk, thus beginning the long connection of the Dukes with Horsham, who, however, did not always descend in the direct male line. The heiress, Margaret de Mowbray, married Sir Robert Howard in 1476 and in 1483 King Edward IV revived the title of Duke of Norfolk in their son John, who was killed commanding the vanguard at the Battle of Bosworth in 1485. Thomas Earl of Surrey who was third Duke of Norfolk of the Howard line suffered attainder under Henry VIII on absurd treason charges, and but for the

Introduction

king's death would have been executed. His estates were seized, however, by the Protector Somerset, who in turn was disgraced in 1549 and the estates became the property of Edward VI. On the accession of Queen Mary the attainder of the third Duke was reversed and his lands restored, but his grandson and heir Thomas, fourth Duke, foolishly tried to marry Mary Queen of Scots and was executed for treason by Queen Elizabeth in 1572. Papers said to have been found in the roof of Chesworth House were used to convict him, and the estates again forfeited. Although Chesworth had seen three kings entertained within its walls and had belonged to persons high in the land, after this time it was left to decay and a survey of 1608 reported that it was very dilapidated 'notwithstanding one hundred loads of wood have been yearly assigned by his Majesty's woodward for the ayring of the same, besydes timber for repayring. The situation hereof is upon marish ground, unhealthy, obscure, and the foundacion sunk at least one foot and mo'. Then the Eversfield family acquired the estate and added it to Denne, where the house may well have been built partly with materials from Chesworth House.

The Significance of the Borough

Although Chesworth had been the 'big house' for some four centuries, Horsham had its own importance as a town from late Norman times when it was established as a borough, returned two members to Parliament from 1295, was the assize town for Sussex from 1307, and had a large church which required the services of a vicar, assistant and two sub-deacons in 1232. We know that 42 persons paid tax in 1296, and a multiplier of 4.5 is usually assumed to derive the whole population, so about 200 people lived in the borough in that year. Assize towns had a larger and wealthier upper class, but the commercial importance of Horsham up to at least the 14th century did not extend beyond trade with local villages. Indeed, the Nonarum return of 1341 states 'there are no merchants living in the borough', and the markets of which we have records show that produce did not go far until the improvement of roads in the 18th century.

Writing of Sussex in 1607, Camden says, 'I have done with the sea-coast of Sussex. As for the inner parts, there is nothing worth the notice, unless I should reckon up the woods and forests'. About the same time Norden observed that the county was 'divided into downs full of sheep, and woodland full of iron mines, and some good pasturate . . . Those who know the Weald well say that the trees have decayed greatly during the last thirty years (from iron works and glass furnaces). But also benefit—unprofitable grounds converted to beneficial tillage'.

The great upsurge of housebuilding in Elizabethan times can still be detected today in spite of the comparatively short life of the timber which largely composed the buildings, but even then Horsham had no special significance among Sussex towns, other than its assizes. Indeed the development of the coastal towns in the late 17th century caused a noticeable decline, but when the railway arrived in 1848 our town was very favourably placed as a junction. As foreshadowed in 1840 by one writer, 'The new and speedy communication . . . .will necessarily tend to swell the larger towns into still greater magnitudes and to diminish the weight of many smaller places, as well as the rural population generally in social affairs'. It is a debatable point whether the railway or motor transport have had the greater effect on Horsham's development.

Modern Expansion

The shortage of food and work in the hungry 'Forties after the Napoleonic wars was felt here as much as anywhere, although the landlords were less unpopular than elsewhere, and agriculture was still the lifeblood of the community. Some manufacturing started in the last century and distribution of the products was helped by railway development, but the biggest changes in our history undoubtedly stem from great pressure on housing since the Second World War in the whole of the south-east of England. Even so, we were

Introduction

described as a dormitory town already in 1880. Electrification of the railway and industrial growth in Crawley intensified commuting and by the 1950s the largest proportion of the population gained a livelihood outside the town. In the 1960s concern was expressed about the decline in trade, and also the deterioration of some property in the central area. As elsewhere, the wisdom of tearing the heart out of the town by laying a large road across the middle will be judged in the process of time.

A resident of not so long ago would have some difficulty in recognising the Horsham of today, notwithstanding unchanged landmarks like the parish church, but what we would find on returning in 100 years time would depend on the outcome of discussions now taking place about the development of the whole of the south-east. Do we want to increase town size perhaps fourfold, or enlarge villages, or even start new towns like Crawley? Such a new town was envisaged in 1547. A document at Magdalen College states, 'There is communication that the Lorde Admirall aforesaid (Somerset) will buylde a toune within the Forest of St. Leonarde, wher increase of tythes may growe to the College . . . whereas now we have but 3s. for the herbage of the forest and 8s. for the parke of Bewbushe sometyme parcell of ye foreste'. But Somerset was beheaded instead.

The church has been chosen for the first chapter because it was in the early days of Horsham the most influential organisation, combining the functions of present-day school, hospital, market, social centre, welfare office, law court, as well as the cure of souls.

Next we consider the way we have been governed or misgoverned over the years, and what the people of Horsham have done about it.

Later chapters take a look at some more aspects of history which have shaped Horsham, but let it be stressed again that in a book of this compass only the barest outlines can be given. Probably the sincere wish of the majority of historians is that their public offerings will stimulate others to push back the frontiers a little further.

Chapter One

THE CHURCH

NOWADAYS it is not often realised how great a part has been played in the history of Horsham by the church, so it is fitting that this should be the subject of Chapter One. We have no real evidence earlier than the 13th century, but it is reasonable to suppose that the earliest Saxon settlement here was by the river, which would be the means of communication in a thickly-forested countryside. Tacitus said that German tribes, which would include the Saxons, were accustomed to place their shrines in the depths of the forest. The community would have a sanctuary and Pope Gregory in 601 gave instructions that heathen shrines should not be destroyed, but converted. We may therefore imagine that Bishop Wilfrid, when he converted the Saxon kingdoms between 681 and 685, would have extended his influence even as far as our remote settlement, and a cross of probable

The Church

wood at first and stone later would have been set up as the centre of worship with services conducted by visiting priests, perhaps from the college of secular canons which is known to have been at Steyning before the Conquest. They might have come along the track which S. E. Winbolt believes runs from the direction of Steyning across a ford at the River Arun and up Denne Road, which he said pre-dated the church.

As the settlement grew, it is possible that a rough wooden church was constructed, but we have to wait until the arrival of William de Braose with the Norman conquerors before both the permanent stone building and the parish structure were established. As to the church, the Normans found Saxon churches both dull and foreign to their ideas of architectural magnificence, and would not hesitate to demolish what they found. There is a tradition, no more, that the first Norman church was pulled down or fell down after about 100 years, and it is a curious fact that the Normans although fine builders above ground were weak on foundations. Certainly the sticky alluvial site was difficult, as was shown again in 1865 when the present building had to be jacked up.

Most parishes can trace their origin to a local lord who wanted somewhere to worship for himself, family and household. William de Braose at Chesworth nearby would find no difficulty in continuing to use the old site, and a look at the functions of a parish at this time will show how it would fit in with the manor of Chesworth. The parish with the church at its heart was both ecclesiastical and temporal: almost all community life was the concern of the parish, with the exception of most administration of justice, which was conducted by the courts of the manor, although even this often used to meet in the church. The relief of the poor, some teaching, minor law and order, repair of roads and bridges, levying of church rates, and many other functions were parish responsibility.

Early Buildings

Returning to the fabric of the church, we know that early in the 13th century there was considerable rebuilding,

probably on a bigger scale to take into account the growing
town. A look at the existing tower of St. Mary's will identify
Norman masonry in the lower part extending round to part
of the west wall and north aisle, and the heavy buttresses
(larger on the south) would support the theory of instability.
Inside, the tower arch is seen to be assymetric, which suggests
enlargement of an existing building rather than complete
rebuilding. The de Braose family was almost certainly
involved, and in 1231 John de Braose granted the revenues
of Horsham church and four other churches to help Rusper
Priory which was in difficulties. Some of the church land
was divided up to endow the vicarage while the rest went
to Rusper. Perhaps soon after the 'second' church was
erected, clerestory windows were added, first in the nave
and then in the chancel. Early churches were much decorated
with paintings as the means of instructing an illiterate congregation, and although the spaciousness of the interior of
our church (unusually there is no chancel arch) was presumably the intention of the Norman builders, it would have
had a very different appearance because of masses of colour,
traces of which have been found from time to time. In 1307,
within half a century of the building of the 'second' church,
the first known chapel was built outside 'within the cemetery'. This was founded by Walter Burgeys as a chantry for
masses for the souls of himself and family, firstly to be said
in the church porch until the chapel could be built. This
Walter Burgeys was one of the two Members of Parliament
summoned in 1295 by Edward I to the first House of Commons. The chapel was shortened in 1884 when the modern
north porch was made and is now known as the Memorial
Chapel. When in 1536 Henry VIII's Commissioners were
unable to discover the founder of this chantry, they merely
called it 'the chauntrie in the porch'.

The next feature in point of time is the monument of
Thomas, Lord de Braose, on the south side of the chancel.
This is the figure of a fully-armed man resting on an altar
tomb, but it has suffered some damage at various times
(in 1640 it cost sixpence 'for setting on ye hands'), and
neither inscriptions nor arms remain. At the time of Philpot

The Church

and Owen's Visitation in 1634 the tomb was adorned with brass shields where only the stone backing can now be seen, but the Puritan despoilation was yet to come. There is an ominous entry in the Churchwardens' Accounts for 1643-44 'Rec. for the Brass taken out of the tomb stones . . . 4s. 10d.'. This member of the Braose dynasty was living at Chesworth when he died in 1395, followed within a few weeks by his month-old son and daughter of two and a half years, who may well be buried in the tomb with their father.

It is likely that there were other monuments dating from the 15th century which have been lost, but there is still an unusual brass in the chancel floor which has been identified from the initials T.C. several times repeated on the cope as an effigy of Thomas Clerke, vicar in 1411. This century probably saw the erection of a carved wooden screen across the chancel which would enable the congregation to see and hear the officiating clergy without

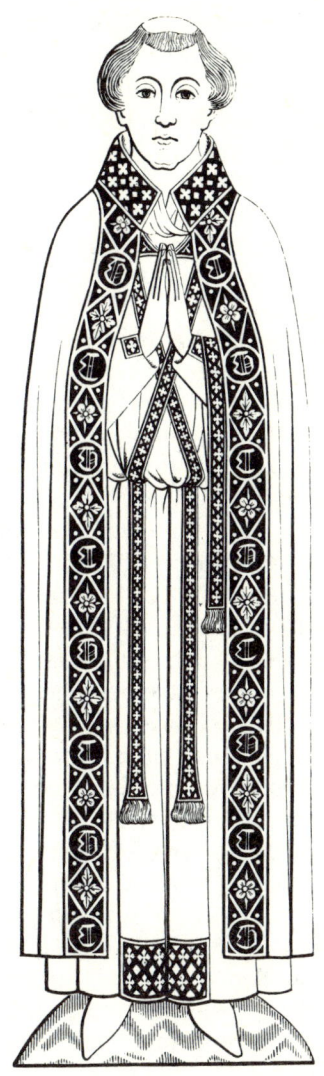

Fig. 1. The effigy (now headless) of Thomas Clerke, vicar in 1411, on the floor of the chancel.

physical access. After the Reformation the gates would have been removed but the screen left. It was not destroyed until 1825 when it, together with the gallery over, was sold for firewood. In 1841 traces were found of 15th-century paintings on the west wall, and it is clear that these have been carefully obliterated at some time. When the 1865 restoration took place these paintings were renewed using the tracings made in 1841, but subsequent deterioration caused them to be painted over in white at the 1965 restoration.

The next chantry chapel resulted from a licence to Richard Wakehurst in 1447 to found a perpetual chantry at the altar of St. Nicholas, north of the chancel, for the souls of Richard Wakehurst, Henry Boteler and Maria his wife, for which lands and rents were assigned so that a chaplain could say masses daily for a salary of £7 a year. These chantries, which were endowments, not buildings, were saleable, and in 1536 Boteler's chantry was sold to Sir Roger Copley of Roughey (Roffey) Manor, hence the later name of Roughey Chantry. The house known as 'The Chantry' near the Church was occupied by the chantry priest, and among other lands which might have belonged to this endowment was the house near the railway station now known as 'Northchapel' although this house may have been part of the lands of the Brotherhood described later on.

One of the striking monuments in the church is the canopied tomb of Thomas Hoo, whose wife's grandmother was the former widow of Lord de Braose, and whose effigy on the opposite side of the chancel has already been described. The tomb is of Purbeck marble in the form of an Easter Sepulchre and was erected soon after Thomas Hoo's death in 1486, although much of the canopy seems to have been restored in Elizabethan times, and there is a tradition that the Queen herself ordered the work on one of her travels into Sussex. Hoo twice represented Sussex in Parliament, and thrice was member for Horsham. He was also one of the grantees for the founding of the Guild of St. John the Baptist and St. Anne, of which an account is given later. There were two persons with the name Thomas Hoo,

The Church

half-brothers, the other being Lord Hoo who was known to have been buried in Battle Abbey.

The Easter Sepulchre was a frequent feature in medieval churches on the north side of chancels and contained a consecrated host placed in it on Maundy Thursday and elevated to the high altar on Easter Day. The Hoo monument was evidently adorned with both inscriptions and coats of arms in brass, but these were removed before 1634, when it was reported that 'the Eschocheons and inscriptions, all taken away', and further damage was done by the Roundheads in 1643.

The Guild or Brotherhood

In 1457 or 1458 a patent was granted for the foundation of a guild for the relief of the brethren, being known as the Brotherhood of St. John the Baptist and St. Anne. Associated with it was a chantry of one chaplain to celebrate mass at the altar of St. John the Baptist, which was located in the 13th-century south aisle. The Brotherhood was to have a master, four wardens and an unspecified number of brothers and sisters. On the sale by the crown in 1548, the guild and chantry having been suppressed by Henry VIII, the inventory has two items of interest. 'Rent of one capital mansion, called "The Broteheddes house", situated and lying in the street called "The Northstreate", in Horsham, with the bakehouse, stable, garden and other appurtenances . . . 11s. 4d.'). This may have been the house now called 'Northchapel'.

The other entry reads:

> The rent of one tenement, with separate chambers for the presbiters, and one garden to the same belonging, situated and being in the Churchyard of Horsham per annum . . . 6s. 8d.'.

This could be the building now numbered 19 and 20 in the Causeway.

The chantry certificate for 1548, detailing the chantries for the crown to seize, called Horsham 'a greate parishe and conteyneth in length 5 myles and within the same about 900 houseling people (communicants) and hathe no preiste but the parishe preiste to serve the Cure and minister which is verie slender to serve so greate a parishe'. Another indication of the state into which the parish had got is given in the certificate of 1550 for Boteler's chantry, which recorded that 'Ornaments, Jewells or any other goods there was none remaineing at this Surveie bicause the said Ribley sumtyme Incumbent had Imbecilled and sold them awaie'. Under Elizabeth I clergy were few and of poor quality owing to the disturbances in earlier times, and the most unsuitable appointments were often made, of which one Ribley was presumably an example. Vigorous measures effected some improvement, but even at the end of the reign more than half the clergy were neither properly licensed nor university graduates.

The remaining chapel to be described was dedicated to All Saints in 1914, but it was formerly known as the Shelley Chapel and before that the Jesus Chapel, and although the actual building dates from the end of the 15th century or the beginning of the 16th, the founder has not been identified for certain. John Michell, of the family at Stammerham, in his will of 1520 asked to be buried in the 'chapel of Jhesu which I of late made', but it has been argued that this refers to a reconstruction or enlargement as there is also a date of 1447 for the original building. The grandmother of the poet Shelley was a Michell, and both Michells and Shelleys are comemorated by monuments in this chapel, hence the name Shelley Chapel.

The remaining portion of today's church building not so far dealt with is the Lollards Tower, now used as the vestry for clergy below and choir in the room above. It was built in the 15th century on the north side of the church next to the chapel of St. Nicholas (Roughey chantry), and is of very solid construction. Tradition maintains that it was used for the incarceration of the Lollards who were the followers of John Wyclif, much persecuted for heresy between the years 1500–1535, and its robust construction was used for many years for the custody of the church records and other valuables. Until 1888 the only means of access to the upper

The Church

storey was a winding stone staircase, and the room contained an oak chest so large that it must have been made on the spot. This is now in the south aisle. Later centuries have of course made this part of the church more comfortable for occupation, and in the 17th century oak panelling was put round the vestry walls. These panels have the names of the churchwardens carved in 1674 and again in 1974.

In the 15th century windows were altered and additions made to the ceiling, but there were no more additions to the main fabric of the church after this period, so that today we see an amalgam of the 13th, 14th, and 15th centuries, with a great expanse of nave and chancel that was doubtless the intention of the original builders, but in the intervening centuries a large amount of woodwork cluttered up the church in the shape of high pews and immense galleries. When the tower grew up to a spire is not known. In his will of 1497 William Forster left 10 shillings 'To the reparacion of the stepill', but as a steeple is a church tower with or without a spire, this is not much help.

Somewhat more is known about the church and its activities from the 16th century onward owing to the greater abundance of records, and Horsham is very fortunate in having a parish register from 1540. Wills giving much detail are more common, and that of John Butler in 1559 includes 'Item I will my wif to sell my blewe coote and with the pryce thereof to burie me honestly'.

The Churchyard

Burial in decent form has always been a Christian concern, but a simple calculation will show that the cemetery round the church would have been filled early on, and re-use of the burial spaces was common. There are at present 1,175 tombstones, the earliest of which is a brick one covered with a Sussex marble slab to Richard Dendy (1690) and his wife Joan (1693). There would have been sufficient space for not much more than one generation in Tudor times, and although in 1640 it was reported by the church wardens that there was one acre of consecrated ground in the churchyard, approximately the same as today, the shape of the churchyard has been altered. The vicarage was from early times adjacent to the Lollards Tower, and in a terrier of 1663 it is described as 'a Vicarage house bordering on the Churchyard on the north side with a Portall southward right against the Vesterie ioyning to the Chancell of the Church', but it became very dilapidated so that Bishop Bowyer's Visitation in 1724 condemned it as 'Mansion house old and ruinous'. In 1840 the Rev. J. F. Hodgson built the present vicarage, using the funds from the sale of the old site to the parish plus a grant from Queen Anne's Bounty. This released a little more land for burials, and customarily bones which were dug up were placed in a charnel house. The curious vault under the Memorial Chapel has been taken to be such a charnel house, but there is no real evidence.

By 1849 it was clear that ground would have to be found elsewhere, so the site in Denne Road, which used to belong to the church from time immemorial, but had been sold, was bought back and consecrated as a cemetery in 1852 and the churchyard closed for burial in 1856. The lych gate (now sadly deteriorating) was decided upon in 1853 by the Vestry, and it is hard to see why the present church authorities will not accept responsibility for restoring what is not only an uncommon link with the past but also valued by many whose family burials have taken place here. In 1884 the cemetery had to be enlarged to an adjoining plot, and here a part was left unconsecrated for other burials.

The priory at Rusper having been dissolved in 1536, the rectorial tithes were granted by Henry VIII to Sir Robert Southwell, Master of the Rolls, and by sale or succession they came together with the nunnery property into the possession of the Hurst family, while the patronage of the vicarage was given to the Archbishops of Canterbury where it remains to this day.

Apart from the suppression of the guild and of the chantries, the Reformation had little material effect on the parish church. Although spiritual ferment was beginning to reach into Sussex, one must not be surprised at the slowness of this occurrence as we were very remote from central

The Church

government in London. Horsham was self-sufficient economically, and except for the officials from borough and county government and for the clergy, the average man was not much in contact with progress. Church life went on much as usual, the sick and needy were looked after, the church buildings were used as parish hall, school, storehouse, courthouse for ecclesiastical cases, and after the Reformation numerous civil duties devolved upon the church authorities such as provision of stocks, pounds, arms for the local defence, relief of discharged soldiers and of the hordes of vagrants resulting in part from the dissolution of the monasteries. All this needed outbuildings, and there must have been many such near the church which have not survived today.

The Bells

There was a bell foundry in the churchyard from 1592 as we know from the parish registers, which refer to the 'Belle House' in the Normandy. The exact location has been a cause of speculation, but as a bell-pit leaves a lot of green-coloured sand around it, the site may yet turn up in someone's garden nearby. When the restoration of 1864-65 was taking place, the Memorial Chapel, then known as Holy Trinity Chapel, was altered, and on taking up the floor 'The furnace and mould in which a bell had been cast, together with a considerable quantity of metal, was discovered'. (Miss D. Hurst's *History*.) It seems extraordinary that casting, which gives rise to a lot of smoke and fumes, should have taken place within the fabric of the church, but it must be remembered that the chapel in those days was virtually a separate building and not as it is now. This could not have been the main foundry site, as records mention a separate building.

The foundry not only cast or re-cast the Horsham bells, but also those for other Sussex churches. The 'greate bell' was re-cast in 1557, and in 1600 a new frame was required for all the bells, which appear to have numbered five at this time. In 1615 the tower was damaged by lightning with sad consequences for 'Eliz. Stroode a mayde yt was killed wth thunder at ye belfery doore', and the tenor bell consequently re-cast by Richard Eldridge who also re-cast the fourth bell in 1621, and his son, Brian Eldridge, carried on re-casting in 1633, 1645, and 1652. It seems that the Eldridges moved their foundry from Horsham sometime around 1623, as there is no further record in the church accounts of their rent for the bell house and the church paid for the 'great bell' to be re-cast at Chertsey. In 1703 there is an entry 'payd for beear when vnloaded ye bell . . . 4s.' which suggests that bells needing attention were taken away. In 1752 they were all re-cast into eight by Lester and Pack in London. Apart from possible over-enthusiasm in ringing the bells, damage has been caused to them several more times by lightning striking the tower. Until 1789 the bells were rung on the ground floor, but the ringers decided to erect a frame at their own expense, which lasted until the 1864 restoration when the bells were moved to the clock chamber. The 1789 frame had hardly come into use when lightning struck and split the seventh bell, which was still rung in this condition until it broke further and was re-cast in 1815 together with the second bell. The tenor bell was particularly fractious and was re-cast yet again in 1751 and 1838. Bell frames, too, gave trouble even in recent times when one would expect more modern materials to last longer. In 1900 the bells were lifted, the bearings levelled and braced up, but by 1921 re-strengthening was necessary, and in 1952 new bearings. Perhaps the most recent work, which was very extensive, will be more lasting. By 1969 there was much concern over the condition of the frame, and when it was decided that it must come down the tower itself was found to be cracked, so concrete was forced in under great pressure (with surprising effects some way from the tower!), and a new cast-iron frame installed. The opportunity was taken to add two more trebles so that a ring of 10 proclaimed joyously in 1973 that all was now well in Horsham belfry, comparable with the great occasion when bells were once again allowed after the silence of the war years. A wonderful amount of work was done by the ringers themselves, who not only dismantled the bells, but also re-hung them, and raised a lot of money for the whole undertaking.

The Galleries

The 17th century saw not only removal of many civil duties from the church, but also a great religious turmoil which had lasting effects. It was a period when much emphasis was placed on preaching, and the growing population of Horsham meant that space in the church was insufficient. To meet this, galleries were erected, enlarged and added to, so that the very fabric of the stonework was endangered. Seating in our church, according to the parish records, was at this time separate for the sexes, and in 1641 there was objection by the Puritans to 'the taking down galleries . . . or restraining the building of such galleries where the parishes are very populous'.

Collyer's School had its own gallery—' a seate or place convenient for the schoolemaister and scollers of the Grammar Schoole of Horsham shalbe built allofte in the church neere the great northe doore', and the whole of the north, south and west sides of the church were thus encumbered, and even at one time so was the entrance to the chancel. A contemporary print shows a preaching gallery extending right into the nave and looking rather like the docking bridge of an Atlantic liner.

Preaching was all, or nearly all, and it may have been the sermons of an hour or more that made popular high pews so that slumber might be less easily detected. The pews were rented or owned outright, so that there is a crop of law cases recorded which went to extreme lengths. The first known rental was in 1625-26, 'Item rd. of Mathew Napper for a seate in the gallery . . . 13d.'. Well before the Civil War it was considered that the standard of preaching must be improved, and 'lecturers' were appointed whether the incumbent liked it or not. In our case, the vicar having died, the Archbishop of Canterbury, who had the right of presentment, put forward the name of one Coniers (or Conyers—spelling was at this time still unimportant). On 19 December 1642, the *Journal* of the House of Lords reads,

'Petition of inhabitants of the Borough and Parish of Horsham, in the County of Sussex; shewing, That one Mr. Coniers hath been presented to that Parish, by the Archbishop of Cant. who is a disserving Man, and unfit for that Place. Hereupon it is ORDERED, That the Archbishop of Cant. shall have Notice, that this House doth not approve of the said Conyers to be presented to the said Parish'. Instead, the Lords were petitioned for one John Chatfield, said to be a 'godly and painful preacher' who had been one of these lecturers for the past six months. Not only was Chatfield appointed, but the Horsham gentry being largely of Puritan sympathies at this time, the vicarage was sequestrated and the proceeds given to Chatfield, who remained minister until 1657, although in the Royalist rising in Horsham of 1648 'Mistress Chatfield advised her husband to withdraw, for fear they should do him more mischief than with songs. The soldiers say that if they had known of their going they would have held their styrrups'. Perhaps John Chatfield was not all that popular in his parish.

By this time (1642) Archbishop Laud was in the Tower for treason, and could be treated indifferently by Parliament, but in the 1630s his policy of revival of the church left its mark in Horsham as elsewhere. He was determined to improve public worship, which had indeed become slovenly, and to restore uniformity, order and decency in the Church. One of his instructions was the provision of rails to guard against profanation of the sanctuary particularly by dogs, who accompanied their masters to divine service. There is a record of 1645–46 'Paid to ould Longe for whiping the dogs for the yeare . . . . 7s.', but a later entry gives the Puritan triumph: '1641–42 Paid to Aldreg for paving of the Chansell when the Communion table was removed . . . 3s. 6d. Payd for writing of a certificate to the Parliament to certefie the Communion table was removed to the antiant place according to an order sent from ye Parliament . . . 12d.'.

Recusancy and the Puritans

From 1603 the clergy were bound by statute to report any recusancy in their parish, and this included Protestant

The Church

dissenters as well as Roman Catholics. The reports had to be made to Justices of the Peace as well as to the diocesan authorities, and we have several records of these reports. Horsham was no different from most parishes in the diocese, the 1676 census of those above 16 years of age giving 2,870 conformists, 30 papists, 100 nonconformists. The General Baptists and the Quakers caused most trouble to the Anglican clergy, and this will be described later in this chapter. Whatever damaging effect recusancy had on the congregation, the Puritan triumph certainly left its mark on the church fabric. Mutilation of churches has been done by many hands, by common thieves as well as well-meaning restorers, so that it cannot always be attributed to Cromwell's soldiers, but the Hoo tomb and possibly the De Braose tomb probably suffered at this time, some corbels were sawn off, and stained glass would certainly have been on the casualty list. There are drawings dated 1634 of some 22 coats of arms and inscriptions mostly in the east window, and these have gone, and when some repairs were being done in 1825 it was noted that an inscription which ran the whole length of the church below the ceiling had been carefully defaced. Mercifully the monument to Elizabeth Delves (1654) on the south side of the chapel of St. John the Baptist was too late for Cromwellian axes. Two brasses escaped as well, the one of a priest on the chancel floor, mentioned earlier, and the other a female figure now let into a pillar in the south aisle, but formerly on the floor of the middle aisle. The inscription has been lost, but a rubbing remains which reads: 'Here lyeth Richard Foys and Elizabeth his wife, which Richard deceased the 25th day of April, the yere 1514: o their soulles Ihu have m'cy'. Although the original 15th-century font of Sussex marble is left to us, the base is modern and the lead lining was sold in 1650 for thirteen shillings. All the early church plate has gone, the earliest piece being a silver-gilt alms dish of 1713. Whatever else the iconoclasts did in the name of Puritanism, they left us the medieval fabric of the church.

Another effect on Horsham of the Commonwealth Parliamentary measures was the abolition of marriages in church, which from 1654 had to be performed before a Justice of the Peace after the production of a certificate saying that the banns had been read in church or market place. Many were distressed at this, and compromised by having a minister of religion present as well, which practice in 1656 was officially recognised.

Eighteenth Century Decline

After the upheavals of the 17th century, when many of the Horsham congregation must have removed to nonconforming meetings, the next century was outstanding for the neglect and religious deadness of the churches. We have seen how the vicarage was allowed to fall into ruin by 1724, and in 1730 a visitor wrote in his diary how much the church had fallen into a bad state of repair. He also noted the wooden grave markers common at that time, but they have of course all perished long since. It is perhaps strange that no mention is made of iron grave markers, often found in Sussex parishes near the old iron foundries.

That the clergy were not of a high standard at this time is evident from several instances. A diary reads, 'I gave a poor man 6d, who came about a-beggin for the prisoners in Horsham Gaol, three of which are clergymen, two of them in for acting contrary to the laws of men, but not, in my opinion, to the laws of God—that is, for marrying contrary to the Marriage Act. The other is for stealing some linen; but, I hope he is innocent'. In connection with Collyer's School, then next to the church, the vicar and churchwardens who had the duty of electing a fit and proper headmaster, sometimes gave the post to a local clergyman simply to add the emoluments to the tithes he already got in his benefice. This was much to the disadvantage of the school, as both duties could not be performed properly by one man, although for 10 years (1712-1722) John Reynell tried to do this while vicar of our parish. He was also notable for having 21 children by his first wife. One of his daughters married the Rev. Francis Osgood, curate of the parish, who obtained the position of headmaster after Canon Reynell and held it for 51 years.

The Church

Pluralities were undoubtedly much of the cause of the church's malaise, just as they are today. The Rev. Francis Atkins was not only vicar of our church from 1769-1796, but also of Madehurst and Clymping, and did not even live in Horsham, while his successor, William Jameson, combined the benefice with that of Clapham in Sussex while being headmaster of Collyer's School for 33 years. Jameson was also noted for meddling in politics as a firm Tory and was proposer of more than one Parliamentary candidate for the old borough of Horsham. Most clergy had considerable interests besides their immediate task of the cure of souls, and curate Osgood was no exception. He had great interest in farming at which he was successful, and spent quite some time as chaplain to Horsham Gaol, while the new turnpike to Dorking was one of his investments. These activities were necessary in the days of large families, poor stipends and difficulties in collecting tithes. In this time of earthly pursuits by their ministers, is it surprising that many looked for salvation in Baptist and Calvinist dissent?

When William Huntingdon, a coal-heaver whose conversion influenced so many people in Sussex that a mile-long procession followed his funeral, came to preach in Horsham market place folk flocked to hear him. As the Whigs had retained the Parliamentary Acts of the previous century, Dissenters were thereby still debarred from any public office, and we find them turning to commerce and building their own educational systems.

The Wesleys did not have much influence in Sussex, and we have to wait until the beginning of last century before the Oxford Movement really stirred the Church of England, with its aim to revive the worship and the institutions of the church; but it took until the second half of the century to complete the change. Much controversy over the amount of ritual in services is recorded in many letters and diaries, but at least religious toleration for all had arrived. An interesting example of this toleration to be seen today is the first gravestone on the right on entering the churchyard from the Causeway. It will be noticed that this faces north and south at right-angles to the usual Christian graves, although it bears a cross. This is the grave of a Moslem woman who lived a recluse in a cottage in the forest for many years under the name of Mrs. Bennett, the 'dark lady', and died in 1854. Her husband, who pre-deceased her, was a French adventurer and when they married she was the daughter of a Persian colonel, and she lies facing Mecca.

The clergy were now much more involved in education with the National and other school movements. It was the Rev. Jarvis Kenrick who, when curate of Horsham, started a National school for boys at St. Mark's in 1840 at his own expense. The setting up of, Ecclesiastical Commissioners changed the pattern of financial organisation, and by the end of the century little remained of church responsibility for public affairs such as health, roads, poor relief and so on. However, it is not to be expected that a vicar of a parish can or should remain entirely aloof from public life other than his cure, and it must be remembered that such an important institution as Collyer's School was still located on the edge of the churchyard. The affairs of the school were anything but placid early last century, and the Rev. H. J. Rose wrote as school governor in 1822 that he would 'rejoice sincerely if it could be shewn that I had no concern with the school whatever'. First politics and then sectarianism had played havoc with the running of the school, but every vicar had a duty to be involved, as he had been since the foundation of the school.

Revival in the 19th Century

The Rev. J. F. Hodgson, vicar from 1840 for the next 43 years, was a fervent Tractarian who had a great effect on the spiritual life of the parish as well as being responsible for the great restoration of the parish church in 1864-65. At first he upset the headmaster of Collyer's School by giving the boys religious teaching which to many seemed too Puseyite, but Hodgson had a great interest in the continuing improvement of the school, and as a permanent governor he was successful in his intention. The biggest task he had to tackle was the condition of the old

The Church

parish church. Neglect in the 18th century had merely postponed the inevitable—that something would have to be done quickly to prevent the total collapse of the main fabric, which was leaning in places as much as two feet out of the vertical. In 1825 some attempt had been made to alleviate the effects that the enormous heavy galleries were having on the structure, and it was then that the 15th-century carved screen across the chancel was removed with the associated gallery, and was broken up for kindling. Removed, too, was the figure of 'Jack o' the clock' which struck the hours inside the church and distracted the congregation. To arrest the leaning of the walls to the north various ugly devices were adopted, such as filling up the easternmost arches of both north and south sides of the chancel with masonry, strengthening the northern buttresses, and placing four beams across the nave and chancel at clerestory level, which effectively blocked any light from several clerestory windows. In addition, walls were built across both north and south aisles. What the church must have looked like must be left to the imagination, and in any case the measures were ineffective and the church continued to lean.

The wind of change was beginning to sweep through the Church of England, architecturally as well as spiritually, and the tottering church of St. Mary's was more than ready for attention. In February 1864 a public meeting was held to determine what was to be done, and a foremost London church architect, S. S. Teulon, was engaged to reconstruct as well as restore. Within less than 15 months an enormous amount of work was done, including removing the roof, jacking up the walls, extending the south aisle, incorporating the chantry chapels into the main church, opening the tower arch, not to mention heating, lighting and seating according to the most modern ideas. The first thing to do was to remove the galleries which had so encumbered the place, and the extended south aisle was to accommodate the seating which had been lost thereby.

The astonishing feat of jacking up the whole church to the upright position is given in a contemporary account in the *Horsham Express* which is worth reproducing in full:

Return of the columns and arches of the south nave to the perpendicular.

On Monday, October 17, 1864, this interesting phenomenon took place in the presence of several admiring spectators, and as perhaps some of your readers who were not present, might be glad of an account of the operation by an eye-witness, I trouble you with these few lines. It may be as well to state that prior to the operation these preliminaries had taken place: first, the roof was supported upon strong balks of timber, and the clerestory walls had been removed as far as the string-course just below the windows. Also four screw-jacks—one for each column— had been arranged, so as to have their purchase on the opposite wall, which (it will be borne in mind) is strong in the support of three solid brick buttresses. In front of these screw-jacks, and stretching across the church, were placed four beams, the opposite ends pushing against another beam, which was laid horizontally against the face of the wall to be moved, and just in line with the points of the arches. In addition to this, the four columns to be moved had been pierced just above their bases, and strong oak needles inserted through the holes. These needles rested on longitudinal beams placed on the ground, and were contrived for a double purpose: first, to assist the throwing over of the column by the insertion of wedges, from time to time, during the action of the screw-jacks above, and thus secure the columns from breaking at the capital; and second, to support the columns afterwards, while inserting the new bases—an operation which has since been successfully performed. These things being all adjusted, exactly at half-past two (every one being in breathless expectation, and some evidently believing the church was about to topple down), the word was given. All the screw-jacks were set going at once, one man taking charge of each jack, and the wedges on either side of the columns were carefully struck. It was a trying moment. Presently the old wall began to quiver and crack, and the plaster flew about in all directions. Another moment, and behold it had gone more than half over to its proper place, the columns having given, as was desired, at their bases. Some little delay then occurred for the re-adjustment of the screw-jacks, and the driving of the wedges; meanwhile your correspondent ascended to the summit of the wall, to witness from thence the remainder of the feat. The word was again given—on went the screw-jacks as before. The wall shook ominously beneath my feet, and I felt and saw distinctly the remainder of the move from this unusual locomotive. The builder and clerk of the works superintended the operation, which was effected, as everyone present allowed, in the most workmanlike manner, so that in less than two hours this wall, which for so many years had hung two feet out of the upright, threatening to bury the

The Church

worshippers in hideous ruin, was set perfectly straight, without any drawback or accident whatever. Thus three great steps have been gained this week towards the complete renovation of our ancient church. First. This wall has been set upright. Second. The clumsy column, heretofore dividing and disfiguring the fifth arch, has disappeared. Third. The unsightly trussed girders, wholly destroying the beautiful perspective of the interior, have been removed.

The next equally astonishing step was to deal with the arcade on the north side in the same manner, after which it was possible to rebuild the clerestory exactly as before, and restore the roof timbers, the Horsham stone roof and the oak ceiling and moulded ribs. As the Trinity chapel was now to be opened into the church, two old windows and an aumbrey in the wall between were removed. In the days when the chapel was used as a school the windows were blocked up by a large plank of oak which was then taken into the almshouses in the Normandy and used as a dining-room table. Today it is to be seen in Horsham Museum.

The present magnificent east window dates from this time, and may be the fourth in line. In the 15th century smaller lancets were replaced with a Perpendicular design similar to that of the 1864 restoration, but on 7 July 1839 this was blown in by a storm and replaced with 'the poorest and commonest style of Perpendicular work', which is shown in contemporary prints as having nine lights at the top over two rows of five lights. It was found that the new window could be made partly from fragments of the 15th-century one which had been built into the east wall. The remaining windows of the church have stained glass dating from the time of this restoration, except for fragments re-used. At the west end of the church, the tower arch was opened for the first time since 1635 when a partition with door had been constructed, and the paintings on the west wall were restored. A new organ built by Willis was presented by Henry Padwick, but it needed repair in 1895 (when it took a year to raise the money), again in 1909, and again when it was restored in 1954. As it is now showing signs of wanting attention (not exceptional after more than 20 years), how long will it take to raise the money this time?

When the area of the sanctuary was disturbed, remains of encaustic tiles were found having eight different patterns, and these were copied by Minton's of Staffordshire so that the pavement was restored as nearly as could be ascertained from similar examples elsewhere. The communion rails of the baluster type dating from Laudian days were replaced with modern ones.

Several of the projected alterations in the church could not at this time be carried out because of lack of funds. The financial organisation of the Church of England changed considerably during the 19th century, when tithes were converted to a money payment in 1836 and church estates (except the glebe) transferred to the Ecclesiastical Commissioners. Church rates, levied from at least the 14th century, were abolished in 1868. It was therefore to private sources that the parish often turned, and in Horsham these were forthcoming in good measure, although it meant hard work on the part of the clergy to get in the pence rather than the pounds. A Church Council meeting of 1884 reported that church supporters among tradesmen were unable to contribute much owing to depression caused by the co-operative store system in London and elsewhere. The customers were not paying cash as they did to London stores. Nevertheless, the list of benefactions to the church in the last century is a long and impressive one, as may be gathered from a glance at the dedications to some of the stained glass windows, for example. The Rev. Hodgson, whose incumbency of nearly 44 years was immensely appreciated by his parisioners, used the retirement present they gave him to build a new porch. The old north porch being almost entirely disused and entry being by the Norman door, it was decided to cut off the Holy Trinity chapel from the porch with a wall and door, rather to its architectural detriment, and make the porch the main entrance to the church. Also, the upper chamber of the Lollards Tower was fitted up as a choir vestry, as the superscription over the staircase reads:

> This 'Parvise' was restored and fitted up, for the convenience of the Choir of this Church, by their friend and former Vicar, J. F. Hodgson.—Michaelmas 1884.

The Church

Church Activities in the Community

The church still played a large part in the life of the town. In 1870 the Literary and Scientific Institution containing a reading room and a chess room was started in the Carfax as a result of church effort, and in the same year so was Horsham Football Club. In 1885 the parish library was opened in St. Mark's School, and it was the vicar (Rev. Charles Robinson) who first mooted the idea of a cottage hospital. He it was also who worked so hard as Chairman of the Governors to re-establish Collyer's School when it was moved to its present site in 1893.

Although no longer a statutory duty since 1834, but a moral one, poor relief has always figured largely among church activities. Allowances on a regular weekly basis to aged persons were supplemented by a winter fund for fuel and food during the winter, and the Maternal Society founded in 1815 for the relief of indigent married women and other similar societies were supported. The working classes were supplied with soup at 1d. a quart in the Bishopric during the winter months every Tuesday and Friday, and to prevent the begging of soup tickets by children it was suggested that these should not be given away during school hours. To encourage self-help, so admired in Victoria's reign, and so deficient today, the Parochial Clothing Club added 5s. annually to each 10s. subscribed by members, tickets for the value being given on one of the town's drapers. Schooling with which the church was concerned will be considered in the chapter on education, but it might be noted here that in 1869 the vicar was concerned with the abuse of charity and noted in the Parish magazine 'Should charitable friends be desirous to assist in the education of children at any of these schools, it is strongly advised that a portion of the schooling be paid for by the parent, or a weekly contribution be made to the Shoe Club; those children whose school-fees are fully paid being generally the most irregular and unsatisfactory'!

The earlier charities of the church, the first of which seems to have been that of Henry Pilfold in 1585 who left lands for the benefit of the poor to the extent of 20s. per annum, were examined by the Brougham Commissioners in 1837. They found seven charities extant, and four lost. That of Henry Pilfold was discontinued in 1805, but Henry Wickens' of 1613 which distributed bread from the Town Hall on New Year's Day was still continuing. John Gorring's charity of 1611 merged with Edward Jenden's of 1828 so that £14 in bread was distributed by the church wardens, and Theobald Shelley in 1689 ordained that bread to the amount of 2s. should be distributed after morning and evening service each Sunday. Other distributions of bread were from Thomas Summers (1808) and Charles Champion (1828), but these various charities were reorganised and consolidated in 1921. A visiting clergyman early last century noted the loaves arranged during the service on a ledge in front of the gallery. 'It was the gift of a singular maiden Lady of fortune and of pity, who left fifteen pounds per annum for the support of certain favorite animals . . . On her decease in July 1799, she was kept for six weeks, agreeable to her own request; fearing, it is supposed, a premature interment. The author of this narrative came down by particular request, to bury her. Her interment at length took place according to her desire, enveloped by the shades of midnight, and it scarcely need be added, amidst innumerable spectators assembled from every part of the county'.

From time out of mind there had been a poorhouse in the Normandy, perhaps once run in conjunction with the Brotherhood of St. John and St. Anne, and in 1842 the Rev. Jarvis Kenrick, who was curate of Horsham, undertook to put up £500 for its purchase and conversion into an almshouse if other subscriptions could raise the same amount. This was done, and St. Mary's Hospital, as it was then known, was opened in 1844.

The Chapel of the Holy Trinity was altered and re-dedicated together with a memorial to the dead of the First World War in 1925 by the Bishop of Lewes. In 1965 it was re-decorated as a memorial to those who fell in the Second World War, and contains the laid-up colours of the 4th Battalion of the Royal Sussex Regiment, hence the modern name of the Memorial Chapel. The dedication

The Church

ceremony performed by the Bishop of Chichester was honoured by the attendance of Queen Elizabeth the Queen Mother. In 1926 Mrs. Laughton laid out the Garden of Remembrance on the banks of the river to the south-west of the churchyard in memory of her husband and son, but this has fallen into sad decay and it would be pleasant to see it restored.

More Church Building

Another consequence of the expansion of Horsham town in the 19th century and the religious revival was the building of more churches. The first addition was St. Mark's in the Carfax, where the site and stone were donated by Thomas Coppard, and the remainder raised partly by public subscription and partly with grants from the ecclesiastical authorities. The 1840 building was not large and was much criticised on architectural grounds, but in 1870 the Rev. A. H. Bridges, who had been the first minister there, built at his own expense in memory of his daughter, the tower, spire, organ chamber, new side aisles and choir vestry. In 1888 the chancel was extended. St. Mark's started with a High Church complexion, the future Cardinal Manning preaching at the consecration service in 1841, and this would have been quite in accord with the Puseyite vicar James Hodgson. Some have said that the parish church was too far away on the edge of the parish, and that St. Mark's was much more conveniently near, but growth of the town between the wars raised the question of provision of a church in the eastern part, and as St. Mark's had never had any endowment and depended for its support on the offertories, the Bishop of Chichester recommended that it be closed to make easier the obtaining of enough money for what was to be St. Leonard's Church in Clarence Road, where the land had already been bought in 1899. During the last war the church was used for storage by the Ministry of Food, and when the question of its re-opening came up again after the war, the vicar and churchwardens were dead against it, but after much petitioning and agitation by the congregation it was re-opened in 1948.

In Broadbridge Heath a mission room was started in 1853 and became St. John's, and Holy Trinity Church in Rusham's Road likewise started as a small corrugated-iron building in 1879.

The Roman Catholics

Turning now to other churches, we find that the persecution of Roman Catholics which started elsewhere in 1563 was hardly known in Sussex, where before the Civil War Protestant and Papist lived peacefully together, but talk of foreign invasion and Popish plots from 1640 onwards began to create fear. However, the census of 1676 showed that only about one per cent. of the parish were Roman Catholic, and their first noticeable presence in Horsham was the celebration of mass in a cottage. In 1845 there was a small chapel entered from West Street, when the Duchess of Norfolk built a chapel nearby in Springfield Road which is now Council offices. The present church dedicated to St. John the Evangelist lies across the road from the old chapel, and was begun in 1919 and opened in 1923.

The Quakers

It was not Papism but Dissent which troubled the Established Church, and it was at Horsham that the Quakers first preached in this part of Sussex. In 1655 'they Declared the Truth in the open market', where they were greeted with violence and mocking. The famous Baptist, Matthew Caffyn, preached a blistering sermon in 1656 entitled 'The deceived and deceiving Quakers discovered', and both civil and ecclesiastical authorities pursued them with fury, some 300 being confined in Horsham gaol at one time or another. Sometimes, however, the gaolers were sympathetic, and for allowing meetings inside the gaol, one of them was sent to the House of Correction in Lewes for several weeks. The celebrated martyr among the Quakers was Ambrose Rigge, who at a meeting in Hurstpierpoint, in his own words, 'at the instigation of Leonard Letchford Priest of that place, I

The Church

was apprehended and . . . they committed me to Horsham Gaol, the 28th Day of the 3rd Month, 1662 . . . where I continued above Ten Years, under many sore Abuses in the Prison, from several Gaolers'. The abuses were unbelievable, as was the venom of Letchford who did not cease his persecutions. Rigge married after two years in gaol, and Letchford arranged for bailiffs to seize what little goods he and his wife had, leaving not even their bed. The Quakers came into conflict with the clergy for not attending church (which they called the steeple house) or paying tithes, and when they did attend divine service they often interrupted it and reproached the preacher, keeping their hats on the while.

Persecution made the Quakers all the firmer, and even the Restoration brought no relief, but in 1672 the Declaration of Indulgence suspended penalties for nonconformity. However, opposition to Charles II forced him to withdraw the Declaration in the following year, and more persecution followed. But eventually toleration prevailed, helped by the passing of the Habeas Corpus Act in 1679, so 1685 was the last year of the Quakers' oppression. The Toleration Act of 1689 removed penalties from Dissenters who held meetings, but they still had to apply to the justices 'for a licence to build a chapel, and as late as mid-18th century the Quakers were still having their goods seized for non-payment of tithes.

The Quakers like other nonconformists had been accustomed to meet in private homes and to preach in the open air, but with easing of restrictions they began to have permanent premises, and the Friends Meeting House in Worthing Road was built in 1786.

The Growth of Nonconformism

While the Church of England slumbered or crumbled, according to the point of view, during the 18th century, the nonconformists were active. The largest body, the Baptists, had split into General Baptists and Particular Baptists, and the former had a congregation in Horsham from 1717 which was influential over a wide area. Earlier they had met in farmhouses in Southwater and Broadbridge in more or less secrecy, but the Toleration Act making meetings legal enabled them to set up a permanent centre in the Worthing Road.

'John Dendy, chirugeon, and John Greeve, mercer, purchased for the sume of Six and Thirty Pounds and Fifteen Shillings of good and lawful money of Great Britaine' a cottage and garden in 1720/21, and with additions the splendid building of today is substantially the same one they made then, lovely mellow brick with a Horsham stone roof. By the beginning of the 19th century a theological change was accepted which denied the Trinity, and today the church is known as Unitarian, although for many years it was called the Free Christian Church, the term General Baptist being dropped in the 1870s.

The congregation was very active in good works and in 1727 the records show 'That after the Conclusion of this present Instant February Bro Thos Caffyn be allowed 6 shillings per month & Old Sister Caffyn 4 shillings per month'. A day school was founded in one of the rooms by the Minister, Thomas Sadler, and later moved to a house in North Parade, and another Minister, Ashdowne, opened Albion Terrace Academy in 1839 which ran a publication, *The Albion Terrace Academy Gazette* from 1839 to 1842. He also started a Book and Tract Society which grew into a library of 4,000 volumes in the Worthing Road building, being the first of Horsham's libraries. Many other societies and groups were started, some of which did not survive the First World War, such as the Elocution class and Gymnastic Society, but one small seed sown in 1893 became the large museum which we have in the Causeway today. Only recently a member of the Marten family, one of whom as Minister thought of assembling a few objects of interest to be brought out of their boxes every now and then, left more books and photographs to the museum.

The tenets of the Particular or Calvinist Baptists were much more restrictive, forbidding propaganda and evangelism, but as the result of the repeal of disabling Acts in 1828,

The Church

the numbers and influence of Baptists spread considerably. The Baptist Union was formed to admit open-communion churches, but Strict Baptists, who believed that church membership should only be granted to baptised believers, went their own way. The Rehoboth (Calvinist Baptist) Chapel in New Street was opened in 1854, the Railway Mission Hall in Oakhill Road in 1896, and the Hope Baptist Chapel also in Oakhill Road in 1903. The Baptist Church in the Brighton Road dates from 1923.

The Congregationalists, or Independents (the names are practically interchangeable) place emphasis on the autonomy of the individual congregation, as do the Baptists, but differ from the latter on the subject and mode of baptism. Congregationalism being a very ancient concept, but one which has been persecuted with other nonconformist ones, there may have been underground links with the Lollards. However, our Independent Chapel in Springfield Road originated with a small building in 1814, replaced by a larger one in 1883. John Morth, a carpenter, after whom Morth's Gardens in the Causeway are named, purchased a cottage in Springfield Road in 1769, and it was here that meetings of the Society of Independents were held. In 1813 the Duke of Norfolk was asked to sell a piece of Swan Meadow for building the new chapel, and it is on this site that the Independents or Congregationalists have met ever since. It had to be trimmed slightly in the name of progress when Albion Way was carved across the town, and some bodies were removed from the burial ground for reinterment.

Although Wesley himself did not visit this area, Methodism after his death in 1791 spread throughout the country, and the Methodist Church in the London Road dates from 1832. The Methodists divided early last century, the Primitive Methodists going their own way. The Pentecostal Church in East Street began as Primitive Methodist in 1891 and later became Swedenborgian.

The Plymouth Brethren are a body of evangelical Christians who began early in the 19th century to try and recapture primitive Christian unity, and they attracted the attention of Charles Eversfield of Denne Park, who provided a meeting house in Denne Road, now called the Gospel Hall. Within 20 years of its foundation in 1865, the Salvation Army came to Horsham, and for many years occupied a building near the junction of Springfield and London Roads which had been the National School. They continue their religious and social activity from their Citadel in Barttelot Road. The Christian Scientists, who believe that 'Spirit is immortal Truth; matter is mortal error', have their church in Guildford Road.

The Church in History

Having traced the establishment and division of the Christian church in Horsham, it would be appropriate to re-stress how important a place it has had over the centuries in our daily lives. Much of the history of England has been made by the relationships between Church and State, and in microcosm this was so in Horsham. The Church laboured for the bodies as well as the souls of the community, and in early times everybody supported it by work, money or goods, while in return the Church relieved the sick and poor, provided a communal meeting place, prosecuted offenders against Church law, provided banks and pawnbroking facilities, schools and fire engines, public-house licenses and soldiers' billets. Now as man is not only incurably religious, he is also incurably social, and an institution which looks after both these instincts has an indefinite power of survival. But there are now more than two dozen places of worship in the town, most of which have their associated social and cultural activities, charitable works, lectures, libraries, and so forth. This great movement into several spiritual paths, whilst illustrating the several aspects of one Truth, would seem a strange thing to the Horsham inhabitant of seven centuries ago, who only knew one church, and that by the river Arun.

Chapter Two

PARLIAMENTARY AND LOCAL GOVERNMENT

WE DO NOT KNOW anything at all about the government of the Horsham settlement in Saxon times, but it must have originated from the estate of Washington under which it came. A Charter of 947 A.D. makes the first known reference to Horsham as a swine pasture or 'dene' in the estate of Washington, granted to Eadric by Eadred, King of the English, and one must assume that Eadric had the fealty of those who lived in Horsham and governed and protected them according to Anglo-Saxon law, under which the freemen of a neighbourhood were responsible for the good conduct of one another. One sometimes reads that Horsham was under the manor of Washington, but this is inaccurate as manor is a French word brought over by the Normans. It is known that the manor of Horsham was given to William de Braose by William the Conqueror, and as de Braose had one of his dwellings at Chesworth, presumably this was the site where our first local government came into being. The lord of the manor had both right and duty to hold a court of justice for all his tenants, and this Court Baron was presided over by the Lord's steward, who was therefore a very powerful man. The main function of the court was economic, dealing with disputes, infringements, and similar matters which affected the economic life of the manor. The King's court for criminal as well as civil matters was called the Court Leet, and the right to hold this court could be given by royal grant to a local lord. When the lord allowed the holdings of his tenants to be turned into burgages and took money rent instead of goods and services, it became a free borough, and that is the origin of the Borough of Horsham. No charter granting this status has ever been found, but for centuries it has been described as a borough by prescription, that is to say by immemorial custom.

The manorial history of Horsham is very complicated as there was a larger manor of the name which contained smaller manors such as Roffey, Chesworth, Hewells, and Tarring-cum-Marlpost, which all had parcels of land right in the middle of the borough. As this book is concerned with the town of Horsham, it is government within the borough boundaries which forms the subject of this chapter. These boundaries run approximately as follows. The southern boundary was the River Arun to a point behind 'Tanbridge House', then north to Springfield Road as far as Rushams Road, across the northern side of the park to a point beyond the railway station, south down New Street, a short way westward along Queen Street to approximately the Iron Bridge, then south again to the river. The extent of the borough is known from documentary descriptions only and not from any map, and is therefore approximate.

The Ancient Borough

Although completely dead today, the borough has been of much importance in times past, and should therefore be described here. It is one of the curious examples of the way in which Horsham loses things without bothering, a trait which will come up several times in this narrative.

How boroughs came into being is uncertain, but they may have originated under King Alfred. One of the chief characteristics of a borough was the granting of trading rights by

Parliamentary and Local Government

the lord, and that we certainly had from very early times in our history. There is some evidence that we were indeed a borough, both inferential and actual evidence. For example, whenever bailiffs have been found to make the Parliamentary return to the sheriff, that has indicated a borough, and at various crucial times when investigation has been made, it was agreed that Horsham *was* a borough. Such were the times when James I, in the midst of his complicated joustings with Parliament, instructed his Attorney-General, Francis Bacon, to check on the rights of certain boroughs, and also when petitions were made to Parliament for the unseating of elected members for alleged malpractices. The process of enquiry by Bacon in 1614 was a challenge demanding to know by what right (*Quo Warranto*) the Corporation (governing body) of the Borough of Horsham had to be a corporate body, using a common seal, making by-laws, holding courts, markets, fairs, and so forth. The Corporation through their attorney claimed that all these things had taken place since the time when the memory of man was not to the contrary, and that was that. Letters Patent were therefore issued in 1617 saying that everything was in order for the Corporation to exercise all the privileges they had enjoyed, and that we really were a borough. It is not without interest that when the town clerk was asked by the Historical Manuscripts Commission in 1837 to list the important documents in his keeping, the only ones he said he had were copies of these proceedings, nothing else!

In later years there were occasions to re-examine these claims in connection with the right to send two members to Parliament, and on 16 June 1715 the House of Commons agreed that Horsham was a borough by prescription, and again when the Parliamentary lawyers examined the Corporation's case on 14 December 1790.

Further evidence that Horsham was a borough at least as far back as 1235 is given in the Calendar of Close Rolls, 1234-37. In 1248 it was recorded that Horsham was represented as a borough by its own jury at the Eyre Court of that year, and from 1295 onwards it was always taxed as a borough. In that year also Edward I summoned the first

Parliament, which included two representatives from every borough, and Horsham sent Walter Burgeys and Walter Randolf. Only about 130 towns and cities in England received such a summons, which gives some idea of the importance of Horsham at that time. But were we not important with a large parish church with four clergy, a fair by royal charter from 1233, and an important baron living at Chesworth? True, we could find no royal charter of incorporation, but charters do not incorporate, they merely record a statement of fact, and in every known case in England where a Court Leet has been held, there has been a Corporation. So why then did Horsham's borough status fade out? This dates from the political control of the borough in the 18th century, when a seat in Parliament was no longer an obligation imposed by the king which many tried to avoid, even though some expenses were paid, but it became the key to preferment and to offices of considerable value, so from the 16th century onward there was increasing interest in the matter of obtaining a Parliamentary seat, accompanied by much bribery and jobbery.

Representation in Parliament

To see how this came about it is necessary to trace the development of Parliamentary representation. The Court Baron, by which the Lord Paramount exercised his authority, became by a gradual process the Corporation, and the corporators were the burgesses who had been allowed to compound for their services to the lord by a money payment. These burgesses were holders of land, with or without buildings, which the lord had granted to them and which were called burgages, and Horsham originally had fifty-two. The earliest known survey of these burgages is dated 1611, and it was made to meet the challenge which was known to be coming shortly from Francis Bacon as described earlier. From this survey it is possible to identify some of the ancient burgage tenements today, and the most prominent is at the junction of Park and North Streets, recently known as 'Greedie's' Cafe.

The burgesses each had votes for the two parliamentary candidates, and what was easier than for an unscrupulous person to buy the freehold of the burgage and thus buy the vote, for what could a humble citizen do when the voting was recorded in an open book for his landlord to inspect? In any case, it was sometimes not even necessary to turn the tenant out, as the deeds could be given to a bogus burgess whose vote was not in doubt, and this occurred with such cynical abandon that the deeds were called 'snatch papers' as they were snatched back after the election for using again at some future occasion. Worse still, as it was claimed that the holder of burgage deeds could have a vote, why should the tenement holding not be split to make two or more votes? This practice became so ridiculous and yet so freely allowed that at the 1705 election Dr. Robert Coe was shown to have leased a pair of gates in a timber yard to his brother-in-law, John Linfield, in 1702 for a rent of a shilling a year.

The first contested election at Horsham was in 1701. By the splitting of burgages the 52 in the survey of 1611 had become 54, and in spite of the Splitting Act of 1696 which said such things were illegal, nevertheless corrupt politicians got away with it time and again. Even before 1701 there was a good deal of competition to get on to the Burgess Roll, which was the list of members of the Court Baron which ran the town's affairs, but where Parliamentary representation was concerned the dust had all settled before election time. However, in 1701 the development of distinct political parties of Whig and Tory produced a contest. There were three candidates for the two seats, and most burgesses probably voted independently, returning John Wicker (who built 'Park House') and Henry Yates. The unsuccessful candidate, Henry Cowper, petitioned the House of Commons against the return on the ground of bribery of some of the voters by Wicker, who was also alleged to have got his brother-in-law made one of the Returning Officers. William III conveniently died, the petition was never heard, and another election ensued, with Yates withdrawing and Wicker and Cowper being returned unopposed. By the 1705 election Charles Eversfield of Denne Park had appeared as a candidate, having just reached the age of 21, and he topped the polling with Cowper next, and Wicker was unlucky. Eversfield was a member of Parliament for the next 36 years and was credited with the erection of a Market House, later the Town Hall. He had his portrait painted which can be seen on the staircase in Causeway House. His career was marked by corruption at the polls—already there were 60 burgages voting—and he made sure of getting both the Court Baron and the Court Leet in his pocket. For the 1713 election Richard Ingram appeared and this marked the beginning of the domination of the town by the Ingram family, a prominent one among the Whigs at Court. Richard was the second son of Lord Irwin of Temple Newsam in Yorkshire, who had married the daughter of John Machell of Hills place and thus come upon the Horsham scene. Richard Ingram made an alliance with the disappointed John Wicker, whom he used to buy votes through the usual bogus deeds, and by the 1713 election there were 67 burgages. He failed to defeat Eversfield or Middleton, and so petitioned on the grounds of bribery, which petition was never heard as frequently happened, particularly if it was inconvenient to the ruling party in Parliament. The year 1715 saw a real party election, Eversfield and Goring for the Tories, and two members of the Ingram family for the Whigs. The Tories apparently won, there now being 70 burgages, but the Ingrams petitioned successfully for them to be rejected, this time because the Returning Officer refused to accept genuine votes and accepted bogus ones. The John Linfield or Lindfield (spellings vary) mentioned earlier in connection with the timber yard gates was an attorney who acted as agent for the Tories, and among his corrupt practices was arresting for debt voters for the other side. The subsequent enquiry into the election caused the Committee to order Linfield into the custody of the Sergeant at Arms for 'divers illegal and unjustifiable practices', from which he was released three weeks later after 'he upon his knees received a Reprimand from Mr. Speaker and was discharged out of custody'.

The Ingrams came to terms with Eversfield about control of the borough, and agreed to nominate each one his own

Bailiff, the importance of this being that the Bailiffs were the returning officers, and when one of the Ingrams succeeded to the Irwin peerage, Eversfield took his place in Parliament unopposed. This cosy arrangement lasted for 26 years, and was further cemented by a marriage connection between the two families. Thus were the voters of Horsham sewn up in helplessness.

Splitting the Votes

Attention having been drawn to the practice of splitting burgages, a survey of the borough was made in 1723 to determine what had been going on, but whether this was commissioned by disgruntled voters or by the Eversfield/Ingram faction, nothing conclusive emerged. The partners in crime wrangled over complicated arrangements whereby Eversfield was to sell burgages he did not own to the Ingrams who had insufficient cash to pay for them anyway, but finally in 1737 in return for £6,000 Eversfield managed to get hold of 20 burgages which he handed over, and he bowed out of Parliamentary representation for Horsham. Just to make sure of enough votes, Henry Ingram, Lord Irwin, split yet more burgages, and the independence of the borough was lost for ever, and it will always remain a puzzle why the good people of Horsham put up with it with scarcely a murmur. In mitigation it should be said that many others among the boroughs became the personal property of the magnates, to be bought and sold by expert borough-mongers as though they were cheese. It is possible that the apparent disinterest of the Lords Paramount, the Dukes of Norfolk, was due to their being Roman Catholics who were under great disabilities at this time.

The stream of corruption flowed endlessly. Lord Irwin made the steward and clerk of the borough agent and steward to himself, and so got hold of the Borough records, his influence with the Duke of Newcastle who was Prime Minister obtained many offices of profit for his cronies, and the Court Baron and Court Leet saw their importance simply withered away. It will be recalled that the original rent of one shilling was due to the Lord Paramount from 52 burgages, but Lord Irwin had so split them up that it was not worth collecting a few pence here and there, and he simply paid the 52s. each year and enjoyed his investment. It is hardly to be wondered at under these circumstances that all trace of the boundaries and details of many of the burgages were lost for ever, which made many fees for the lawyers when subsequent elections brought up the matter of voting rights again. By 1764 the 52 had become 85.

No election was contested until 1790, the Ingrams being put in without opposition, even in one case when Charles Ingram was yet a minor. The Patronage Secretary in 1783 reported to King George III that Horsham's two seats were doubtful, and that 'Horsham is Lady Irwin's Borough (Lord Irwin died in 1778); has generally been got for the friends of the Government by attention and will probably be so again, but will require now a little more management'. So now even royalty was up to the neck in it.

The Duke of Norfolk Intervenes

Probably the reason why the 11th Duke of Norfolk began to consider the question of breaking the Irwin hold on Horsham was the arrival of Thomas Medwin as steward of the Court Baron. As a lawyer he had already acted for the Duke in various matters, and for Robert Hurst, a barrister who also had done business with the Duke. It is to the Medwin collection of papers, left to Horsham by William Albery and now in the Museum, that we owe so much for a picture of Horsham at the end of the 18th and beginning of the 19th century, as Medwin had his fingers in every conceivable pie in the town. He made a confidential survey for the Duke in 1787 which concluded that all his Grace had to do was to choose the returning officers by means of Medwin as steward, who only had to call for the election of a Court Leet jury such burgesses as he thought would favour the Duke. Simplicity itself, and the plot came to a head at the election of 1790 when the Duke, aided by Hurst and Medwin, ran two candidates who were elected because of

Parliamentary and Local Government

meddling with the Burgess Roll and with the Courts, and because the Duke had purchased the votes of some hitherto independent burgesses. However, his triumph was not to last as the unsuccessful candidates petitioned to upset the election, and they won the day. How far cynicism had gone in these matters was shown when the returning officers, sworn by oath to be impartial, obtained an indemnity from the Duke against any harm that might come to them as a result of anything they might do at this election. In spite of Medwin's activity as political agent to the two candidates of the Duke, as steward to the Court Baron, steward to the Court Leet, chief clerk of the poll, and for good measure town clerk as well, the rejected candidates were declared duly elected by the House of Commons Committee, who censured the returning officers, which unfortunates were also mulcted £800 in damages by the Judge of Assize, although as will be recalled they were indemnified by the Duke.

For 16 years there was again no contest when election time came round, but the Duke had not given up after all, and he took a leaf out of Lady Irwin's book by splitting up as many burgages as he could acquire, while the Lady on the other hand was doing exactly the opposite by piecing split votes together to make them more genuine and therefore more valid, albeit it made them also fewer. The election of 1806 was remarkable as the returning officers lost their nerve, making a double return on the grounds that on the one hand the Duke's candidates, who appeared to have most votes, were duly elected, and on the other, the Irwin candidates were also elected owing to the fierce objections of their supporters to alleged bogus votes for the Duke's men. So the House of Commons had to sort that one out, and it took then 11 days of sittings to conclude that the Duke's candidates were duly elected. Parliament only endured six months, so there was another election in 1807 at which the Duke's candidates again triumphed, but this time on petition were unseated. Nothing had changed except the constitution of the Committee of the House, but this was enough to tip the balance in Lady Irwin's favour.

Ironically one of the unsuccessful candidates was Sir Samuel Romilly, who went on to a great career of reforming the abuses of the criminal law and of slavery. Of his candidature for Horsham he wrote in his memoirs, 'This buying of seats is detestable; and yet it is almost the only way in which one in my situation, who is resolved to be an independent man can get into Parliament'.

The Duke Triumphs

Lady Irwin died before her petition was heard, and her estates went to her son-in-law, the Marquis of Hertford, who was quite happy to sell the lot to the Duke of Norfolk for over £90,000, including the Hills estate and all the burgages with their attendant votes, thus enabling the Duke to do what he liked with the Borough of Horsham, of which he was now both Lord Paramount as well as the parliamentary patron. Always a good man of business, the Duke got a good deal of the money back by simply enclosing Horsham Common for his own purposes. His friend Robert Hurst managed to get a Bill through Parliament along the lines of many such at this time, the basic argument being that land could be far better cultivated in large amounts than in small holdings, and the Enclosure Act of 1813 removed about a square mile of land from the ownership of the people of Horsham to that of the Duke, Robert Hurst, and a few others who were given 'awards' of various parcels, without any cost to themselves.

The successor to the 11th Duke, his cousin, took just as much interest in his pocket borough, and persuaded Robert Hurst to vacate his seat in 1829 so that the Duke's son, Lord Surrey, could represent Horsham. At the next election in 1831 both Surrey and Coulborn, the ex-members, did not have sufficient respect for Horsham to bother to turn up in the town all day, such were the depths to which Parliamentary representation had sunk. It is good to know that there was some resentment shown at this behaviour, as the *Brighton Gazette* reports:

> There was no Election, no dinner, no church bells, no anything; to the great mortification and discontent of the patriotic

Parliamentary and Local Government

Electors, and so indignant were the Band that they covered their instruments with crepe and marched round the town playing the Dead March in Saul.

Reform came at last in 1832, when rotten boroughs were swept away after the *Times* had suggested putting the culprits in Newgate gaol for breach of parliamentary privilege, but this was not the end of corruption. The townspeople were indeed glad that the Reform Bill was passed, and celebrated with a march round the town followed by a dinner in the park with 3,000 sitting down to cold beef, presided over by Thomas Sanctuary who had been High Sheriff of Sussex. Under the terms of the Bill, Horsham lost one member, the franchise was extended to every householder of £10 annual value, and the boundaries of the constituency were extended to include the whole parish rather than just the borough, so that 257 voters were now concerned and not just the burgesses, although still over half the householders of Horsham were ineligible to vote.

The first member elected under the new arrangements in 1832 was Robert Henry Hurst, son of the member from 1812 to 1829, who easily defeated Edward Blount, a member of the Duke of Norfolk's staff, as there were too many memories of the Duke's domination of the old borough. Hurst was unsuccessfully opposed by Thomas Broadwood (who built 'Holmbush') in 1835, although it was not such an easy run as Hurst's parliamentary performance had come under fire—he was not so radical in the House as he had professed to be. It was said that with a view to controlling votes as in the bad old days, Hurst bought numerous properties in and around the town. The increase in the franchise meant that it was no longer a matter of buying a majority of votes, but having 20 or 30 tenants to vote, for one might tip the balance. The voting in 1835 gave Hurst a lead of only three over Broadwood, and as the latter was alleged to have spent £10,000 on the election, he was not going to give up without a demand for a scrutiny, but this only reduced the Hurst lead to one. Voting was still open, and there was beginning the appalling practices of enticing voters away from the town on some pretext so that they

THE INDEPENDENCE OF THE BOROUGH OF HORSHAM

Exemplified.

(Copy note sent to the DUKE OF NORFOLK'S Tenantry.)

"Arundel, June 20th, 1841.

"Dear Sir,

"His Grace is anxious to assist Mr. Hurst in his Election for Horsham, do all you can to procure Votes for him.

"Yrs. truly,

"R. WATKINS."

Qy.---Who is *now* the Duke's Nominee?

Printed by C. Hunt, Horsham.

Fig. 2. Typical of the election handbills, this one endeavoured to identify the Duke of Norfolk's continuing interest in the borough.

Parliamentary and Local Government 53

could not vote, or getting them too drunk to mount the hustings, which customs were even more prevalent in later elections.

Death of the Court Leet

Although the Reform Act had done something to revive genuine political life in Horsham, its effect on the Corporation was literally fatal. The Duke of Norfolk, no longer interested in manipulating the Court Leets and the Bailiffs appointed thereby, did not bother to see that the Court Leet was held again, and as new legislation enabled the Sheriff of the County to appoint returning officers, bailiffs were no longer necessary for this purpose and simply ceased to exist.

Much the same contest took place at the 1837 election, when Hurst beat Broadwood by two votes, and this is the last we hear of Thomas Broadwood's parliamentary hopes. Hurst withdrew from the 1841 contest just before nomination day, after an immense amount of bribery to buy votes by the opposing candidate, Robert Scarlett, but when the latter succeeded to the peerage in 1844, Hurst came forward again, this time much more Tory than Radical, and was returned unopposed, having done his best to satisfy all political complexions.

By this time Hurst was in financial trouble, and in 1845 he went abroad without resigning his seat, and never again attended the Commons, thus leaving Horsham unrepresented for two years until the General election of 1847, one which will for ever be infamous in the history of Horsham. Hurst put up for sale his Holbrook estate, and it was suggested that the purchaser might also have the parliamentary representation of Horsham, so Seymour Fitzgerald bought Holbrook with just that idea in mind. His opponent was John Jervis, son of the Attorney-General who was incidentally related to Thomas Broadwood, and both sides set out to make this the most drunken election that Horsham has ever seen, Fitzgerald having his headquarters at the *Anchor* and Jervis at the *King's Head*. In the subsequent proceedings to untangle the allegations and counter-allegations of bribery and corruption, which fill many pages in the official report, evidence was given of enormous quantities of liquor being made available on every occasion, and Horsham's lone constable reported, 'I never in my life before saw such a drunken and riotous scene', while the *Brighton Gazette* said Horsham was deluged with drink. The stories of corruption at every level make astonishing reading. Henry Padwick, agent to the Hursts, was accused of offering the parliamentary seat to Fitzgerald for £1,000 to be paid on top of the price for the estate, after success at the election. There may have been some truth in this as a Speaker's warrant had been issued against Padwick on a previous occasion elsewhere on exactly the same charge, which Padwick avoided by going abroad. Nearly every publican in Horsham was instructed to give free drink to all comers, and at the first meeting of Fitzgerald and his supporters at the *Swan* it cost the candidate three dozen bowls of punch and 124 bottles of wine.

Besides treating practically the whole town to free drink, the candidates just as freely offered bribes to buy votes, and in evidence at the House of Commons it was stated that James, agent to Jervis, sat at the *Crown* with bags of gold in front of him to impress the voters, while Jervis's father, the Attorney-General, went around offering offices of profit. The Albery papers include lists of these bribes, about which there does not seem to have been the slightest fear of prosecution. It is refreshing to learn that Sir Henry Fletcher, a landowner on some scale in Horsham, refused to influence his tenants to vote either way.

The *Sussex Advertiser* described Fitzgerald's politics as 'amphibious', and said Jervis was standing for the independence of Horsham, but plain ambitions without political theory had never been so naked in the history of any of our elections. Jervis got in by 164 votes to 155, but his opponent lost little time in petitioning to upset the result, which was duly done by a House of Commons Committee declaring that Jervis was guilty of treating. Even in an age when elections were frequently corrupt, Horsham was the talk of

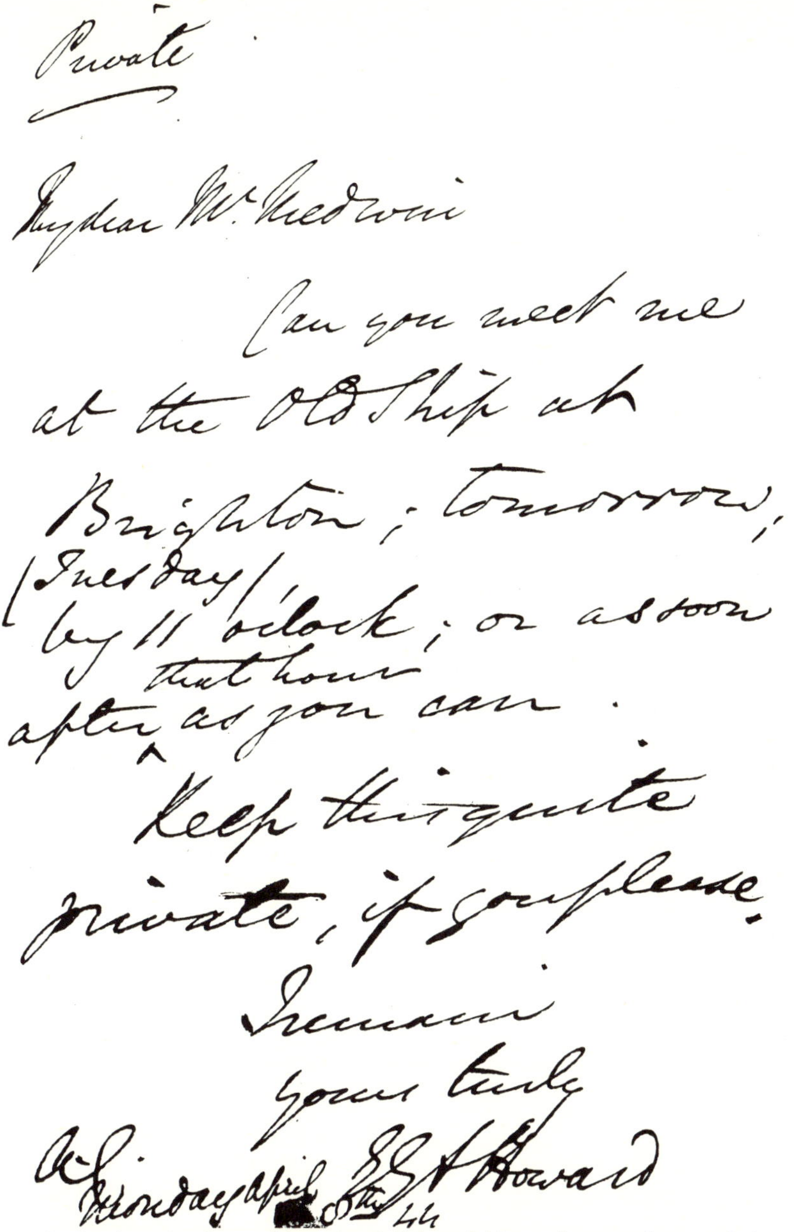

Private

My dear Mr Medwin

Can you meet me at the Old Ship at Brighton; tomorrow; (Tuesday) by 11 o'clock; or as soon after that hour as you can.

Keep this quite private, if you please.

I remain
yours truly
Monday April 8th /44   E J A Howard

Fig. 3. Intrigue in the making. Lord Edward Howard, second son of the 13th Duke of Norfolk, was elected M.P. for Horsham in 1848 by *not* bribing anyone. Pilfold Medwin, the addressee, was as deeply involved in political jobbery as his father, T. C. Medwin, had been.

the kingdom, even moving the Prime Minister, Lord John Russell, to introduce a Bill 'To promote further enquiry into Bribery and Corruption alleged to prevail in the Borough of Horsham', but it was not proceeded with as there were a number of other boroughs in the same state, and no one knew how far such an enquiry might go. A writ was issued for another election in 1848, when Lord Edward Howard stood instead of Jervis, again with Fitzgerald on the other side. It was cleverly contrived that Lord Edward Howard would bribe or treat no one, so when Fitzgerald obtained 182 votes and Howard 115, it was comparatively easy to petition successfully against Fitzgerald, who had spent something like £80,000 in vain, although remarkably enough he was elected eventually on four occasions.

A Widening Franchise

The Representation of the Peoples Act of 1867 widened the franchise considerably, every householder now being able to vote. Horsham politics were still not crystallised into ideologies, and the party organisations were personal to the candidates. In 1868 Major Aldridge, a landowner from St. Leonard's, was persuaded to try and turn out Robert Henry Hurst, junior, who had got elected in 1865, but on no real policy grounds. Hurst had the support of the majority of Horsham town voters, but Aldridge was backed by the country districts, and the result was a dead-heat with 380 votes each. Both candidates challenged the other over bribery, and various forms of cheating, which undoubtedly took place, but in the end Major Aldridge withdrew his petition and Hurst took his seat as Member. One wonders why a petition would be withdrawn in these circumstances, when time and money had got the candidate so very near his goal, but at the time it was said that Major Aldridge would have risked disqualification on account of malpractice anyway, whereas if he withdrew he could always fight again.

In the 1860s politics were beginning to be more defined in party terms. A 'Constitutional Association' was formed in 1869 for the Conservative Party, while the Liberals formed

Parliamentary and Local Government

their party under the presidency of Henry Michell, a successful brewer who had been Hurst's election agent earlier. The voting after 1868 was no longer open, and polling at least reduced the amount of intimidation and corruption, so that the 1874 election brought a most unaccustomed quiet. Gone, too, were the hustings in front of the town hall which had been the scene of such tumult, as the 1872 Ballot Act also stipulated several polling places with sealed boxes, as today. Seymour Fitzgerald had returned to Horsham, and stood as a Conservative against Robert Henry Hurst the Liberal. The result was a majority of 200 for Fitzgerald, in line with the rest of the country, but a year later Fitzgerald was given a lucrative office which necessitated his resigning, and back came Aldridge, now a colonel, as Conservative opponent to Hurst. Although on national issues there was no difference between them, on local matters Hurst was in favour of adopting the new Local Government Acts which would mean a Board to run much of Horsham's affairs, while Aldridge with the majority of the people was against this. In any case, the voting was going to be split four ways, as the famous temperance man, Jury Cramp, himself a Londoner, was giving his support to a temperance candidate from London, and an extraordinary person called Worth declared himself a candidate against Conservatism, Liberalism and Temperance, and in favour of nothing but Worth. This individual did manage to get going quite a number of local activities such as a local newspaper, the *Sussex Herald*, and various horticultural and poultry shows, and led a sizeable agitation for the revival of borough status for Horsham, but where he came unstuck was his dubious use of other people's names as his alleged supporters, and he soon faded from the scene, leaving only three candidates for the election.

Hurst managed to beat Aldridge by little more than a dozen votes in a poll of more than 800, and Richardson, the Temperance candidate, supported Horsham's reputation for having as many beershops as anywhere in the country by only getting five votes. There was the usual bribery and treating before the voting, and both Hurst and Aldridge made the inevitable charges against the other, although on consideration Aldridge thought it safer to rely only on the charge of paying certain expenses, and the following letter gives an example of how imprudent even lawyers can be on occasion:

> Dear Sir, We find your name on the Register. We shall be glad to hear if you will give your name to Mr. Hurst, in which case we shall be glad to pay your travelling expenses.
> We are, dear Sir, Yours obediently Medwin & Co.

So Robert Henry Hurst was unseated, but Colonel Aldridge still thought it safer not to claim the seat, and the Conservatives put up Sir Hardinge Giffard, who, although Solicitor-General, had tried four unsuccessful times to get a seat. The Liberal candidate was James Clifton Brown, not well known, but assured of support from all the Hurst party which included Henry Michell, and he was successful by a majority of over 50, there not being enough corruption this time to warrant the usual petition.

The 1880 election, at which Sir Henry Fletcher beat Clifton Brown by over 100 votes, was the last of the series. Constituencies were reorganised and the Horsham seat, based on the Parish of Horsham, became the North-west Division of the County of Sussex, thus ending a tradition of 600 years, and thus also putting a further nail in the coffin of the old Corporation, as its function in electing Bailiffs who would be returning officers had now no purpose. Gone also were the opportunities for the many kinds of jobbery such as tampering with the town hall clock to allow extra voting time, jailing voters for debt just before the election so that the other side had to pay their debts and get them released, or seeing agents arrive openly at the House of Commons with orders from the Duke of Norfolk to his puppet M.P.s on how they were to vote.

Some Horsham M.P.s

One way or another Horsham has had some remarkable Members of Parliament, famous and otherwise. Those elected in 1333, 1345 and 1421 were all indicted for burglary, assault, or deer-stealing, but largely escaped punishment. Henry Husse (1529) was one of the Commissioners sent round by Edward VI to list all the valuables remaining to the church after the Reformation, and Peter Osbourn (1563) was Keeper of the Privy Purse to the same monarch. John Middleton (1624) bought 'Hills Place' in 1608, and his son, Thomas (1640) at first took sides with Cromwell and became Deputy Lieutenant for Sussex, but later hindered the Commonwealth Committee in Horsham, for which he was imprisoned in 1648 and his estates seized. However, his appeal in 1651 was successful and by an amusing muddle he got back more than he lost, as he was repaid not only by Parliament for lost rents, but also by the man who was ordered to receive these rents. Always on the Royalist side was Sir John Boroughe (1624, 1625 and 1626), who was a trusted member of the court of Charles I during the Civil War. Sir John Covert (1661), one of the biggest landowners in Sussex, was captured when the parliamentary forces stormed Chichester in 1642.

When popular democracy was unknown it was much easier to establish dynastic successions. Three members of the Ingram family sat between 1715 and 1761, all becoming later Lords Irwin, but the most famous parliamentary family was that of the Hursts, recorded as property owners from an early date in Horsham. Until the restoration of the parish church in 1865 there used to be a memorial stone to Robert Hurst of Hurst Hill, who died in 1483. He lived in the 'Moated House' under Hurst Hill, and this considerable mansion has now disappeared. Three of his descendants represented Horsham between 1812 and 1875. First, Robert Hurst, elected 1812, 1818, 1820, 1826, and 1827, and becoming Father of the House; his son, Robert Henry Hurst sat in 1832, 1835, 1837, and 1844; and his grandson, Robert Henry Hurst, junior, in 1865, 1868, and alas! was unseated on petition in 1875.

The Burgess Vote Fade-out

One result of the manipulation of votes that went on for a century or more was the loss of identity of true burgess votes, as the burgage tenements had been split and rejoined so many times, with the deeds being forged and handed round among numerous individuals. The gates of a timber yard have already been mentioned as purporting to allow a vote, and the House of Commons Committee enquiring into the matter in 1715 were also told of 'a certain narrow way, being a wain-way' as having the same privilege. Several voters did not even know where their property was supposed to be, never having set eyes on it, and merely obliging their patrons by accepting the deeds and a few guineas. The last known genuine burgess vote was exercised by Pilfold Medwin in 1880, who as the second and only surviving son of Thomas Medwin, agent to the Duke in electoral battles a century before, had inherited his father's burgage.

How the Borough Died

The origin of the Borough of Horsham may have been obscure, but its demise was clearly seen, and the greater part of the responsibility for this must be laid at the doors of various Dukes of Norfolk and members of the Irwin family. In the 1530s the then Duke said, 'In times past, I could have made burgesses at Horsham', an early example of patronage, but the real trouble was in the 18th and 19th centuries when the burgesses were so nobbled that the usual borough machinery for election of officers was simply a waste of time, and everyone lost interest in their own local government as there was nothing they could do about it any more than they could about parliamentary representation; the municipal and parliamentary franchise went together. The steward presiding over the Lord Paramount's Court Leet was the town clerk, and when this Lord was the Duke of Norfolk he saw to it that the annual feasts of the Court Leet were sufficiently sumptuous as to stifle any possible resentment about the impotence of the Corporation until the next feast came around, but after the Reform Act was passed in 1832 the Duke lost interest and the 1834 Court Leet was the last. With its usual habit of letting things go, Horsham failed to use the Municipal Corporations Act of

Parliamentary and Local Government

1835 to revive the Corporation. The Government realised that boroughs were oligarchies riddled with corruption, and by this Act imposed a uniform system for all boroughs. But Horsham preferred to muddle on, having already seen its Corporation decayed and its other privileges of holding punitive and administrative courts removed to the Sessions, while the Vestry adopted the Lighting and Watching Acts, which at any rate was something in line with the changing political scene everywhere else. Lighting consisted of gas lamps round the town, which were a great improvement on the lanthorn which John Baker's boy carried to light him from 'Park House' to the 'Manor House' in 1770. Watching involved a force of watchmen, appropriately clothed and armed with staves, and the provision of a town fire engine for the first time. Both Lighting and Watching were supervised by inspectors elected by the ratepayers, who now had four separate bodies regulating their daily lives—the parish organisation embodied in the Vestry, the Parish Highway Board, the Poor Law Guardians, and the inspectors. Further local government acts in 1848 and 1858 continued the programme of municipal reform but they left Horsham quite unimpressed until the Home Office in 1858 held an enquiry into the extent of the town boundary, and this stirred things up. Robert Henry Hurst, junior, whose father had been M.P., for some time had been concerned at the backwardness of Horsham's local government arrangements, and he chaired a committee to investigate the desirability of adopting some of these new acts, which endeavour was furthered by an outbreak of scarlet fever in 1862 which highlighted the public health situation, but still the point of doing anything about the matter was not reached.

There then ensued a situation not unlike the present day, when the ratepayers living outside the town saw no reason why they should contribute to schemes carried out inside it. Sewers and paving in Horsham were paid for by ratepayers in all the parish, and the country people overlooked the fact that their highways were also being paid for by the town's ratepayers, to the extent of 40 per cent. If the Acts were adopted and a Local Government Board set up in Horsham, the expenditure would be separated, so by 1874 Robert Hurst, as one of the churchwardens, obtained sufficient support from his fellow churchwardens and others to call a public meeting at the Town Hall to consider whether or not to try for a warrant of incorporation for the borough. He seems to have had second thoughts about borough status, because before the meeting was held he said it was not worth while trying for it, and it would be far better to adopt the local government acts, so the meeting took place without the presence of Robert Hurst or indeed either of the other two churchwardens. However, enough public interest had been engendered, and after a poll of the inhabitants showed 518 in favour and 222 against, the Local Government Board for Horsham was set up, consisting of 15 members headed by Robert Hurst, who received the largest number of votes. The first task the Board tackled was drainage, which as elsewhere at this time was one of the biggest causes of disease. Wells and open drains existed near each other throughout the town, but in 1878 the site at Hills farm was purchased for a sewage works, and in the same year the Horsham Water Works was bought by the Board.

Horsham Town Hall

The Town Hall used to be known as the Market House, and clearly that is what it was from time immemorial. The lower portion was an open arcade in which stalls were set up, and the upper floor was used for the town's public business. There was more than one occasion when the judges sitting upstairs complained of the noise downstairs. When the Eversfield family came into Horsham in the 17th century they were anxious to move up the social scale. John Eversfield in 1574 was the owner of some prosperous ironworks in Kent, Sussex and Surrey, and lived at Worth. His son, Thomas, bought the Denne estate for £5,500 in 1604 and soon after built a mansion there. He became Sheriff of Sussex, and his son Anthony was Horsham's M.P. four times between 1678 and 1688, and the latter's nephew and heir

Parliamentary and Local Government

was M.P. eight times between 1705 and 1741. At some time unknown the Eversfield family appears to have given the Market House to the town, and all the various courts met there—assizes, the Lord Paramount's Court Baron and Court Leet, sessions, and others. Like any other building, the Town Hall, as it had become, needed maintenance, but the local government machinery being so much in thrall and inactive, as we have seen, nobody undertook the task, and a meeting of the justices in 1808 seemed largely in favour of demolishing and rebuilding. As with many such matters, nothing was done, and the complaints multiplied until at the 1812 assizes the Lord Chief Baron joined his voice to those of the many other complainants, and it was proposed to remove the assizes altogether to Lewes, which had a fine new hall.

This is where the Dukes of Norfolk enter the Town Hall story. In order to prevent the loss of the assizes to Horsham, the 11th Duke offered to do up the Town Hall provided he could continue to hold his courts as Lord Paramount, having become such by his purchase of the Marquis of Hertford's Irwin estates. The site may have been rightfully the Duke's, but the building was supposed to belong to the town as a gift from the Eversfields, although the town seemed to be unaware of this.

The Duke spent a great deal of money on the enlargement of the structure, placing the three coats of arms on the north end, the royal arms being flanked by his own and those of the borough (the latter being derived from those of de Braose). The clock was added in 1820. The inscription on the large bell reads:

> His Grace the Duke of Norfolk presented the new Town Hall clock Anno Domini 1820. R. Hurst Esq., and J. Torne, Bailiffs: R. Steadman, gent., Town Clerk: Sir John Aubrey, Bart., and Robert Hurst, Esq., Members of the Borough.
>
> Whose praise and fame I'll speak and tell,
> As long as I remain a bell,
> And after death I hope and trust,
> They'll all be numbered with the just.

Those responsible in later years allowed the supporting timbers to rot, rendering the bells unsafe, and there has recently been such lack of interest in the town's heritage that a suggestion was made in the District Council that the bells be sold for scrap! However, they have been removed from the Town Hall and rescued by those who have a better sense of responsibility, and they may be seen in the Museum.

Even the Duke's measure did not quieten the complaints from the legal gentry, and in spite of the thousands spent on the place, real decay of the structure set in so that there was great fear of the roof falling, or of the judges being precipitated through the floor into the cells beneath. Only 20 years after the rebuilding, in 1832, a committee was got together after much discussion to consider what was to be done about it. Plans were drawn up for a very large building, about three times the size of the present one, done by a London architect named Abraham, who captivated the authorities with his 'Saxon' style. The site was to be in the Carfax about where the bandstand is now, the land being presented by the 12th Duke of Norfolk, although it was not really his to give. Deeds back to the 14th century show that there was not a single burgage tenure in the whole of the Carfax area. which meant that it must have been an open space belonging to the town as a whole, but once the Corporation started quite unlawfully selling off parcels of land in the 17th century or earlier, there was nothing to stop the Duke of Norfolk or anyone else subsequently buying up those parcels.

The committee which was supposed to do something about the tottering Town Hall met and met again, and achieved nothing except to decide that as the assizes had been wholly removed from Horsham by 1830, there was no need for judges' rooms and so forth, and such a large building as Abraham's was not needed, quite apart from the question of cost. Nevertheless, the committee made a report at the Epiphany Sessions 'expressing their thanks to His Grace the Duke of Norfolk for the handsome manner in which he has offered the proposed scite (in the Carfax) and old materials'. In the end the Duke offered to present the Town Hall as it stood (just) to the town, but such was the state of local government there was no town council or any similar authority to receive it. In 1867 a public meeting agreed to accept the gift in trust on a lease of 99 years for £1 a year, three local worthies being appointed as trustees to act as a committee of management until such time as there might be a proper town authority. But funds had to be raised, because the building had at least to be patched up, so private subscriptions were obtained and the building mortgaged to the Horsham Building Society for £288 15s. 0d. Thus the Town Hall was in full and unshored use again for quarter sessions and any other public use, and in 1888 brought even more distinction to the town when the West Sussex County Council, formed in that year, met within its walls. Just before this the Duke agreed to sell the freehold to the town for £25, and the building was demolished except for the north front with its coats of arms, and entirely rebuilt much as it is today.

Could the Borough be Revived?

To return to the matter of the defunct borough, there have been some attempts to revive it, but none even within sight of success. Probably the best chance of achieving this was in the days of Robert Henry Hurst, junior, whose influence on the town's affairs and whose public activities were considerable, but although he was much concerned with bringing into being a proper town government by adopting public acts such as Public Health 1848 and Local Government 1858, he thought it not worthwhile obtaining a new charter of incorporation, and without his support there was insufficient interest in the matter to do anything about it. The question was brought up in 1862 and 1874, but it largely lost its original significance in 1894 when the Urban District Council was formed and took over the powers of the Local Board. In 1911 the Council was moved to consider the possibility once again, but in view of a majority in favour of only one vote, it was dropped. This was not good enough for the newly-formed Chamber of Trade, which was strongly in favour, and was somewhat jealous of the Council. Once again the Council considered the matter, and, produced the same voting result, and again nothing was done, and there the matter rested.

What, it may be asked, would have been the advantages of re-establishing borough status for Horsham? After looking at other boroughs, a case may be made that the civic pride which ensues from possession of a mayor and corporation does instil in a town a community spirit greater than Horsham possesses. We should perhaps be more aware of what Horsham really means, and what it has lost through lack of self-interest. On the other hand, the Urban Council during its life from 1894 to 1974 did provide a lot of service for the town, but without at any time appearing to know what sort of town it wanted. Perhaps this is the reason why Horsham has lost so much in its history—lack of any real idea of what it wanted to be, and lack of firm enough leadership to counteract apathy. Only at the time of the Civil War was Horsham really politically aroused (the food riots in the 1840s were economic). As a market town, we had one of the County Committees appointed by the Commonwealth Parliament meeting here, and powerful it was, but as the majority of Sussex gentry were Royalist, it will be seen in Chapter Five how the town was threatened with burning, and how the townspeople guarded the store of arms in the Market Hall against possible seizure by Cromwell's men. In 1673 one report spoke of Horsham as the 'shire town', and indeed for centuries the assizes were held here, so were quarter sessions. Up to the 1920s the town hall was the meeting place of the County Council, and the 1832 report on the town hall had used the term 'Shire Hall' for the old building, so we have been the administrative capital of West Sussex. We had the County Gaol for 300 years, and now we have lost the lot, even the public lavatories in the Carfax where the bus terminus is said to have 1,000 bus movements a day. Perhaps in another generation we shall not be the ancient and much respected town of Horsham, but a suburb of Greater Crawley.

Parliamentary and Local Government

Courts and Justices

Quarter sessions having been superseded together with the assizes by crown courts in 1972, they have become relegated to the history books, but their importance to Horsham was considerable. They were quarterly meetings of Justices of the Peace, which office is an ancient one replacing the manorial court functions in Tudor times. The justices had administrative as well as criminal responsibilities and in fact were our local government. A Tudor commentator said of them in 1583, 'there was never in any commonwealth devised a more wise, a more dulce and gentle, nor a more certaine way to rule the people, whereby they are kept alwaies as it were in a bridle of good order'. Appointed by a county commission, they were practically rulers of the county until the 19th century, when the local boards for health, highway, guardianship of the poor and so forth replaced quarter sessions, leaving only the licensing and criminal functions. Alehouse licences were granted by a single Justice, so the opportunities for corruption and for playing off one against the other were tremendous, but in 1650 licensing became part of the duty of petty sessions.

The justices gradually replaced the sheriff as the organ of local government, but Sussex did not have its own sheriff until 1565, there being only one appointment of the king's executive officer for Surrey and Sussex jointly. In the middle ages the office was one of great profit as the sheriff collected money due to the king, but as far as Horsham is concerned he was responsible for the gaol, for looking after the justices, he acted as returning officer for elections, and he was particularly in the 18th century a figure of considerable social distinction, which explains why Sir Charles Eversfield and others equally ambitious were keen on holding the office. Honours have not always been sought after, that of knighthood in medieval times meant supplying men, arms and services to the king at one's own expense, and as late as 1630 Charles I raised some badly needed money by fining three Horsham worthies who declined the honour. They were Richard White (£10), Hall Ravenscroft, who lived in the Manor House and was later a prominent Puritan

(£10), and John Lintott (£12). Today we may grumble at the amount of money raised from us by rates and taxes, but at least they are not so inequitable as earlier taxes on hearths, windows and soap.

We have a lot to be thankful for in that our local government today is neither a feudal lord of fickle temper, nor a corrupting oligarchy. The measures which control our affairs have been democratically decided, even if we do not like all of them. If only more interest were taken in what was going on, and if more votes went into the ballot boxes . . . Horsham, like any other community, gets the government it deserves.

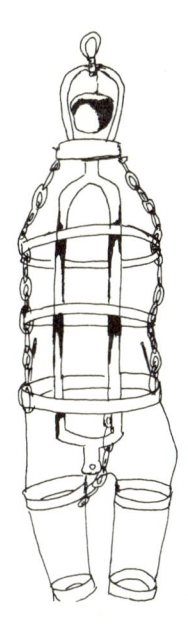

Chapter Three

CRIME AND PUNISHMENT

WHATEVER ONE'S FEELINGS may be about the crime rate nowadays, it is difficult to maintain that there were no periods when crime was not very much worse. In Anglo-Saxon times, civilisation and Christianity had at least modified the ancient 'eye for an eye' concept so that instead of personal vengeance the injured party had to accept a pecuniary redress, but for some centuries after that, if the sovereign or feudal lords wanted to punish a rebellion, for instance, wholesale hangings of guilty and innocent alike were not unknown. Offences against authority were the most heavily punished, but offences against property were the most severely condemned by the community.

The Constable

The unfortunate who had the first responsibility for law and order was the constable, an unpaid man who was compelled to take the duty for a year, although later on it was permissible to pay someone else to perform the task instead. A report to Quarter Sessions in 1646, 'Hy. Michell chosen last Friday as one of the Constables of the Borough departed to avoid serving the office' is typical of many, and it is little wonder that law and order was most inefficiently maintained by means such as this. So little regarded was the constable's office that it was considered a joke to make a dissenting minister a constable. The method of choosing the constables in Horsham from medieval times was appointment by the Steward at the annual Court Leet of two men from a list of four burgesses prepared by the bailiffs, but after the 17th century the bailiffs made the appointments themselves. Broadly, the duties of the constables were to keep watch and ward within the confines of the Borough, and to do this they had the assistance of petty constables called headboroughs or tythingmen, who had a sector of the town each. Customarily an appointment was made for each of the four streets, North, South, East, and West, and another for the Carfax.

The constables were responsible for looking after the instruments of punishment such as the stocks, whipping post, pillory and tumbril, and they were expected to deal with vagrants, rioters, and any other offenders as ordered by bailiffs or justices. They also had charge of the arms kept by the borough in case of tumult, and reference to Chapter Five will show how difficult this was in the time of the Civil War. In the 18th century the degree of lawlessness was such that people took the law into their own hands and in 1785 formed the Horsham Society for Prosecuting Thieves and Felons. This organisation issued handbills and put up posters offering rewards for the arrest of persons accused of a variety of offences, mainly robbery in some form or another. The rapid dissemination of information into the surrounding districts was undoubtedly a factor in the success of the Society, but the appointment of a paid constable under the act of Parliament of 1839, and subsequently the establishment of county police in 1857, made the Society redundant, and it ended more as a social club in 1858.

Crime and Punishment

The Court Leet

The Court Leet of the Lord Paramount, established under Norman rule, dealt only with minor offences. It lost a lot of its importance when assizes were established in the 13th century, at which any indictable offence could be tried. It still continued to punish minor offenders for such things as neglecting to keep the highway in front of their doors in good repair, for depositing rubbish and ordure on the highway, for assault and battery, for selling produce outside the market, for short weight or measure, for refusing to take up public offices such as juror. Towards the end of the 18th century the Court Leet ceased to have much significance and met but infrequently. This was because the entire lack of interest in the borough on the part of the Lord Paramount the Duke of Norfolk, his rival Lord Irwin having completely sewn up the borough politically.

Quarter Sessions

The next court of law in order or importance was the meeting of the justices in quarter sessions, begun in 1362, although minor charges could be dealt with by two or more justices at petty sessions. The administrative side of quarter sessions has been dealt with in Chapter Two, but mention must be made here of the judicial work of the Horsham sessions which took place from 1626 to 1939, but not continuously as they were also held at Chichester, Midhurst, Petworth, Steyning, and Arundel. From 1940 they were held at Chichester only until they, together with the assizes, were abolished and replaced by crown courts. The sessions were social occasions as well as judicial ones, and brought much trade to the town, so that when there was reluctance to hold them in the Town Hall at the beginning of last century because it was in imminent danger of collapse, there were many townspeople in favour of the rebuilding.

Quarter sessions dealt with a wide range of offences. In 1647 Richard Gander and Agnes his wife were fined 3s. 4d. for eavesdropping, and in 1649 'Jana Hatkins spinster alias wife of Abraham Hatkins guilty of stealing a shirt worth

10d.—whipped'. Until the 18th century quarter sessions could impose the death penalty, but most such cases were reserved for the assizes. The first assizes were in the 12th century, but they were sporadic until 1285, when travelling judges visited certain towns on circuits. The first recorded assize in Horsham was in 1306, when 22 criminal and 57 civil cases were enquired into, which underlines the fact that many people had to wait unduly long for their cases to be heard. There are records of assizes in Sussex before this at Lewes and Chichester, and as there was only one Sheriff for both Surrey and Sussex until 1565, some Horsham miscreants were sent to Guildford assizes. The first recorded crime to our discredit was noted at Lewes assizes in 1248: 'Unknown malefactors came by night to the house of Lucy de Chichester and bound her and her two sons and carried away their goods', but no criminal, no trial or punishment.

Like quarter sessions, the assizes brought much trade and many people to Horsham and the opening of the assizes was a great occasion marked by a ceremonial entry of the judges into the town with a retinue of javelin men, trumpeters and footmen. They were met at the borough boundary by the Sheriff and officers of the borough and the procession entered the town to the ringing of the church bells. The javelin men were local farmers who dressed up in gay uniforms and carried painted staves with steel tips, one of which was presented to the Museum. That they made an impression is noted by the *Sussex Weekly Advertiser* in 1804: 'Sheriff J. Dent, Esquire, made a remarkably neat appearance, his javelin men all young yeoman were dressed in handsome blue coats, buff striped waistcoats, buckskin leather breeches and top boots'. John Baker's diary in 1772 shows how the uncertain state of the roads made the time of arrival of the judges erratic. On the first evening the vicar preached an assize sermon before the knights of the shire, the judges and other notables, and on the next day the business of swearing the juries took place.

The amount of civil and criminal business at each assize could vary considerably, but one of the unhappy features

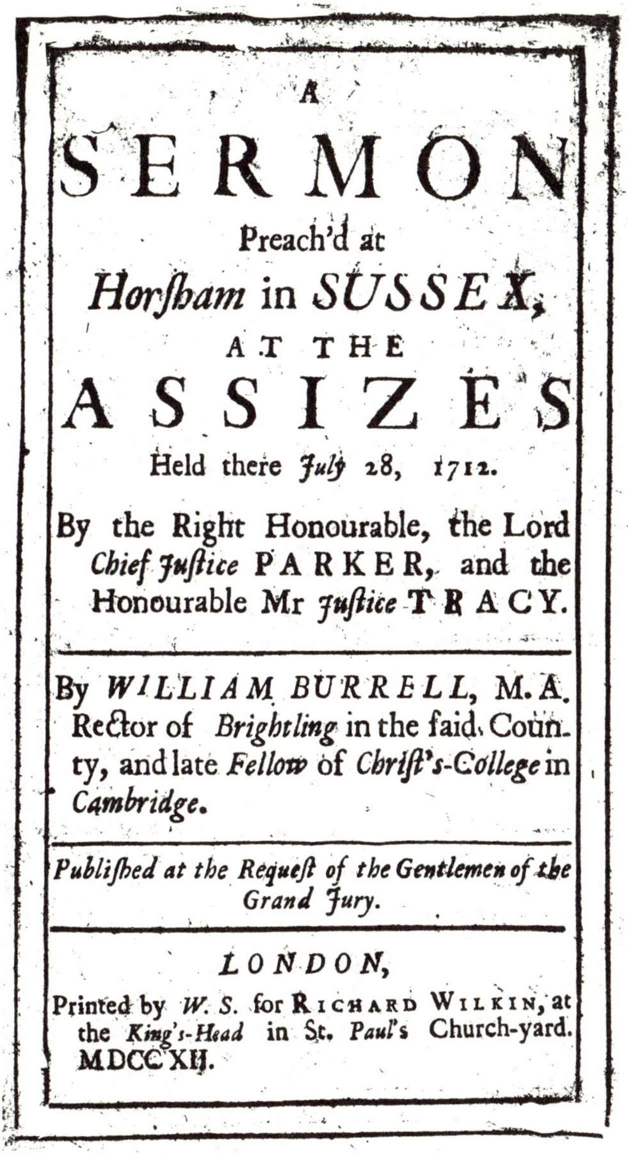

A SERMON

Preach'd at *Horsham* in SUSSEX,

AT THE

ASSIZES

Held there *July* 28, 1712.

By the Right Honourable, the Lord Chief *Justice* PARKER, and the Honourable Mr *Justice* TRACY.

By *WILLIAM BURRELL*, M.A. Rector of *Brightling* in the said County, and late *Fellow* of *Christ's-College* in Cambridge.

Published at the Request of the Gentlemen of the Grand Jury.

LONDON,

Printed by *W. S.* for RICHARD WILKIN, at the *King's-Head* in St. *Paul's* Church-yard. MDCCXII.

Fig. 4. It is doubtful how ardent the request of the Grand Jury was for the printing of this Assize Sermon, or indeed whether many of them could read it.

was the retention in gaol for six months or more from one assize to another of those who were remanded for some reason. With so many crimes liable to be punished with death, bail was rare.

The courts were held in the building now known as the Town Hall, but until not much more than 100 years ago it was called the Market House, as this is what it started out to be. The lower floor was open as it consisted merely of arches and pillars, a commonly found design for markets, but when the assizes were held the arches were boarded up so that one could meet upstairs and one on the ground floor, but it must have been very draughty and there were many complaints. The cells were below the ground level, and may still be seen. Horsham kept its assizes for nearly 500 years, but when the turnpike roads improved in the late 18th century there was less opposition on the part of the judges to going as far into the Sussex mud as Lewes, and that fact together with the dreadful state of the Town Hall, described in the last chapter, settled the matter and the assizes were not held in Horsham after 1830, much to the disgust of all those who profited from all the extra business. From 1800 the assizes were divided between Lewes and Horsham, and the final factor was the building of a new county hall at Lewes, in spite of a temporary reprieve when the Duke of Norfolk spent a good deal of money on the Town Hall on enlargement, permanently closing in the arches and so forth. There were always problems over sufficient accommodation, which prudent persons arranged well in advance. Besides the witnesses, lawyers, jurors, prisoners' families, court officials and so on, there were hosts of hangers-on who looked to picking up a bit of business from holding the carriage horses of the bigwigs to printing ballads about the condemned, to be sold at the execution site to the crowds who always attended such occasions.

Hanging the Only Remedy

Punishment under Anglo-Saxon and Norman rule was often brutal in the extreme, but the more barbarous

Crime and Punishment

mutilations had largely died out by Tudor times. Nevertheless the punishment for any serious crime until the 17th century was almost invariably hanging, and what constituted serious crime 200 years ago seems strange to us today. Again the concept that property is sacrosanct comes through strongly. At the peak of the desperate legislation against lawlessness last century there were 223 crimes on the statute book which could be punished by hanging. It was only in 1828 that petty treason was abolished, and this crime included coining and killing of husband by wife or master by servant, death by burning being the penalty sometimes used for females on the curious ground that a female body should not be publicly mangled. In 1598 Robert Johnson, a labourer of Horsham, was sentenced to be hanged for making two twopenny pieces from tin, and forgery of a £5 note was similarly dealt with in 1808. Juveniles were not immune—a boy of 14 was sentenced to death for stealing a banknote from a letter, but the sentence was commuted to transportation for life. Edith Lavendar, an unmarried mother of 17, was hanged for killing her baby in 1799.

The Wages Riots

The hungry '40s in the last century produced a crop of sentences for rick-burning and smashing of agricultural machinery, two boys of 15 being sentenced to death in 1821 for firing a rick, although they were transported to Australia instead. The wages riots had subsided by 1869 when we find a youth was merely fined £1 and costs for a similar offence. The fear of farmers and other property owners was heightened by the absence of any effective means of keeping law and order other than constables and special constables reluctantly sworn in for the occasion when things got really hot, so the sentences at the assizes were correspondingly savage, in spite of occasionally sympathetic juries. The genuine mobbing for higher wages also cloaked extortion rackets when bands of men went round the Horsham houses demanding money, which in view of the high state of tension in the town, was usually given, but Lord Melbourne, the

Home Secretary, wrote strongly to the Horsham magistrates observing 'with great regret that the Justices of the Peace and others have in many instances (been) under the influence of intimidation', whereupon the magistrate felt constrained to fill the gaol with men waiting for the assizes on charges of arson, robbery, and machine smashing. Five were hanged.

The Gallows

Executions took place on Horsham Common until 1775 at a spot about halfway up the King's Road until the new gaol was built in Queen Street, when the gallows were located at the 'Hanging Plat' between Hernbrook Drive and Sandeman Way, off the Brighton Road and again on the Common, which extended right round the north of Horsham from Rusham's Road to the Brighton Road. In 1822 the system was adopted of a special gallows erected for each occasion outside the walls of the gaol in Queen Street, where the last execution in Horsham took place in 1844. These public executions (there were eight in 1790) were supposed to be a deterrent to others, but they also drew forth from the people the most appalling exhibitions of depravity. Fictitious confessions were printed and circulated among the crowd, pedlars offered food and drink, the whole atmosphere was a carnival one, and the authorities usually managed to order the execution either on a fair day or at least on a Saturday market day. Sometimes people paid a penny to see the body afterwards, occasionally females with scrofula would ask the executioner to touch their necks with the dead man's hand for a cure, an ancient nostrum. The bodies were sometimes claimed by relatives, but between 1752 and 1832 they were given to doctors for dissection; after this time they were buried within the precincts of the gaol. In earlier days the bodies were buried in the south-west corner of the churchyard, the Parish Register not always mentioning the names, but just the fact that they were executed criminals. Until 1834 the practice of hanging in chains or gibbets was used for particularly bad murderers or cases of highway robbery, especially if the mails were involved.

Crime and Punishment

The End of Public Executions

Apart from the unhealthy interest taken by the people of the town in the executions, there were some revolting scenes when attempts were made to revive the hanged men (and women, two of whom were among the five hanged on 29 June 1606). Perhaps the worst occasion was the execution of the soldier, Edward Broadbent, in 1819, who had shot dead a bullying sergeant. The rope to hang him was too long, and his feet touched the ground when the cart moved away, so a hole was dug beneath them to complete the slow death of this unfortunate. Legislation in 1837 reduced capital crimes to murder and treason only, which at least reduced the number of executions, but Horsham was at last freed from these atrocious spectacles after 1844. It was at the last execution that the Rev. Jarvis Kenrick preached a sermon in St. Mark's church at which he vehemently condemned public hangings, which had the effect of encouraging some of the teachers to take their pupils for a walk up Denne Hill while the execution was taking place.

That the whole grisly process did not only affect spectators is shown by this extract from the *Sussex Daily News* of 29 January 1749. 'We hear from Horsham that one Day last week, Robert Clarke, Executioner there, hanged himself with a Bridle, in the Hayloft belonging to the *Anchor Inn* at Horsham. The Cause of his committing this rash Action, was his being entrusted with half a Guinea to pay for a Pig, which money he lost at All-Fours, instead of paying for the Pig. The place is vacant and will be conferr'd on them that can make the best interest'.

Burning at the Stake

Not every execution was by hanging. The penalty for *petit treason* was sometimes burning at the stake, and in 1752 Anne Whale poisoned her husband with the aid of her cousin, Sarah Pledge, resulting in the former being burnt after strangling at Broadbridge Heath, and the latter hanged there. Ann Cruttenden, a widow of 80 years, was burnt after being hanged on Horsham Common in 1776, the diary of John Baker recording that she was such a small woman and the crowd so great that he could see nothing of her as she was carried past 'Park House' on the way to execution.

Other Punishments

At one time every felony except petty larceny (theft of property less than a shilling in value) was punishable by death, but certainly by the 18th century about half of the condemned were reprieved. The early assizes, therefore, either sentenced to death or acquitted in the majority of cases, but there were other punishments inflicted at quarter sessions and assizes, the commonest of which was whipping 'until the back be bloody'. This was applied to men and women alike, after 1772 the sentence omitting the sanguinary details, but the last man to be whipped at the cart's tail was in 1805. An order was made in 1819 that Scottish and Irish paupers should be passed on to the ports for shipment home instead of being whipped, which was the fate of most vagrants. The pillory was a particularly unfair mode of punishment as it depended on the feelings of the crowds whether the victim was assaulted and pelted with filth or whether if the mob was sympathetic he would not be well looked after and even feted. It was awarded most frequently for libel against authority (perhaps here the crowd was favourable), false weights and measures (here the populace would exact its own vengeance), perjury, and forgery. Branding on the hand or cheek was found to have no effect on the crime rate, and was discontinued towards the end of the 18th century. The truce between Church and State in medieval times allowed the clergy to be tried by ecclesiastical courts which were much more lenient, and anyone could claim the privilege of clergy by simply proving that he could read. This device was often used by accused persons, but to prevent a layman getting away with it more than once, which was not permissible, he was burned on the hand to record his first conviction. Sussex assizes dealt with 'Foster, John, of Horsham, husbandman, indicted for grand larceny. On 15 Oct. 1580 at Handcross, he stole £22 in money

Crime and Punishment 79

from Richard Curtis, bishop of Chichester. Guilty; allowed clergy'. Although now subject to the bishop's court, Foster would not have been hanged as he certainly would otherwise have been by the assize verdict. Benefit of clergy was finally abolished in 1827.

Transportation

The most usual consequence of a reprieve from capital punishment was a sentence of transportation for a term of years, or for life. For over 100 years until the loss of the American colonies in 1776 the convicts were transported thither, but when that was no longer possible they were kept in the hulks of old ships moored in the Thames under the most dreadful conditions of squalor. The discovery of Australia gave a welcome opportunity to get rid of the convicts from 1787 onwards, and very many were transported there either as a sentence in the first instance or as an alternative to hanging. The cruel part of the punishment was the tearing away of the convict from wife and family, who were often consigned to the poor house as a result. Even children of 11 years and upwards were transported, and about one-tenth of all convicts so dealt with were female. Two boys of 15 were sentenced for stealing from the *Anchor* inn in 1816, and another of the same age for stealing a watch, and yet another for theft of a handkerchief. The Establishment was indeed anxious to protect its property.

Pressing to Death

Horsham gained notoriety as the last place in England where pressing to death, or *peine forte et dure*, was practised. The man concerned was John Weekes of Fittleworth, who was arraigned in 1735 for murder of Elizabeth Symonds and for robbery. By ancient law, those capitally convicted had their goods forfeit, but if they were to die under this punishment, a survival of trial by ordeal, then theoretically they were unconvicted and their dependants could inherit their property. The punishment consisted of putting weights on the man until either he agreed to plead or he expired. In the case of John Weekes in Horsham gaol he died mute. To show how confused legal thinking was about this time over the question of pleading, the Act of 1772 made him guilty if he refused to plead, and the Act of 1828 made him not guilty, as is the case today.

Imprisonment of Debtors

For very many years justice was indeed blind over the question of debtors. Anyone could allege that another owed him a debt and get him committed to prison until the alleged debt was discharged, but quite often the mere fact of commitment to prison meant that the debtor was unable to earn and therefore unable to pay. More especially, a perfectly innocent person who had been discharged as not guilty of any crime at the assizes could not obtain his freedom until he had paid fees to the gaoler. There were not statutory, but fees paid only by ancient custom, and no one could escape them. These are some ludicrous cases where persons have lingered in gaol for year after year because they had no means to pay these fees; also debtors were not included in Elizabethan prison regulations which said that an allowance for bread was to be made for felons, so they depended on outside help or starved, and nobody in authority seemed to mind at all. The quarter sessions of 1671 fixed a table of fees which stipulated that a debtor should pay £1 to the gaoler on his commitment and four pence to the turnkey, two shillings a week for his accommodation and various amounts for food, drink and fuel, and finally a fee of two shillings to the gaoler who released him. There were even fees to be paid each time a prisoner was shackled and unshackled.

The Greenfield Case

A mass of papers in the Museum archives describes the celebrated case of Zephaniah Greenfield, who was utterly ruined and committed to Horsham gaol in 1782 for no fault

Crime and Punishment

of his own. His brother Daniel had been an overseer of the poor 56 years earlier, and with his colleagues had borrowed money to provide a workhouse for the poor. Years later the creditor sued for repayment, by which time Daniel had died and Zephaniah had become his executor, and the only person available for proceeding against. A series of complicated and lengthy legal actions reduced him to penury from having been a master maltster, and he went to prison unable to pay either the original debt, which was not of his incurring, or the considerable legal fees. Fortunately for him he was eventually released, but others in the same situation were often kept in gaol until they died.

At parliamentary election time the debtors used to raise funds by sending congratulatory messages to the successful candidate, whoever he might be, and were in turn rewarded with a guinea or two. Amusing though this might seem, it was often life or death to the debtors to obtain some kind of subsistence from outside the gaol. The farcical nature of the laws about debtors is shown by this account in *Gentleman's Magazine* for 1765:

> A middle aged lady in Sussex, happening to be much involved in debt, married a felon, who was capitally convicted at the last assizes for that county, but had his sentence changed to transportation. The marriage was celebrated in Horsham gaol, the bridegroom being in his irons, and consummated in the same place: but his irons were taken off in a few days. His lady, being by this stratagem freed from the prosecution of her duns, is to furnish him with cash sufficient to transport himself to any part of the globe.

Smuggling

Another absurdity of the law was smuggling. This practice flourished in Sussex as a maritime county, and far from being universally condemned as a social outrage, it was more than condoned by all walks of life, and brought to an end by the simple process of lowering or abolishing the duties so that it was just not worth while to smuggle. In 1745 it was reported to the House of Commons that at least three-quarters of the tea consumed in this country was smuggled, and two-thirds of the tobacco. At its height, smuggling reduced the labouring population who were better paid by the smuggling gangs than by the farmers, and it became really a major industry. Tales innumerable are circulated to this day, and the aura of romance associated with the crime usually ignores the fact that many murders of a horrific nature were committed together with other assaults on those attempting to preserve law and order. Troops were often called upon to assist the revenue officers, but it was a hard task when the gangs were able to call upon so much assistance and sympathy from the populace. Once a parson declaring his intention to hold a service was told by the sexton that he could not possibly do that as the pews were full of kegs of brandy and the pulpit full of tea. It was said that tombs in Horsham churchyard were used for concealment of contraband, but an inspection today tends to discredit this typical story as none of the tombs offers much capacity compared with the innumerable cellars and barns which were more usually employed. St. Leonard's Forest contained many tracks and hiding places used by the smugglers, or owlers as they were called, and Owlscastle, near Roffey Park, is said to be connected. Hawkins Pond in the Forest was the site of meetings of the Hawkins gang.

Magistrates were reprimanded by the Secretary of State in 1721 as they were afraid to take action against the smugglers, or often unwilling as they too drank brandy, but the appointment of a revenue officer called Thomas Walter in the 1780s was successful in suppressing smuggling in the Horsham area. He had his own troop of uniformed men on horseback and earned a good deal from his labours until removing to Ewell in 1793.

The 1745 report to the House of Commons said that 'men called duffers who go about on foot have coats in which they can quilt a quarter of a hundredweight of tea . . . Duffers supply it to hawkers who sell it to consumers'. Is this the origin of duffel coats?

The virtual end of smuggling came after the Napoleonic wars when much better coastguard and customs services could be organised, and the profit was largely taken out

Crime and Punishment 83

of the smuggling racket by Sir Robert Peel's reduction of customs dues.

Few Sussex Witches

It is a curious thing that a county like Sussex, never backward in creating and fostering folk tales and superstitions, had a creditable record when it came to persecuting witches, unlike some counties where a veritable reign of terror operated in the 16th and 17th centuries. It seems to be a fallacy that witches were usually burned to death, as in the whole of the 17th century only 18 out of the 514 witches prosecuted in the Home Counties were in Sussex, and of these, four were convicted and only one hanged.

The Gaol First Mentioned

The origins of Horsham gaol are lost, but it must have been in existence by 1541 when the Parish Register has this entry: 'Richard Sowton of Nuthurst for coining money was hanged at Horsham and buryed 15th June 1541'. This is the first explicit reference to the gaol, and the fact that in the previous century prisoners from Horsham were lodged in Guildford gaol (there was only one Sheriff for Sussex and Surrey) does imply that the county gaol came into existence early in the 16th century, perhaps as a result of instructions to the justices in 1532 that they must provide gaols to be kept by the Sheriff. The gaol until the 18th century was not a place of incarceration as a means of punishment, it was a place of detention pending trial and punishment, this last being execution, whipping, branding, pillory, or transportation.

The House of Correction

The usual petty criminals were confined in a house of correction controlled by the justices, not a Sheriff's gaol, and these small fry included rogues and vagabonds, disorderly persons, beggars, absconding servants, trespassers, and the like. Horsham's house of correction was at the corner of Springfield Road and London Road from some time in the 16th century until 1700 when the justices at quarter sessions directed that a house of correction should be built on the site of the old gaol, namely the first site described below. John Howard in his tour of gaols visited it in 1773 and reported that it consisted of only one room about 10ft. by 7ft., so it could not have been of much significance.

Gaolers and Their Fees

Although by the Act of 1532 justices were responsible for constructing and maintaining gaols, in practice they were farmed out to individuals who ran them as a means of livelihood on whatever could be extorted from the prisoners. Besides the fees, an income could be obtained by supplying food and other essentials, so that gaolers had arrangements with suppliers which ensured them useful commission. In the case of the first gaol, it was located opposite the *George* which was the taproom for the gaol, and was actually owned by one of the gaolers. These gaolers, as might be expected under this system, were often of the lowest type, and there are many accounts of their cruelty and rapacity. The gaoler in 1645, Richard Luckens, had 11 charges made against him including fighting, swearing and blaspheming, drunk and disorderly, allowing prisoners to escape, using witches to get them back again, encouraging his prisoners to deal in stolen goods, siding with the king's cause and not parliament's, and others of the same nature. Unfortunately it is not known what happened to him, but it is noticeable that all the charges relate to offences against authority, not against his prisoners, who must have suffered to a great extent from such a man.

Gaol keepers seem to have been frequently fined for allowing their prisoners to escape, so frequently in fact that one wonders whether it was not often made worth their while. In 1814 a visiting parson said, 'the prisoners have a habit peculiar to themselves—made of differently coloured cloth, which gives them a grotesque appearance',

1. Interior of the Parish Church in 1862, from the altar, showing the extra tie-beams. The lean to the north can be clearly seen.

2. The *Normandy* about 1870. The old almshouses are on the left, and in the centre of the picture is the Priest's House, a very early building.

3. Charles Howard, 11th Duke of Norfolk (1746-1815). 'If in his cups he was quarrelsome, when sober he was an agreeable companion; his conversation was pithy and full of a cleverness which even the strongest port failed to eliminate.'

4. The whipping post (and bull ring), once in the Carfax, now in the Museum.

The Cottage Hospital, Horsham.

5. The Cottage Hospital about 1900.

6. 'E' Company, 2nd (Volunteer) Battalion, Royal Sussex Regiment, in 1888.

7. One of the armoury buildings in the Depot, built in 1804.

8. Some of the hundreds of horse bits, no two the same, collected by William Albery and presented to Horsham Museum.

9. The Town Mill early this century. The large building (now much dilapidated) still remains.

10. With the abundance of local clay, bricks were often made on site.

11. The cricket field at the top of Denne Hill (the house can be seen on the left).

12. After 1850 until the present day cricket has been played on the ground which was part of the barrack fields.

13. Bands have been popular in Horsham for over a century. This one was the Borough Silver Band in 1937. William Albery did much to ensure its success in competitions.

Back row: F. N. Walder, E. Streeter, C. Walder, J. Clark, W. Nightingale, E. Short, E. Ballam, J. Carter, C. Farley, R. Burgess, R. Brackpool. *Middle row:* F. Turner, F. Capon, H. E. Voice, H. Garman, W. Grady, R. Richardson, H. Potter, J. Streeter, R. Buckman, R. Pullinger. *Front row:* F. T. J. Walder, E. L. Woods, W. Albery, F. Walder, H. R. Woods, H. Woods, A. Ballam, G. Sainsbury, H. Gorringe.

14. Water-colour painting (late 19th century) of Collyer's School on the old site. In the exact centre is the Vicarage, and on the right is the steam mill in Denne Road, now the bus depot.

15. One of the equipages of the Eversfield family at Denne, about 1740.

16. West Street about 1868, looking east. Most of the buildings still exist behind modern accretions. The paving was Horsham stone.

17. The Mechanical Age reaches Horsham.

Crime and Punishment

presumably to make it difficult to get away, although the report of a visiting committee in 1812 said that 'a party coloured prison dress is given only when the prisoners' clothes are worn out'. It follows that any escape would be better attempted early on!

Various Gaol Sites

The first known site of Horsham gaol was in North Street about where Linden Road used to be, a few yards north of the Mecca. The property is first referred to in the survey of the town dated 1611, and it was used as a gaol until about this time, after which the gaol moved to the north-east corner of the Carfax. Early town gaols were small buildings, not specially built, but merely stone houses strengthened as necessary at the doors and windows, and they required no complicated administrative system as they merely kept the prisoners until the next step of trial or execution.

The third gaol was located from 1640 to 1779 where the Post Office now is, moving finally to the Queen Street site just by the north end of the Iron Bridge. The Post Office site was most unsatisfactory and quarter sessions noted in 1649 that it was 'not of sufficient strength to hold the prisoners by reason whereof divers have made escapes'. There had been complaints anyway about the previous site on the corner of Carfax, and the judges had ordered something to be done, but the rebuilding on the new site was done very badly, and a lot of additional work had to be carried out. The notebook of the antiquary John Warburton for 1729 shows a sketch of a three-storeyed building with a note 'At the North end of the Market place stands the Gaole built of Free Stone and Crenelled on ye Top'.

John Howard and Reform

Gaols in the 18th century were still universally dreadful, and the reformer, John Howard, on his visit in 1774, found Horsham to be no exception. 'The wards are dark, dirty and small . . . There is not the least outlet for felons or debtors,

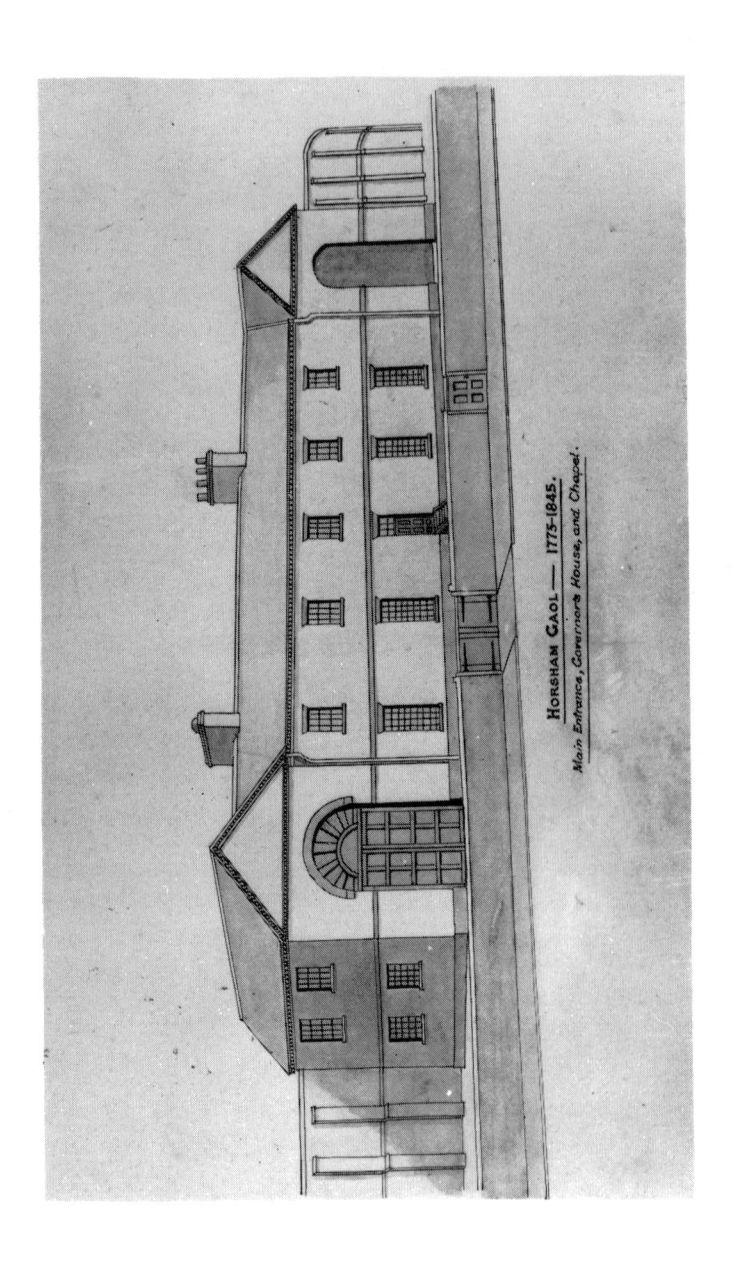

Fig. 5. A sketch of the gaol on the north side of Queen Street, approximately where the Iron Bridge now is.

Crime and Punishment

but the poor unhappy creatures are ever confined without the least breath of fresh air. Rooms in old gaol too small, except the free ward for debtors. No straw; no court; and yet ground enough for one behind the gaol'. Howard had a powerful supporter in the Duke of Richmond, who as Lord Lieutenant of the County carried great weight when on three occasions he persuaded the Grand Jury at the assizes to present 'that the common Gaol, or prison of the County is insufficient both as to the security and health of the prisoners'. Quarter sessions, whose responsibility it was, had to agree to the building of a completely new gaol, and the Queen Street site was chosen. Lady Irwin, ever anxious to acquire burgage tenements for the votes attached to them, bought the gaol site and the vote which had previously been vested in the justices.

The new gaol excited admiration from all who did not have to serve time in it. The youthful Howard Dudley enthusiastically wrote that it was a 'neat and handsome structure and entirely appropriate for the purpose'. John Howard's view was also that it was 'particularly well suited to the purpose. The gaol is kept very clean. I do not omit the old table of fees, though this county has set a noble example of abolishing all fees, and also the tap: in consequence of this I found the goal as quiet as a private house'. Compared with the stinking and corrupt gaols he had visited up and down the country, including Horsham, the new gaol was indeed an advance. It was the first to have individual cells, each with a brick arch over which was supposed to be protection in case of fire, and proper segregation was arranged for male and female, debtors and felons, and the condemned. When Lord Chief Justice Mansfield visited Horsham the gaoler told him that there were only half the usual number of prisoners for trial and the gaol was three-quarters empty, because in the last 12 years only one person had returned to prison because of the new idea of solitary confinement!

The Treadmill and Other Employment

The theory last century that hard physical labour was an essential part of the prison system was exemplified by a huge treadmill or hard labour machine, in which pedal cranks futilely beat the air to exhaust the pedallers. At least stone-breaking had an end product which this machine did not. Employment in gaols had always been a problem. The conditions of life for the inmates depended entirely on the gaoler whose aim was to make as much for himself as he could, so if the prisoner could pay for luxuries he was reasonably well off, but those who could not were dependent on the small allowance for bread and small beer made by the county authorities. Certainly there was nothing comparable with the present-day system where prisoners can earn by their labour, although in 1835 Horsham gaol did introduce a small manufactory for mops and mats. As far back as 1669 the justices were empowered to provide materials for the prisoners' work, but it was not mandatory and seems not to have been applied to any extent. Those who were destitute, particularly debtors, depended to a measurable extent on private charity, and several local people made regular donations of food and money.

The lack of provision for keeping body and soul together was matched by the lack of medical and spiritual care. Occasionally one of the clergy would attend at the gaol if specially required, for which he was paid a fee, and he would also attend at executions, but towards the end of the 18th century there was a proper appointment of prison chaplain and surgeon. In 1841 the Rev. Henry Allen complained of strong malt liquor coming into the gaol through the debtor Lazarus and of prisoners drinking and smoking instead of attending chapel.

Enlargement and then Disuse

The end of the Napoleonic wars saw a great increase of both crime and debt because of the discharged soldiers and sailors and the very bad state of agriculture; consequently the gaol had to be enlarged in 1819. The growing agitation over the unsatisfactory state of the Town Hall for assizes brought into question the continuance of the county gaol, but the Duke of Norfolk's improvements of the Town

Crime and Punishment

Hall in 1812 brought brief respite. The improvements were not enough, however, and in 1830 Lewes managed to get the assizes away from Horsham, one of the outstanding among many examples of how Horsham lets things go. This meant that the gaol was almost redundant, or at any rate it no longer had the status or activity of a county gaol, and the committee appointed to examine the question in 1835 reported that it should be used only for debtors, for prisoners awaiting trial at the Horsham sessions, or for condemned criminals. Legislation having abolished capital punishment for many offences, and debtors being dealt with otherwise than by endless imprisonment, there were few occupants of the gaol, and a suggestion was examined of converting the old and nearly disused gaol into a lunatic asylum. Fortunately, expert opinion was sufficiently enlightened to turn the proposal down.

The Prison is Sold

The decision was taken in 1845 to sell the prison together with the land to the highest bidder, and the astute Henry Michell, who had made a lot out of brewing and malting, bought the materials of the gaol which amounted to two and a half million bricks, 15,000 square feet of Horsham stone, and a great quantity of iron and timber. This cost him £2,560 and netted him several times the amount when he disposed of it, the land going to build another Michell malthouse, to the Waterworks Company, and to other building. The site of the gaol became Park Square until the new railway cut through the middle, when it became Park Square West and Park Square East.

Michell agreed to build a lock-up in Queen Street from the materials of the old gaol, but such was the curious arrangements of those times it had to be paid for half by the magistrates and half by the town and sessions jurors. The townspeople were told that if they could not find the money they would lose the midsummer sessions, and with the memory of the loss of the assizes still rankling, the town paid up.

The bulk of the iron from the gaol was used to build a railway bridge over the Ouse at Lewes, some material went to construct most of the railway works between Horsham and Three Bridges, and bricks were also used for numerous buildings such as 'Northlands' at Warnham. (Probably Warnham bricks were used in the gaol originally before being thus re-cycled.) After 300 years the county gaol was no longer in Horsham.

Chapter Four

HEALTH

THE CHIEF CHARACTERISTIC of medicine from medieval times until late 18th century was that it dealt with disease and other bodily damage after it occurred: preventive medicine had not yet arrived. Similarly, public health had little meaning until the 1830s, and for Horsham not until a generation later. Yet as early as 1443 there was flourishing in this town a celebrated physician, one Nicholas de Horsham, who was said to be 'a very learned Man, and so famous a Physician, that the Nobility coveted his Company on any conditions, so high an Esteem they had for him. It seems it was something of a peculiar Art in him to cure and yet please his Patient, which he would not do nevertheless, unless it was consistent with the Disease, for his Aim was to cure and please, if possible, but displease if unavoidable. He was of a middle Temper, neither so rough as to affright, nor so gentle as to humour a Patient into his Destruction, so that he was almost two Physicians in one Man'. (Cox, *Magna Britannia*).

Ignorance and the Plague

The great ignorance of medicine about the causation of the diseases which ravaged the population from time to time meant that only a few measures, and those empirical, were taken to combat the menaces which were often carried by lice and rats, both very common pests. The Parish Registers show that burials took place from plague outbreaks in 1560, 1574, 1608, and 1609. The economic effect of these occurrences was a shortage of labour with an increase in wages, and the landlords and farmers suffered. Those who were poor or diseased were not treated well by their fellows. A monthly meeting of the Vestry in 1665 decided that all in the poor book should wear 'on the right Arme in open view as a badge of their Poverty Two letters, vizt. H.P. of the coulrs yellowe and blue, each letter to be fower inches in Length & one inch in breadth at the least And that every of the said poore people of the said parish which shall refuse to weare such Badge constantly in view as aforesaid shall have no Releife out of the Poore booke untill he or she shall conforme to the said order'. Elizabethan medicine made some advance, but anti-plague measures were vague and incomplete—quarantine was partly understood, and vinegar was much used as antiseptic. The centres of plague were in the crowded towns, and those fleeing the plague used to go into the country where they were far from welcome—'seeing that we have sent our children forth three weeks past into a good air and a sweet country, let us follow them'. Strangely enough, the Great Plague of 1665 which so devastated London does not seem to have reached Horsham, for which we can perhaps thank the very bad communications. The ship-borne rat which carried plague would arrive at the port of Shoreham from the Continent and spread its infection along the trade route to Horsham.

An Insanitary Town

Plague was followed by smallpox in 1659 and not much more was known about dealing with this either. Until the 18th century medicine was still of the nature that it could

Health

be said of one doctor, 'his inattention was of great value to his patients'. Some attempts were indeed made to keep the streets and ditches of the town clear, but the mere frequency of presentments to the Court Leet and later to petty and quarter sessions suggests that the general state of the town was always bad. In 1622 seven townspeople were presented for allowing privies to be 'filthy and unclean for want of cleansing and scouring for a general nuisance', 10 more for decayed and broken ditches, and four others for blocked gutters. Three more allowed dung heaps to be on the king's highway. All were fined and put under further penalty if they did not do something about the nuisances by a certain date. In conditions like these it is not surprising that the Registers show an excess of burials over christenings in the 17th century, although caution has to be used when interpreting such data as the population was affected by other factors such as refugees from France, whose names also appear in the Registers.

Polluted Water

Associated with the absence of proper drainage as a cause of disease was the water supply. In this area it is not necessary to dig wells very deep to obtain a regular supply of water, and each dwelling had at least one shallow well which was only a matter of feet from ditches and drains, a state of affairs that was to last until only 100 years ago. The Court Leet of 1627 heard a presentment 'that the public well called Comewell in the North Street is defective for the want of a new curb, therefore it is to be repaired by the next Court', so there was some public supply, but it was no safer, nor was it much advantage when the water from the river was pumped by to the town by the operation of a water-wheel, as the river received most of the town drainage anyway.

Growing Enlightenment

Even a century later the assizes of 1766 imposed fines for keeping hogs near the public streets and feeding them with offal, which caused 'divers unwholesome and hurtful smells'. In the 18th century medicine was moving from superstition towards science, and together with a great increase in philanthropy and improved feeding this meant a much lower death-rate. In the early part of the century smallpox was again prevalent, and there were outbreaks in 1803 and as late as 1832, particularly among the poor, because vaccination was only partly adopted. One effect of the growing attention paid to medicine was the enormous expansion of commercially promoted remedies, often quack and bogus to a degree. The newspapers carried a lot of advertising matter, the *Sussex Weekly Advertiser* of 30 October 1797 extolling Dr. Williams' Worm Cakes and Nervous Cordial among others sold by the famous Horsham chemist, Thomas Mann.

Treatment of mental disease was only now beginning to emerge from the superstitious aura which enveloped it for centuries. John Baker mentions a Doctor Waggett who kept a sort of madhouse near the *Lamb*, but this would have been a private institution, and the poor insane would be found as often as not in the gaol or workhouse. The era of gin-drinking from 1720 to 1750 which was held to have been responsible for so many deaths in London does not seem to have affected Horsham unduly, and the very numerous cases of drunkenness in this and the next century were usually attributed to beer rather than spirits. Everyone drank beer from toddlers upwards, which was often just as well as it had been boiled, when to drink raw water was to drink germs. But there was a lot of difference between small beer and strong ale.

The gaol accounts in 1707 and 1719 show that a woman doctor attended prisoners, who paid tribute to her skill in a petition to quarter sessions: 'We the poor unhappy Prisoners in your County Gaole of Horsham have laboured under our calamaties of sickness and lameness but by the assistance of the Widow Briggs, Surgeones by her dayly attendance with God's Blessings hath restored us to our former health by Her Medicines and other necessarys'.

Health

The Struggle for Improvement

For most of last century enlightened men were battling for improvement of sanitation in Horsham, but it was a very uphill fight and we were far behind other towns in Sussex. One of those who did a lot of work in urging anti-cholera measures was Doctor Gideon Mantell of Lewes. He is best known for his discovery of fossil mammals in St. Leonard's Forest, but he also enters our story as the man who saved the life of Hannah Russell, condemned to death at Horsham in 1826 for poisoning her husband with arsenic, but Mantell proved that he could not possibly have died so quickly from this cause. Quarantine was applied by regulation in Sussex in 1805, but the borough had its own ideas about refusing to be 'druv'. Much was still accepted as 'act of God', and the entries in the burial register of the barracks around the turn of the 18th century showing that 50 per cent. of the deaths were of children would excite little comment. The Public Health Act of 1848 advocated, but did not compel, sanitary services and provision of pure water supplies, so it was ignored, as was the Local Government Act of 1858 which gave more powers. A town meeting in 1859 rejected the proposal to adopt the Acts by 160 votes to six. Robert Henry Hurst, junior, thrice elected M.P. for Horsham, made great efforts to get the town to see sense, but the fear of having to pay for all these marvellous proposed improvements was too strong, so disease and death quite unnecessarily prevailed. Scarlet fever was epidemic in 1862, so Hurst tried again, and in this he was helped by the Literary and Scientific Institution which produced figures to show how much worse off Horsham was in its death-rate than were other towns in Sussex.

An Action Committee

A broadsheet was issued with the heading 'Health of Horsham' and the names of a committee which was pressing for action. These included the Rev. J. F. Hodgson, vicar, Hurst, and 10 others. The general defects of the drains were glaring, it said, the cellars being infested with rats and

NOTICE.
WATERWORKS

THE
BOARD OF HIGHWAYS

Invite the attention of all the Inhabitants who propose to have Water laid on from the Waterworks, to take the *present opportunity*, whilst the Public Roads are about to be opened for laying the Mains, to have the necessary Service Pipes attached for conveying Water to their Houses, in order that as little obstruction or inconvenience may be caused to the Public as possible.

(By order)

RICHARD LAKER,

August 19, 1865.   Clerk to the Bo

R. LAKER, PRINTER, HORSHAM.

Fig. 6. The apathy of the public towards a proper water supply was very great, and this handbill demonstrates the constant urging that was required to get it accepted.

inundated with sewage which was leaking through the soil into adjacent wells. Almost the whole of the town was supplied from shallow wells usually 14 to 24 feet deep, and these produced specimens of water which had a greasy film on top and smelt abominably when heated. Horsham well water had 49 grains impurity per gallon compared with only two for Glasgow, for instance. Deaths from fever were 15 per cent., 10 per cent. being reckoned a high national figure. Total deaths per thousand were 25 in Horsham, but only 16 in the rural districts, and 24 in the country as a whole. The remedies they urged were deep main sewers, deep enough to take full drainage from houses, and a pure water supply.

Whose Responsibility?

But the trouble was that there was no public body to carry this out, and the committee pressed the townspeople to take the legal power under the local government legislation and spread the payment over the next 30 years as was permitted, so that future generations would be paying for the benefits they enjoyed. Water supply should be ensured by forming a private water company. Their efforts were fruitless for another 10 years. The cry 'we can't do it if it costs money' is not peculiar to authorities in 1977. In 1872 the Public Health Act compelled the appointment of medical officers of health, and in 1874 Hurst had the support of Dr. Kelly, Horsham's first M.O.H., in raising the matter again. Dr. Kelly not only reported that the health of the town was very bad but the death-rate was 24 per thousand population against 9.4 in the surrounding parishes, and 19.5 nationally. In the face of these facts, over 500 ratepayers objected to any scheme to better their health, and still little was done, although the Horsham Water Company, a private concern, did start up in 1866 and the gypsies with their insanitary encampments were no longer allowed to pollute the Carfax at fair-time after 1870. At least one citizen was conscious of hygiene, for he wrote to the *Horsham Advertiser* in 1875 that he had bought pork chops from a butcher which were wrapped up in two smallpox certificates, and might that not spread the contagion?

Sanitation at Last

Suddenly, in 1875, the town reversed its ostrich attitude. On 12 April a public meeting decided to adopt the local acts, and a subsequent poll showed 518 in favour and only 222 against. This opened the way for the first and most important task to be tackled—the drainage system. There followed a long and complicated tangle involving a farmer, Stanford of Broadbridge Mill, suing the Local Board for pollution in the river which passed through his land, and the Board trying to buy the land from him for a sewage works, costs rising so that the final figure for the drainage scheme was nearly double the original figure (history is repeating itself a century later), and the whole affair was the major issue in the first elections to the Urban District Council in 1894. In 1896 the Council bought more land at Broadbridge Heath for extending the sewage works and also for an isolation hospital. The 'pest houses' had long been in New Street on the west side near the junction with Oxford Road. The gaol had its infirmary, and so did the workhouse, but there was no hospital for the town until 1892.

Horsham Hospital

The Rev. C. J. Robinson, vicar of the parish who did so much to rehabilitate Collyer's School, said in 1890, 'The experience of the two years that I have spent in Horsham has taught me that what is most wanted to promote the material welfare of our poor—and, indeed, of other classes also,—is some sort of *Cottage Hospital,* in which more skilful nursing and, perhaps, isolation can be given to patients than are possible in their own homes. Even in Horsham many of dwelling houses are over-crowded, unventilated, and ill-adapted for the treatment of the sick, while there is no place within the county nearer than Brighton for the reception of "accident cases".' The idea caught on at once, funds were raised, and by July 1892, a little over two years from the vicar's original suggestion, the hospital opened with its first two patients. R. H. Hurst gave the land, C. J. Lucas of Warnham was president of the fund, and Horsham showed not for the first time that it cared about its hospital.

The architect's intention was to produce a building of cottage-like appearance, and it had a male ward of three beds, a female ward of three beds, and another two unspecified beds, total eight. Each bed was reckoned to cost £40 a year. The cost of building was £1,350, and it opened free from debt and complete with a wine and beer cellar. Miss Edith Harrison from Westminster Hospital was the first superintendent. In 1923 it was necessary to have a larger building and the maternity unit was opened in 1944. The fight put up by the people of Horsham in recent years to save their hospital must surely go a long way to make up for the lethargy of earlier generations.

Chapter Five

MILITARY

THE MILITARY SIDE of our history has not been a great part of the whole, neither has it been inglorious. The pre-Conquest system of the *fyrd*, by which the local lord could call upon any able-bodied men to bear arms as required, was the earliest form of militia. The Norman Conquest was a comparatively peaceful invasion as far as Sussex was concerned, although there was much ill-treatment of the inhabitants when resistance was shown, and we have no record of this in the area. William I started the system which continued for centuries of a feudal levy based on a quota of men to be supplied by the county. They were organised in bands to be trained at the county's expense, hence the term 'trained bands' which remained in use until after the Civil War.

The earliest record of armed men dates back to 1242 when Hugo de Cumbe of the manor of Hawkesbourne (just north of Horsham) supplied four knights to do service. In 1320 one thousand horse-shoes were sent from the forge at Roffey to the port of Shoreham to be used by Edward's troops against the invaders from Scotland, at a cost of £4 3s. 4d., plus 5s. carriage charge to the port. During the French wars Sussex provided a good deal of war material through the ports of Shoreham and Portsmouth, and the king's commission levied 16s. from the borough of Horsham

Military

to pay for archers to be armed for 'service beyond the seas'. By the Sheriff's order, Horsham produced 150 sheaves of well-sharpened arrows, 25 to the sheaf, about the time of the battle of Crecy in 1346, and they were to be sent to London on five horses at a cost of 5s. for onward transmission by sea to Portsmouth. The Exchequer Accounts also show that Thakeham provided scaling ladders for the assault on Calais. The left wing of Henry V's army at Agincourt was composed of Sussex men, but we do not know for certain whether any came from Horsham.

Liability for Local Defence

For local defence, or for dealing with riots and tumults, the constable appointed by the borough had charge of the arms until the end of the 16th century, and as the constable was an impressed man, often of poor calibre, one wonders what his store of arms really amounted to. The Militia Act of 1662 stated that all property owners must provide horses, arms and men as required, but the 1757 Act removed this liability from the individual to the parish. Sir Francis Drake's famous advice, 'look well to the coast of Sussex', was taken in 1586 and the county was ordered to provide 600 men against the expected Spanish invasion, together with gunpowder and other necessary stores. The warning system, apart from Drake's small and fast ships, consisted of beacons ready for lighting at a moment's notice and swift post-horses to carry the news to London. In the year of the Armada there was also a financial levy on the county, and a muster of able-bodied men between the ages of 18 and sixty. The great enthusiasm aroused in her subjects by Queen Elizabeth facilitated the raising of the levy, but the defeat of the Armada in July 1588 soon enabled a stand-down, much to the relief of those anxious to get in the harvest.

The Civil War

The unsettled state of the country in the reign of James I led to a statute establishing a stock of arms and gunpowder in each county, and these stocks were to be of use to both sides in the forthcoming Civil War. When tension between Charles I and parliament reached boiling point in 1642, one of the points at issue was the militia. Parliament, quite unconstitutionally, passed a Militia Bill which transferred the nomination of the Lords Lieutenant who commanded the militia from the king to parliament, and on the refusal of the king to agree to the Bill, parliament drew up an Ordinance for the training of the militia, and hostilities began in August 1642.

Sussex was divided, but then so were families everywhere when it came to taking sides, but the parliamentarians were better organised. Some indication may be given of where Horsham stood from the fact that the male population of the borough was 509, and in the second year of the war a parliamentary commander reported that he could rely on 200 Roundheads from Horsham. Service in the militia was not popular: training might be about one day a month, and the men were not supposed to serve beyond the county boundaries so that they did have some opportunities to till the land, but their wage was only slightly above the normal agricultural figure, and they had to pay for their own subsistence from pay constantly in arrear. Disruption of ordinary life was made much worse by the system of free quarterings which could be imposed at will, although Cromwell did end this in 1645. Another cause of dissatisfaction was the interruption of trade caused by skirmishing in many parts of the country, and a petition was sent to the king at Oxford to allow the safe passage of the cattle from Wales which had always formed an important part of Horsham's market activities. By the time the war had been in progress for two years, the local feeling was a hearty dislike of the activities of both sides, which is not difficult to understand when one considers that the victory of either would not have made much difference to Horsham's fairly sleepy isolation.

Some of the gentry of Horsham were much affected by the Civil War, notably the Eversfields of Denne, and the Middletons of Hills, although the latter came out of it best as will be recounted. In September 1643 the estate of Sir Thomas Eversfield was sequestered when he was accused of deserting the parliamentary cause, although he had himself been one of the commissioners for sequestrating other peoples' estates and was member of parliament for Hastings. Some of the proceeds of the Denne sequestrations were taken by the parliamentary commander, Col. Morley, to pay his troops. The case of Thomas Middleton was more complex. He, too, had apparently been favourable to the parliamentary cause at the outset, but the Articles submitted in 1644 to the Committee conducting the war at 'Derby House' stated that in the previous December, when the king's forces invaded Sussex, he 'pretended himself sick and would not in any ways show himself against the King's forces . . . in all probability consenting to the bringing of some of the King's forces to take Horsham'. At the time of the outbreak of the war, Middleton was our member of parliament and was a Commissioner for Sussex to sequestrate the estates of the malignants, in which capacity he headed the signatories for the sequestration of Horsham vicarage in March 1643. Exactly what caused his disillusionment with the parliamentary cause is not clear, but he was able to talk his way out of trouble on this occasion, but not the second time in 1648 when he was arrested and brought to London charged with complicity in the rising of Horsham. Released temporarily, he was tactless enough to record his vote in the House of Commons in favour of the proposition that the king should be reasoned with, and was imprisoned again and his estates confiscated.

The sequel to the confiscation was unexpected as it resulted in a net profit for Middleton. He was ordered to pay £1,000 to a nominee of parliament, as half of the total fine, and when he appealed successfully in 1650 the Barons of the Exchequer ordered him to be repaid £2,000, the whole amount of the original fine, so that he ended up £1,000 the richer. Middleton seems to have got himself involved in bizarre situations; on one occasion he and a colleague, two 'persons of great bigness',. stood up in the gallery of the House of Commons to hear better, and the resulting cracking of a board made members think 'that it was a plot indeed; and an alarm of fire, of the house falling, and of a malignant conspiracy, spread rapidly over the town so that a regiment of trained bands was collected in the city upon beat of drum, and marched as far as Coventgarden to meet these imaginery evils'. Nerves must have been taut in those days.

The Rising in 1648

The skirmishing in 1648 was the only time that there was fighting in Horsham itself. With Chichester and Arundel secured four years before by the Roundheads, Sussex was not considered to be a danger, but in fact disaffection and war-weariness had done more than the parliamentarians realised, and the anonymous 'Letter from Horsum in Sussex, relating the present state of this country' reported that 'the country is risen about Horsham, and protest that they will fight for King and the country'. Realising this danger, it was ordered that the store of arms in Horsham should be carried to the safety of Arundel castle, but the people of Horsham resisted in some force, and mounted a guard over the magazine in the loft of the Market House. On 22 June 1648 the Horsham parliamentarians wrote to 'Derby House' 'We endeavoured to remove the magazine at Horsham to Arundel Castle on the 9th, but were resisted by the Bailiffs and Constable and disaffected party there, by whom the arms and magazine are still kept with a strong guard'. After a few days, however, the townspeople decided that it would be better to help themselves to the swords and muskets if they were going to fight for the king, which they did, and then proceeded to Horsham Common to train in their use. Here then was a force reckoned to be about five or six hundred with horses, and the parliamentary command was alarmed indeed. An urgent message was sent to Sir Michael Livesay who commanded a Kentish regiment, and his forces were first met with near Knepp castle, the resulting skirmish ending with the death of John Michell of Stammersham and the wounding of his son. There was a small

Military

engagement in the town itself, recorded in the Parish Register under the burials of 'Edward Filder, by the soldiers thrusting a sword through the window of his house in the back lane (now Denne Road); William Baker in the hop gardens belonging to Nicholas Sturt (now the site of the Mecca); and Thomas Marshall, Gent., who followed into east Street, and killed near Thomas Michell's door'. One Roundhead was also killed; that ended the fighting in the town, and the Civil War was over for Horsham, except that the resulting plundering caused a lot of dissension. The iron-workers, too, had cause to complain, for in 1644 after the capture of Chichester and Arundel the Roundheads destroyed the iron-works in a good number of places, as it was feared that they might continue to produce armaments for the Royalists.

At the Restoration, King Charles had in mind to reward his followers with the Order of the Royal Oak, after the Boscobel oak in which he hid, although this came to nothing, but three local people to be included were Thomas Middleton and two of the Eversfield family.

The Napoleonic Wars

Although Charles II is sometimes credited with the formation of England's first real standing army, it was not legalised until the time of William III, and Horsham was not involved again in military matters until the 18th century, when an Act of 1757 reorganised the Sussex militia so that men were chosen by lot, or had to provide a substitute, and no doubt some of Horsham's menfolk were involved. The fear of a French invasion in 1778, followed by many others until Trafalgar in 1805, brought into action denial measures whereby cattle were to be driven away, mills and provender destroyed, and the enemy also deprived of horses and carts. A corps of gamekeepers was to be organised 'to attack and annoy the enemy', foreshadowing both the Home Guard of the Second World War and the underground force to operate if the Germans invaded. Although not in the immediate front line of an invasion, Horsham at once played its part, and the *Sussex Advertiser* relates how the Volunteers Associated

Company (formed 1779) fired 12 exceeding good volleys in front of the *King's Head* on 17 June 1780 in honour of the local M.P. being reappointed Attorney General, and several hogsheads of beer were subsequently distributed.

During the period when France was occupied with the Revolution, the volunteers lost their significance and were kept in abeyance until 1792 when Pitt called out the militia because of unrest, and in 1793 France declared war on Britain. New companies of volunteers were formed in all the towns of Sussex during the Napoleonic wars, Horsham raising a corps of cavalry and a corps of infantry in 1798 with the Government providing arms, horses and accoutrements and the men's services being given free. As in the times of the Armada, service was not required beyond the confines of the county. Alas! Horsham's Loyal Volunteers lasted three weeks. Timothy Shelley, who had chaired the original meeting to set up the Volunteers with himself commanding the cavalry and Edmund Smith the infantry, was required by the Lord Lieutenant to find 20 persons more respectable than those in the list Shelley had submitted, and failing to do so the movement was at an end.

The Barracks

The chief part played by Horsham at this time was as a military town, as among 22 other towns it became a centre for troops, horses, arms and stores. For these purposes first the barracks were built on the south side of the town in 1796 and then the depot on the north-east in 1804. Before this troops had been quartered on the Common to the north and east, and in the town itself. The remarkable feature of defence plans was a constant moving of troops about the country, and this shows up in the records of quarter sessions as the justices were responsible for payment, for conveyance, commandeering horses and carts for baggage, which was on such a scale that it was said that 'the baggage waggon of a militia regiment resembles more the removal of the household furniture of a family than that of the military stores of an army'. William Albery made an analysis from the

Parish Register of the regiments at the barracks at one time or another, and this shows that 69 moved in and out between January 1797 and June 1814, an average stay of three months each. They came from Yorkshire and Denbighshire, Essex, and Derbyshire, in fact from all over the country. We did have the Sussex militia for a short stay once, but never the Sussex Regiment.

Profiteering

It may be imagined how profitable it was to own a haulage business at this time, and other fortunes were made by suppliers of all kinds of stores and foodstuffs to the barracks. The number of men quartered there constantly varied, but it was usually somewhere between 1,000 and 2,000, and there were good contracts to be had. One butcher was said to have made £80,000, leaving £20,000 to each of his four daughters without making one of them respectable, and this was at a time when many of the poor could not afford meat at all. There was of course the debit side, as the soldiers were frequently on the rampage, waylaying and robbing, particularly when in drink, which was frequently, and causing great damage in public houses. The chief trouble was lack of anything to do in their spare time, or organised means of saving their money, and there are many stories of soldiers lighting their pipes with banknotes, eating them in sandwiches, and buying watches in the town to take back and cook in a frying pan when they got tired of them. Apocryphal many of these yarns undoubtedly were, but the criminal records of assault, murder, robbery and so forth were real enough, and the townspeople were often much relieved when a particular regiment marched away.

The barracks had been built of timber on brick bases and roofed with tiles, the timber sections being prefabricated. About 12 acres of ground were occupied by quarters, hospital, magazine, stables and other buildings, the land having been leased from the Denne estate for 21 years. After the Battle of Waterloo had put an end to any threat from Napoleon, the barracks were evacuated, the stores sold and the buildings demolished. The Government surrendered the lease of the land to Tredcroft, the owner of Denne, three years before its expiry, and part of it became the cricket ground. One effect of the removal of the barracks was a considerable loss in trade, still remarked on by the *Universal British Directory* in 1839.

The Depot

To return to 1804, it was felt then that 30,000 stand of arms in Horsham barracks were not enough, and negotiations were opened for the acquisition of land on Horsham Common for the storage of more arms. The Office of Ordnance wrote to Thomas Medwin as Steward to the Duke of Norfolk and town clerk: 'Sir, His Grace the Duke of Norfolk having signified to the Board of Ordnance his consent to the Erection of an Armoury to contain 10,000 stand of Arms, on Horsham Common', would Mr. Medwin make arrangements accordingly, to which Medwin replied that 'He fixt upon an Acre of Ground . . . His Grace expects the Board to pay 100 guineas for the purchase of the Ground'. This was remarkable cheek as the Duke had no right whatever to the Common, which belonged to the people of Horsham.

The depot was built substantially to last, unlike the wooden barracks, and upon stone foundations were erected brick buildings, and the whole area of over three acres was surrounded by a high brick wall with spikes on top. In spite of their robust construction, no use for them was found after the war was over, and the stores were removed in 1809 and the property sold in 1827.

Raising the Forces

The system of raising troops at this time consisted of bounties for enlistment, and throughout the emergency the voluntary system continued, whereas the Navy Act 1794 and the Army and Navy Acts 1796/7 required the Sussex justices to raise 400 men for the navy who were chosen at meetings of the principal inhabitants, and the notorious press gangs were used as well. There was some compulsion on the county to take further anti-invasion measures when the war flared up again in 1803, by making comprehensive returns of stores, transport, livestock, and arrangements for their evacuation, and warning beacons were prepared, including one on the high ground of St. Leonard's Forest. The Volunteers were re-formed with a high rate of response, the basis of organisation being the north and south divisions of each rape. The Horsham Company amounted to 120 men, but they were maintained for only a few years and that under difficulty as the threat of invasion receded. Appeals were made from time to time for donations to buy clothes for the Volunteers, who were constantly short of money, and in 1815 they were disbanded.

The Crimea War of 1854 found the army quite unprepared, and when in 1859 Napoleon III was thought to be planning an invasion, the Volunteer Movement received fresh impetus. Territorial battalions were formed under the Cardwell reforms and the Horsham Company was called the 7th Sussex Volunteer Corps, a unit of the 2nd Administrative Battalion Sussex Volunteers. Amateurs in the best sense of the word, their discipline was maintained by fines such as one shilling for loading contrary to orders, or firing out of turn, and irregularity in the ranks such as laughing or talking cost sixpence.

At first the Volunteers had their headquarters and armoury in Market Square, but in 1873 Captain W. Egerton Hubbard built a fine headquarters (still to be seen in Park Street as a furniture store) which contained besides the large drill hall, recreation facilities and canteen.

The headquarters of the 2nd Administrative Battalion Sussex Volunteers was at Horsham from 1869 to 1874 when amalgamation took place of the 1st and 2nd Battalions to become the 2nd Sussex Rifle Volunteers, and the latter moved to Worthing. In 1880 the 7th became 'E' Company, 2nd Sussex Volunteer Regiment, and in 1887 the Regiment was incorporated with the Royal Sussex. Introduction of a more powerful rifle (the Lee-Metford) about this time meant

A CALL TO ARMS!

4th (Home Service) BATTALION
ROYAL SUSSEX REGIMENT.

This Regiment is now being raised at Horsham to form a Reserve to the 4th Battalion Royal Sussex Regiment, which has been accepted for Foreign Service. A recruit (subject to the conditions stated below) can decide whether he will enlist for Foreign or Home Service.

CONDITIONS.

TERM.—Duration of the War, or not exceeding 4 years.

AGE.—(a) Foreign Service, 19-35 } Height 5ft. 2in.; Chest 33in.
(b) Home Service, 17-35
Ex-Sergeants up to age of 50 years; Ex-Corporals up to age of 45 years.

PAY.—7s. per week (exclusive of board and lodging).

ALLOWANCES (for upkeep of Kit).—1s. 2d. per week.

SEPARATION ALLOWANCES.

Wife, 9s. a week.
Wife and 1 child, 10s. 11d. per week.
Wife and 2 children, 12s. 10d. „
Wife and 3 children, 14s. 9d. „

Wife and 4 children, 16s. 9d. per week.
Each additional child, 2s. per week.
Each Motherless child, 3s. per week.

A child means a boy up to 14 years and a girl up to 16 years.

Enlist at once—delay is dangerous.   Apply at nearest Police Station or at THE DEPOT, THE DRILL HALL, HORSHAM.

Hon. Recruiting Officer for this District
Who will enlist men and give all information:

J. A. MINCHIN, Esq.
"WANTLEY," HENFIELD.

HORSHAM, OCT^r 1914.

PRICE & Co., PRINTERS, HORSHAM.

Fig. 7. This poster of October 1914 called for Reserves for the 4th Battalion.

Military

that the range at Horsham had to be closed and the Steyning one used instead.

The Royal Sussex Regiment

Horsham's chief connection with the Royal Sussex Regiment was through the 4th Battalion, formed at Horsham in 1908 out of 'E' Company of the Volunteers. In 1910 the Sussex Territorial Force Association acquired the old drill hall in Park Street, so Battalion headquarters moved there from Worthing. The outbreak of war in 1914 saw the 4th Battalion quickly organised on a war footing and it served first of all in Gallipoli, then Egypt, Palestine, and finally in 1918 the Western Front, during which time 489 of all ranks were killed.

War, 1914-1918

The First World War affected Horsham as much as any town in England, and the intense mobilising and recruiting efforts not only involved the enlistment of the men of Horsham in the services, but also called on much civilian contribution to the war effort. At the end of 1914 the Royal Fusiliers (22nd Battalion) had encamped at Roffey in wooden huts and they contributed a lot to the social life of the town before moving on to Nottinghamshire in June 1915, to be followed by many other troops just as a century before.

After the war Captain Middleton, who was Adjutant of the 4th Battalion, built the *Capitol* cinema to give employment to ex-servicemen, particularly bandsmen, of the Battalion. This scheme, called the 'Blue Flash' presumably from the regimental facings, merged with the British Legion in 1924. The Territorial Force had become the Territorial Army in 1921, and it was decided to build a drill hall in Denne Road with money obtained privately by the Battalion, perhaps an event unique of its kind. The architect was Lieutenant-Colonel Godman, then commanding the Battalion, and the hall was opened in 1927.

Between the wars the Battalion was noted for its athletic meetings, which before 1930 had become one of the principal athletic events in Sussex. When 1939 came the Battalion concentrated here, and was serving in France by April 1940.

War, 1939-1945

The Second World War once again saw Horsham as a military town as in Napoleonic times. In every way necessary the people played their part, and perhaps the most astonishing civilian contribution was the Horsham Scheme of Patriot Engineers 1942-1945. This started with a broadcast in 1942 by Sir Stafford Cripps calling for an end to alleged complacency in the country and for an all-out effort to win the war. The Chief Air Raid Precautions Officer, Captain J. E. Pugh, M.B.E., was so impressed that he considered how his own volunteers could use the hours of waiting on duty. With others of like mind he organised a machine workshop in a garage at the corner of Bishopric and the Worthing Road which turned out millions of parts for armaments, using almost entirely volunteer labour, which included a retired rear-admiral in his seventies. The project was so successful that a film was made of it for propaganda purposes, and the *New York Times* featured it. Besides the material output, £4,800 was donated from the profits to the Exchequer.

Another distinction we had was a Y.M.C.A. canteen which served between seven and eight million service men and women, including almost every Canadian soldier who came to England during the war. The services of the 3rd Sussex (Horsham) Battalion Home Guard must not be forgotten, together with thousands who made their contribution and sacrifice in our defence, let us hope for the last time.

The war memorial in the Carfax was erected in 1920, and those memorials in the parish church (where the colours of the 4th Battalion Royal Sussex Regiment have been laid up) were described in Chapter One. Many of the surnames on the memorials of both wars are the same, and many of them occur time and again in Horsham's history.

Chapter Six

INDUSTRIES AND TRADE

CLEARLY there is no space for describing all Horsham's industries and trades, but those which have had particular significance in the history of the town will be touched on. There is no doubt about Horsham's first industry and trade—it was the manufacture of stone implements on a scale too great to be for local use only, so they must have been traded elsewhere. The period was Mesolithic, that is to say about 7,000 B.C., and the style of flint manufacture is sufficiently distinctive to be given the name Horsham culture. The objects found, as described in the Introduction, were the working tools of everyday life, and the finds so far show that the Horsham district was prominent in this manufacture and trade.

There is now a gap in our economic history until medieval times: the Roman tilery discovered in 1964 only two miles away at Itchingfield, and the Roman iron workings at Broadfield are outside our story. In the 11th century the manor of pre-Norman origin was becoming the borough, and essentially both manor and borough must have a market. In the case of Horsham, the market would necessarily cater for a small area because of the difficulty of travel in the clay, but as settlements developed the importance of Horsham market increased as the town was the only one of any size in this part of the Weald.

Fairs and Markets

There is nothing more than tradition for the statement that the weekly Saturday market was granted by a charter of King John, but equally there is no reason to suppose this unlikely even though the lord of the manor, William de Braose, did quarrel with King John in 1208. Naturally, fairs as well as markets did some trade, and we have records of fairs for horses, sheep, cattle, pedalry, and toys, but at all markets and fairs many everyday necessaries would be sold, in early times made locally and then, with improved communications, from elsewhere in England and abroad. Fuller's earth, for instance, was essential for clothmaking when almost every village had its plantations of flax and hemp. (The fulling mill pond at Chesworth was mentioned in documents of 1650.) The fuller's earth could have come from Baynards, and a chemically-similar import to Horsham would have been 'Talc . . . in Latin Talchum . . . maketh a curious Fucus for the Ladies Faces, which they justify to be lawful, because it only clears, does not change the Complexion'. Until the roads improved in the 18th century almost everything that people needed would be made locally, making communities self-sufficient.

Two references to Horsham market have been sometimes misunderstood: the Nonarum report to the king in 1340 said there were no merchants in Horsham, but a merchant was then a man who traded on a wide scale, and any town must always have had petty merchants, which underlines what has been said about Horsham being self-sufficient and insular. The second reference is Camden's description of Horsham as an 'indifferent mercat', which again suggests small-scale, but still it must have been very important for the town and surrounding villages.

Appropriate to the name of the town is the horse fair recorded from 1233, although there does not seem to have

Industries and Trade

been a great deal of horse-dealing after medieval times. Cattle, on the other hand, have always played a major part, and it has been suggested that Horsham's comparative nearness to London made it an important market. Good roads were not necessary for the movement of cattle, and many of them came on the hoof from Wales, as Cobbett noticed in his *Rural Rides.* Welsh names are recorded in the Parish Register in the late 16th century, and in 1609 one 'Roger Lewis, a Welchman, a drover of cattell' was buried. For centuries this trade with Wales was carried on, there still being stories in rural parts of local cattle being caught up with the Welsh droves, and angry farmers having to recover them, but in 1870 the trade was transferred to the railways. The route into Horsham was over the North Downs, using byways to avoid tolls, coming from Guildford, Albury, Shere and Ewhurst.

The sheep fairs were in April and July, horses and cattle at Whitsuntide and the end of November, and the big Welsh cattle fair on 17 November. This was called St. Leonard's Fair, as it was held in the Forest, and then on the Common until this was enclosed in 1813. The First World War saw the end of cattle fairs.

Horsham market has had considerable ups and downs. In 1581 there were complaints about higglers raising prices. These people bought poultry and other produce direct from the farms and supplied the hawkers and shops, thus bypassing the market and preventing poor people from taking advantage of fixed market prices. The famine in 1630 compelled the justices to order that the poor might be allowed to buy corn in the market for two hours before a bell was rung, and there were many similar controlling measures respecting the market. In 1703 John Wicker, M.P. for Horsham, petitioned Queen Anne for a new monthly market for cattle and other produce, and this was granted in 1705, but it declined and ceased to operate before 1750. The bailiffs and burgesses attempted to revive it in 1790, but although weekly markets continued, the monthly one faded out. The markets were losing a lot of trade to independent dealers outside, and a public meeting was held in 1756 to determine what should be done. The result was 100 tradesmen binding themselves by deed not to trade outside the market, and to prosecute any who did, who were called forestallers. 'The Town also is and has been served with a great Deal of the Poor and very indifferent Meat to the Great Disappointment of the Gentlemen and Tradesmen who are able and willing to pay for good Meat if the same could be had in the same Market and to the Great Oppression of the poorer sort of People who are obliged to buy such Poor and Indifferent Meat at High Prices Which Greivances being duly considered by us this Day at this Present Meeting in order to redress the same and restore the said Markets to their former State and Condition as much as may be done by us . . .'.

Another complaint was cattle being driven to London, presumably for higher prices. This was no new problem—in 1350 the mayor, aldermen and commonalty of the city of London wrote to the bailiffs and good folk of Horsham that John de Farnham had complained that two of his merchants having purchased some cattle to bring to London for the king, the great folk and the commons of the land and of the said City, were arrested by the bailiffs of Horsham and made to swear that they would purchase no more. The bailiffs were desired to release the men—or else!

The Livestock Markets

There was a revival in the cattle market when it was established in the Bishopric in 1852, but increased traffic, particularly motor, drove it into the railway yards, where it finally expired a few years ago as a result of centralised marketing at Croydon facilitated by improved road transport. The cattle market which was in Horsham for many centuries has been allowed to go elsewhere.

In 1882 the Aylesbury Dairy Company bought Stammerham Farm and went in for cattle breeding on a large scale, but its investments in farm buildings were on such a scale that it went bankrupt, and its position was not helped by the murder of the managing director at Monte Carlo. The resulting low price of the land enabled Christ's Hospital to acquire

Industries and Trade

the estate, so a business failure brought this great school to our doorstep.

In spite of frequent legislation by the Court Leet and quarter sessions, there were innumerable breaches of the rules of trading, the earliest we have being the visit of Edward I to Horsham when he fined the bakers 15s. for short weight on 30 June 1299, and the township also had cause to remember the visit as it was fined 40s. for 'transgression of measures'. In 1790 parliament ordained that boroughs must specify what weights they were using, and Horsham reported back that two Tasters were appointed who keep standard weights and measures, and if on examining the ones used by shopkeepers and publicans they find them faulty, they are destroyed. Inspection for disease was imposed by quarter sessions in 1866 after an outbreak of cattle plague, with compulsory powers of slaughter and compensation.

Other livestock of importance at Horsham market included poultry, although in 1724 Daniel Defoe says that Dorking market got its poultry from as far away as Horsham. The poultry market ceased in 1907. There have always been deer in numbers in the area, and they were sold like cattle in the markets. Rabbits were said in 1813 to be going to London in considerable quantities. The small weekly markets of today are a pale reflection of the considerable activity that once used to be, and attempts to hold other general markets have not succeeded, reflecting the power now possessed by the shops in gaining and holding custom. It is of interest that the weekly market of the Women's Institute in the Carfax was the first of its kind in the land when it started in 1932.

The Importance of Corn

Until the iron industry developed, Sussex was purely agricultural (even as late as 1947 agriculture accounted for 23 per cent. of labour in the Horsham area), and the market reflected this accordingly. Corn was important as food, for man and animals, and for brewing, and a corn market was granted by Henry VI in 1460 to the Archbishop of Canterbury. As a directory of 1866 says, 'the corn market at Horsham has from time immemorial held a high place amongst the markets in Sussex and the neighbouring counties, supplied as it has been by the produce of a district celebrated for its corn growing qualities'. It was in this year that the Corn Exchange in West Street was designed by the local architect Edward Burstow and built by a public company, but this building ceased to be used for its original purpose with the decline in the corn trade in the first few years of this century, and in 1913 the building was sold and became part of the *Black Horse* hotel, now demolished. In earlier centuries a good deal of trading in corn took place in inns, and this also was concerned with the avoidance of market tolls. Once again the Sussex roads played a part in corn prices, as Daniel Defoe observed in 1724, corn was 'cheap at the barn, because it cannot be carry'd out, and dear at the market because it cannot be brought in'. Yet again in 1787 the *Gentleman's Magazine* said that 'the market for corn used to be very considerable (at Dorking), but is now transferred in great measure to Horsham, since the turn-pike road has been made from London through that place to Brighthelmstone'.

The corn mills in Horsham go back at least to 1231 when John de Braose gave the rectorial tithes to Rusper Nunnery, including the rector's water corn mill. Deeds locate this on the river below the church, but at some time later it was moved to the present site of the town mill. Prewett's mill dates from 1861 and was originally a steam mill, as was the one in Denne Road (1852), now the bus depot. There are no records of any wind mills within the borough, although just outside at Wimblehurst, King's Road, Compton's Lane, and Millthorpe Road there were once mills. Wimblehurst mill, dating at least from 1724, was blown down in 1861. Champion's mill was a post mill blown down in 1860, although the miller's cottage still stands today. This is a site well known to Horsham people of earlier generations as the gallows was nearby. Compton's mill was a smock mill and is shown on maps between 1759 and 1823. The

Industries and Trade

Star mill in Millthorpe Road was also a smock mill, but was pulled down in 1795 when the machinery was removed to a steam mill in the Crawley Road. Until modern times the price of corn has played a vital part in the country's economy, although it was not so vital in the feudal economy when the lord provided some food for villeins and freemen, supplemented by what they could grow themselves. It was when labour became paid and farmers sought to obtain a livelihood from the land that corn and other market prices became so important. The 1630 famine has already been mentioned; this was caused by the weather, there being no lack of work because of the flourishing iron industry, but it was a case of actual shortage of corn and not lack of wages. Part of the measures taken by the authorities against possible disorder due to famine included vigorous harassing of rogues and vagabonds, whipping them and passing them on to their home villages, and also apprenticing poor children from the age of 10 upwards. The Poor Relief Act of 1601 permitted the parish overseers with the consent of two justices to bind as apprentices children whose parents were unable to maintain them.

Riots and Rick-burning

The really bad time was from mid-18th century to the 'hungry forties' of the next century, caused firstly by maladministration of the poor laws and exacerbated by the economic effects of the Napoleonic wars, and also sheep-rot and over-cropping. Many reasons have been put forward to explain how the trouble was caused, including political ones about the radical teachings of William Cobbett and economic ones about farm machinery putting men out of work. Depression during the war coupled with rising prices compelled labourers to seek higher wages, and for this purpose they combined together, a heinous crime at this time. In 1793 the demand was for 2s. a day, but in 1830 2s. 6d. was not enough. Violence was not so bad in Horsham as elsewhere, but cases of rick-burning and machine-smashing in the surrounding districts were of course dealt with at the Horsham assizes, so the town was made well aware of the strength of feeling in the country. The constables were quite unable to cope with the unrest, and Horsham's hand fire engine was quite inadequate for the fires. Troops had to be called in. The worst year was 1830, when mobs went about compelling workers to join them on pain of destruction of their dwellings, and threatening also the gentry, magistrates and various officials, besides the parsons who collected tithes. No wonder the magistrates called Horsham 'a hotbed of sedition'.

In November 1830 a mob of between 1,000 and 2,000 marched on Horsham, evidently well organised and determined to get their demands of a minimum 2s. 6d. day wage and reduction of rent and tithes. A letter from the High Sheriff to the Home Office gives one version of what occurred, and a lady writing to a friend in London gave another. The Sheriff said that the complaints of the mob were attended to, thought reasonable, and the meeting dispersed quietly. The unknown lady gives an entirely different account, in which she says that the mob forced the worthies to come to the parish church, where the gentlemen stood at the altar and the labourers in the body of the church where they were encouraged by the farmers. 'Mr. Hurst held out so long that it was feared blood would be shed, the doors were shut until the demands were granted, no lights were allowed, the iron railings that surround the monuments were torn up and the sacred boundary between the chancel and the altar overleapt before he would yield'.

The result of the meeting was an agreement by the vicar to reduce tithes by 10 per cent. and by the magistrates that wages should be a minimum of 2s. 6d. per day, as Mr. Hurst reported to Sir Robert Peel.

The Home Secretary's response was chilling. 'I cannot concur in the opinion of Mr. Hurst that it was expedient or necessary for the vestry to yield to the demands of the mob'. He may have been right, but when a magistrate attempted the next day to swear in special constables he found that only four out of 63 were prepared to take the

Industries and Trade

oath. There was so much trouble in the south of England that providing troops to keep order was a problem. Cavalry from Dorchester and 100 infantry from Portsmouth were ordered to Horsham.

The magistrates were powerless to resist the labourers' demands, but the cost of living went up and up. Rents rose as much as 90 per cent., and distress was such that some farmers paid no rent at all. The poor rates were of course greatly increased, and there was much unemployment and decline in cattle rearing and crop growing. In the 1830s there were several wet seasons, thus causing the loss of sheep as well as crops. To crown it all, taxation to pay for the war had grown alarmingly—taxes on salt, soap, candles, leather, malt, sugar, tea, just about included everything necessary to the working man, within whose lifetime the cost of living rose 500 per cent. Those paid by the hour tried to work longer hours to keep their families alive, but this was not in their interest as it had the effect of bidding against each other and actually lowered their wages.

The attitude of some local gentry was sympathetic to the labourers, which accounts for the smaller number of rick fires in the Horsham area, but central authority was grimly callous. In 1800 an Act was passed instructing the justices to substitute rice and herrings in place of wheaten bread when corn was short, and the reaction of the House of Commons to the following petition from a public meeting in Horsham in 1817 was merely to order it to lie on the table:

> The Land, that real source of national wealth, is rapidly receding from that high state of cultivation to which it lately attained, and no longer yielded profit to the farmer. Trade is daily declining . . . The petitioners therefore address the House in the full hope and confidence that they will afford them relief by lessening the enormous burden of taxation which has brought that misery upon them; which burden has been much increased by the sudden depreciation in the value of every description of property, occasioned by the fluctuating paper currency. But they humbly beg leave to express their conviction that a reduction of the taxes to any beneficial extent can only be effected by enforcing the most rigid economy in every department of the State, instead of the present shameful extravagance.

The last part has a curiously modern ring, and the sentiments were strongly supported by the *Times* with phrases like 'shamefully have the poor been treated' and 'the Corn Law—that most flagitious of monopolies—has contributed largely to this unnatural and cruel evil'.

The savage sentences of hanging and transportation eventually suppressed the more violent manifestations of discontent, but not before the mob threatened to attack Horsham gaol and release the inmates, only desisting in the face of troops. As a result of Lord Melbourne writing to the magistrates reproving them for not being firmer with the rioters, prosecutions increased, and the January 1831 sessions saw 60 magistrates in attendance. The Poor Law of 1834 was bitterly resisted as it broke up families, children being sent away to be apprenticed and adults being kept at bare subsistence level in grim workhouses. There were cases of Horsham children being sent to factories in the north of England, and the fierce resentment can be imagined, in spite of a pamphlet circulating in the area which advocated this practice. Mobs outside the town hall in 1835 had to be dispersed by troops called up from Brighton, and once again men refused to be sworn in as special constables and were fined £5 each.

Poverty continued to be widespread during a large part of the 19th century, about a third of the agricultural population being permanently unemployed, and as Horsham was still largely dependent on agriculture the town was much affected. Many people did try to help in their private capacity. The Sussex Agricultural Society of 1796 was started to improve the breed of cattle, but it had other activities like prize-giving for thrift and industry. 'Five labourers who had brought up the greatest number of children exceeding the age of two years, in habits of industry, with the least proportionate relief from the Parish' were awarded 10 guineas down to one guinea. The winner had 13 children. The Mechanics Institute in the Carfax opened in 1829 to encourage young men to better themselves by attending evening classes in the rapidly-growing

Industries and Trade

practical sciences, and more on such bodies will be found in Chapter Eight.

Employees in the Household

The biggest single category of employee in Horsham until the present century was the household servant, using the term to include outside workers such as those in dairy, brewhouse, garden, stable, and so forth. Such employment was highly regarded by many because of the security it appeared to give, because, however low the wages might be there was always board and lodging provided. In Elizabethan times everyone had to work, and wages were fixed; both the hired servant and the apprentice was subject to control, and over-payment brought fines to both employer and employee—£5 and 10 days imprisonment for the one, and 21 days for the other. Servants were bound to continue in their employment until released, or suffer imprisonment again, and before leaving the district had to obtain a testimonial to avoid being whipped for being a vagrant.

To give some idea of what was expected of the indoor servant, here is a reference dated 1744:

> This is to certifie to all whome it may concern that ye bearer hereof Mary Chitty at times have lived with me 2 or 3 yeares and that her behaviour during that time have been discreat prudent and orderly—That twas for no misdemeaner we part'd with her but twas her choice—That she is a nonperil for house wife'y and a Phinexe for cookery for washing, getting up linnen, stiching of Bedds or Pettycoats making of Tae and washing up dish's not to be outdone by any of her sexe—That she will come when she is bid and shut ye door after her—and that she have amongst many other Quallifications to numerase to perticulize a very exterordinary one to be found among here sexe viz. not given to fond of ye fellows.

Shop Assistants

The powerful bond which tied an employee to the job is not perhaps realised today. In Tudor times it was a legal bond, at other times it was an economic one—work or starve. Shop assistants had notoriously long hours until legislation in the 1930s, and this is reflected in an appeal to customers issued as a handbill round the town at the end of last century. Mentioning that certain named shopkeepers were insisting on remaining open until nine o'clock during the summer months, the appeal continues, 'It is said of Assistants that they are a dissipated class. The Mechanic whose day's labour ceases at six o'clock, has every inducement to improve his mind; while the Assistant leaves *his* shop at eight or nine . . . often too late for the Lecture Room or the Library, is it to be wondered at that they should so often be attracted to the Tavern, by the course (*sic*) excitement of a Free and Easy Club, or to the Theatre at half price, where a lower order of entertainment is expressly provided for the *sufferers* and *victims* of late hours. The Public are earnestly requested to visit the Shops before seven o'clock in the Winter and eight in the Summer'.

Whether this softened the customers' hearts is not known, but a similar appeal in a trade journal in the 1930s also asked the public to shop earlier, but this time it was before six o'clock on the first three days of the week so that the shop assistants could have the evening free. Before the Second World War there was one shop in Horsham to every 47 persons, compared with 71 in the rest of the country, and the town was well patronised from a wide area. This was partly due to a vigorous Chamber of Trade (founded 1909), but of late years this body seems to have been unsuccessful in getting shops to agree on an early-closing day.

Timber

In this age of plastics it is difficult to realise that almost every conceivable thing was once made of wood, from houses to food plates, from carts to malting shovels, from arrows to ploughs. Sussex is still the most thickly wooded county in England, having almost three times the national average of plantations or natural forest, and this in spite of the enormous toll taken by the iron industry in the 16th and 17th centuries. It says a lot for the conservation programmes of our forefathers, and from at least the time of King John who used Knepp as a hunting lodge, there must have been skilled foresters in the neighbourhood. Two thousand oak trees were cut down on the Chesworth and Denne estates in the 18th century, and the Surveyor General wrote to the Lords of the Treasury on 2 October 1770 recommending that because of the great shortage of timber any lease granted to Sir Charles Eversfield of Chesworth Lodge should contain a clause for the absolute forfeiture of the estate if even one tree be cut down without a licence.

Horsham used to be pre-eminent in broom making, six out of the 17 makers in Sussex in the 1862 directory being in the town, although this hard to credit. These directories, said to have originated in the Middle Ages when registry offices were kept by nuns to help country girls look for places as domestic servants, were notoriously inaccurate and often copied each other's misinformation, but nevertheless there must have been quite a brush and broom business here, the materials being at hand in the forest. All carts and most carriages would be of local manufacture, J. and E. Heath's Carriage Manufactory being much advertised in the 1820s.

Tanning and Leather

An industry associated with timber is of course tanning, and Horsham was important in this field, there being in the 16th century at least 10 tanners at any one time, reducing to about eight in the next century, but by the end of the 18th century the London tanyards were competing. The availability of oak bark and cattle hides proved of no avail when chemical processes took over, and the industry disappeared from the county at the turn of the present century. Gibbings, Harrison and Company had the tanyard in the Brighton Road until 1912, when it ceased and became Margetson's the leather dressers for a year only, but it is now a council depot and is an interesting building of cast-iron construction, and the site of one of the last tanneries in Sussex. Another tanyard was near Tanbridge, sometimes mistakenly identified as 'town bridge'. Most shoes and harness were locally made until last century, so there was plenty of demand for the products of the tanyards. Our most famous saddler and harness-maker of recent times was William Albery (born 1864). After attending Collyer's School, where he began a lifetime of fine calligraphy, he succeeded to his father's saddlery business, and spent much time in politics as a rabid Liberal, in building up the borough band, in researching and writing a *Parliamentary History* of our town, and then the *Millenium of Facts* about it. In addition he stood successfully for election to the Urban District Council in 1929 solely on the platform that some of Park House should be available to the public for reading rooms, museum and library. When he died in 1950 he left all the papers resulting from extensive researches to the town, so he is owed a debt of gratitude not only for his many good works, but also for finding out so much of our past.

Brewing

Horsham has always had plenty of beer-shops, except when the Puritans reduced them to two official ones in 1636, although in 1644 the churchwardens complained that there were 27 unlicensed ones! The heyday was probably in the last century when the cattle market was in the Bishopric and practically every house was a public one. There were three breweries at this time, and the most prominent brewer was Henry Michell, who also made money trading in malt, with coal and brick-making businesses as well. He acquired the West Street Brewery in 1840 and the Fountain Brewery in the Carfax in 1853 (behind the present Post Office). His house next door was rebuilt in 1868 and called 'Grandford House' from a previous owner of the land called Henry de Graunteforde, and is now commemorated in a new building of the same name.

There was a time when practically every farm had its hop garden and brewed its own beer, as did many households.

Industries and Trade

At the back of Henry Michell's Carfax brewery was a hop garden which extended to where the Mecca is in North Street, and in a deed of 1683 a close called a hop garden in the Bishopric was conveyed from John Wicker, brewer, to Samuel Blunt. This would have been associated with the West Street Brewery.

Cider making was once a considerable industry in Sussex from the 13th century, and cider was sent from Sussex to the siege of Calais in 1349. As earlier records show it was brought from Normandy in considerable quantities; the custom of making and drinking it presumably came from there. There was a clause in a lease from Chesworth in 1628 which included a covenant 'to plant or graft six crab stockes or perrye stockes yearly', but by the end of the 18th century cider seems to have been replaced by ale. In 1869 there were two ginger-beer factories in Horsham, and Michell produced a mineral water containing iron from a local spring which at one time had a good sale. But the 'authenticall drinke of Englande' is the one which the people of Horsham have most enjoyed throughout their history.

Water, Gas and Electricity

The success of a brewery naturally depends on the quality of the water available, and in both quality and quantity Horsham has always been fortunate even in times of great drought, such as 1976. The story of the fight to discourage people from confusing their wells and their drains has been told in Chapter Four, and although the value of uncontaminated sources was known from quite early on, the public were hard to convince. Water was supplied for the town from the river, using a pump driven by a water wheel and wooden pipes which are sometimes still found on excavation. There was a public fountain in North Street, where Comewell House is today, still in use in 1735, and in 1745 the justices made a contract with the proprietors of the waterworks to lay on a supply for the gaol, then in Carfax.

By the middle of the 19th century the growth of popultion was such that an additional water supply was needed, so an artesian well was sunk to 75 feet in Park Terrace East, and a reservoir constructed near the Forest Hospital. The well was deepened later, but even this was not enough, and now water comes from the borehole at Hardham. The quality of the water was an important factor when C.I.B.A. decided to establish a factory in 1938. In 1880 Horsham was nearly involved in a madcap scheme which never got off the ground to pipe sea water from Lancing to London by way of this town.

Henry Michell was one of those who found it so difficult to persuade the townspeople that pure water was essential, and in his diary he says, 'This year I invested £1,500 in the Horsham waterworks. I have taken a great interest in this matter as I think it is very much wanted and I have no doubt but in the end it will pay very well, but the ignorance and prejudice one meets with in offering this, one of the great necessities of nature both in a physical and moral sense, from those who ought to hale it as a great boon, is surprising and disheartening, but there was just as much ill-feeling against Gas when that was first established here'. This was in 1836, the gasworks being on the north side of what is now Albion Way, and Michell was chairman of the company for over 25 years. The usual pedestrians' complaints were made when the gas pipes were put in just after the Highways Board had made up the streets, to be followed not many years later by the laying of sewers.

The town's electricity supply began in 1901 with the erection by the Council of a generating station in Victoria Street which burned refuse, and was said to be the most economical in the country. Street lighting was changed from gas to electricity at this time.

Iron Manufacture

The iron industry in this area was important for the employment it gave, for the value to the owners of timber and ore, and for the availability of the finished product for making agricultural and other iron implements. The industry was at its peak between the years 1550–1650, Sussex having

Industries and Trade

49 furnaces out of 73 in England, although the recently-discovered Roman works at Broadfield demonstrate that iron-working was practised on a large scale in the first and second centuries. There would then appear to have been a lull until the 14th century, when the forge at Roffey was ordered to send 1,000 horseshoes to Shoreham for onward transmission to Newcastle for the Scotch wars. Although the industry carried on, it was not until Tudor times that it became of really national importance. In 1602 Queen Elizabeth leased practically the whole of St. Leonard's Forest to Sir John Caryll, who made a lot of money out of iron, and his ornate tomb may be seen in Warnham church. John Eversfield was noted in 1574 as owner of numerous ironworks in Surrey, Sussex and Kent.

He lived at Worth, although his father came from Poyle, near Staines, and it was his son who bought Denne in 1604 and became the first of the Eversfields who have played quite some part in Horsham's history.

The only other nearby forge besides Roffey was that on the site of the present mill at Warnham, which dated from the Stuart period, but Horsham would have supplied labour for the ore pits in St. Leonard's Forest, and for the works at Birchenbridge, Bewbush, and elsewhere. The locations of iron activity may often be spotted on the map from names like Cinderbank, Hammer Pond, and similar. The Cromwellians were concerned about the ironworks supplying arms for the Royalists, and so were ordered to destroy the Ifield works, but there were other reasons for the general decline in the industry after the Civil War. First, better and cheaper iron was coming from Sweden, and deposits of worthwhile ore were being worked out in our area, and by the 18th century the discovery had been made of how to smelt iron using coal instead of wood, so the industry in Sussex had vanished by mid-18th century. The roads, which had been much cut up by wagons employed in iron-making, were no longer repaired with the waste slag, and the forests were no longer devastated by the huge demand for fuel.

Glass Manufacture

Glass-making was another old industry, but it did not concern Horsham a great deal. The Parish Registers mention four glass-carriers and one glass-maker buried between 1590 and 1621, but the industry was in the Chiddingfold-Loxwood area. Perhaps too much has been read into these records as some have tried to establish the existence of a glassworks in or near Horsham, citing drops of molten glass being found in the Causeway and at Hills Place, but one way of producing glass drops is to burn down a house, so these drops can be found almost anywhere.

Brickmaking

Brickmaking died out after the Romans left, but revived in the great rebuilding between 1560 and 1640, when many of Horsham's important houses were constructed. It was a common practice to build a house from clay dug and fired on the premises, so plentiful is the material, as any gardener in Horsham knows, but some land conveyances specify that this shall in fact be forbidden. Brown clay is better than blue for hand manufacture, and even firing was effected by burning furze cultivated for this purpose on the Common until it was enclosed in 1813. Old maps show little brickworks dotted all over Horsham. Henry Michell not only sold two-and-a-half million used bricks from the old gaol, but he also made new ones on the site and sent half a million to the Crystal Palace at Sydenham. Commercial brickworks were small until recently, one example being the Horsham Engineering Works which was acquired by H. and E. Lintott from Steele and Dodson in 1897. Besides engineering the business included an iron foundry and a brickworks. The Lambsbottom brickworks closed in 1914, but numerous small brickworks such as those next the Forest Hospital run by the Dinnage family, and another in Depot Road belonging to the Nightingales for several generations, were closed at the outbreak of the last war, not for economic reasons, but because of the blackout, the burning being in open clamps.

Industries and Trade

Canal and Railway Transport

When the canal fervour was waxing at the end of the 18th century Horsham was not unaffected, and a meeting in the town hall in 1782 resolved that 'the extending of the Navigation of the River Arun from Newbridge to Slinfold will tend to improve the lands and estates adjoining . . . and will also be of great public utility and of particular benefit to the inhabitants of the said town of Horsham and the trade and commerce thereof'. The scheme collapsed, as did several others to bring water transport nearer to the town, but even so Horsham's economy was aided by cheap carriage of coal and other heavy cargoes on the canal at Newbridge. Enthusiasm for canals having waned, attention turned to the new railway, and in 1834 and again in 1838 petitions were organised in Horsham pointing out that goods went to London more cheaply from Guildford as they were carried by water, and Horsham market was being adversely affected. The railway did come in 1848, but as always with such matters it proved a double-sided benefit, as the livelihood of local producers was harmed. Instead of being a market town for local products, Horsham became a distributing centre of food brought in by railway; and cheap manufactures, from the Midlands and North, of metalware and other household and agricultural goods meant the destruction of local industries. Another effect the railways had was to damage the retail trade as increasingly people went to London for their shopping. Local tradesmen complained that co-operative shops in London were too competitive, and urged Horsham customers to pay cash more often and in their turn they would render accounts more promptly.

However, we owe some industrial development to the railways, as it brought Agate's timber yard in 1860, Lintott's foundry in 1861, Boxall's in 1862, and there were two more iron and brass foundries by 1900. The railway has always been a mixed blessing; around 1800 the town was growing fast, and a directory of 1839 said it had 'an air of liveliness superior to most other towns in the neighbourhood, but this advantage of situation will doubtless be materially impaired when the railway shall be opened throughout from the metropolis to Brighton'. As we have seen, others felt the same, but undoubtedly the biggest single factor in the very rapid development of Horsham since the war has been not the motorcar, but the railway. Figures show that the proportion of commuters has shot up in the last 20 years.

Banks

Increase in trade together with reaction to the high incidence of robbery at the end of the 18th century brought into being Horsham's first bank, opened by Messrs. Lanham, Price, Shergold, Harben and Scutt. Other banks followed, and they drew on the large London houses, but by 1812 Horsham Bank, run by Lanham and Richard Grinsted, was comparatively large, and issued its own banknotes. In 1819 a Savings Bank started, and soon all the modern operations of finance had arrived, including an office of the Inland Revenue in the *King's Head* (Officer—Mr. Thrift) from 1855 to 1881, which accounts for the sign still visible on the building.

In the latter part of the 17th century there was an acute shortage of copper coins, so local tradesmen produced their own tokens which also had advertisement value. Examples include William Hamper (1653) with a picture of candles being dipped, William Shortt (1677) *King's Arms* and Richard Barnard (1669) also candles.

Printing

Printing has always been a small industry in Horsham, and indeed presses have been literally a one-man concern, not worthy of a place in trade directories of the early 19th century. The first known book to be printed in Horsham was *A Journey from Bassora to Baghdad*, printed in 1784 by Arthur Lee, who was the first printer of any note. He was followed by Charles Hunt (1839), John Clarke (1845), Zechariah Kennett (1845), and William Laker (1845). The first newspaper was the *Horsham Mercury*, printed and published by John Tugwell in 1864, and at least one newspaper has been printed here ever since that date.

A JOURNAL,

KEPT ON A

JOURNEY

FROM

BASSORA TO BAGDAD;

OVER THE

LITTLE DESERT,

TO

ALEPPO, CYPRUS,
RHODES, ZANTE, CORFU;

AND

OTRANTO, IN ITALY;

In the YEAR 1779.

By A GENTLEMAN,
Late an Officer in the Service of the Honourable EAST-
INDIA COMPANY:

CONTAINING

An Account of the Progress of Caravans over the
Desert of ARABIA;
Mode and Expences of Quarantine;
Description of the Soil, Manners and Customs of the
various Countries on this extensive Route, &c. &c.

HORSHAM:
PRINTED BY ARTHUR LEE;
AND SOLD BY
J. F. and C. RIVINGTON, *St. Paul's Church-Yard*
M.DCC.LXXXIV.

Fig. 8. The first book known to have been printed in Horsham. The author was Samuel Evers, who later became clerk to T. C. Medwin. *(Courtesy, British Library Board.)*

Clay Pipe Making

A local industry of some importance was making clay pipes. This was certainly a skill, but it might be thought to have been carrying it a bit far when a Bill was introduced into Parliament in 1677 to encourage the trade, which 'shall be adjudged an Art, Mystery, and manual occupation'. Seven years apprenticeship was suggested, but fortunately the Bill failed. Henry Burstow tells of his family making pipes in their house in the Bishopric, and it was indeed a cottage industry. The chief Horsham makers were William Collis (1715), Thomas Clarke (1754), Thomas Bright (1754), James Petter (1839), James Swinyard (1845-62), William Swinyard (1850), and Jn. Harrington (1860-70).

Horticulture

Horsham once had several nursery gardens in the town. Allman's started in 1828 and was at the north-east corner of Park Street and East Street, covering some 10 acres, and Riley Scott behind the station dates from 1866. Industries like this have their day and disappear without leaving any trace. Who now remembers that Horsham was once famous for its gingerbread? When Shelley was nine years old he wrote to a friend in Horsham to bring him some gingerbread when there were no less than eight shops in the town making it.

Chapter Seven

SOCIAL LIFE

WHAT WE IN HORSHAM have done with our time out of working hours has been determined more by the economy than by the current social structure, as elsewhere in England. When the average working man toiled for nearly 100 hours a week, as he did in the 15th century, he must have had little appetite for anything but rest. From March to September he worked from five in the morning until eight at night, and during the other months from sunrise to sunset. If he did not, his family starved. When the opportunity did come for a break, such as a church feast or a fair, then he thoroughly enjoyed himself. When the church played such a large part in everyone's daily life in medieval times, besides the religious festivals there were church ales, where the drink was brewed on the premises, and churchyard fairs and markets, although these last were forbidden by papal decree in 1291. The markets were even held on Sundays as that was the time most parishioners were gathered together! But church porches and churchyards were no longer big enough, and in any case the Statute of Westminster in 1295 decreed that henceforth neither, fairs nor markets were to be kept in churchyards, for the honour of the church.

The Fairs

Even before this, we have record of a charter being granted by Henry III to William de Braose for a three-day fair each year on 7 July, and this was held in the Carfax for 553 years. Only the king could grant the franchise for a fair, for reasons of public order and because the grant was valuable—the tolls and revenues went to the grantee. The fair was important for economic reasons at first, with pleasure second, but later the commercial changes with the advent of warehousing, travelling chapmen and salesmen with their samples, meant that the fair was losing its economic importance by the 18th century.

Our July Fair brought both profit and trouble to the bailiffs who ran the town's affairs. The profit was probably much greater when the Fair was an economic necessity for the community, but when the Fair became merely a collection of sideshows and pedlary, it was more of a public nuisance than anything else,. and eventually had to go. By the last century the first day had become enough for any serious business purposes, and the remainder was given up to pleasure and fleecing the simple folk. Originally the Carfax was open space for these fairs and markets, but gradually it became occupied by stalls which were left up from day to day, these became a little more permanent structures, and before the town (or most of it) had realised what was happening, building took place and various people laid claim to the sites and the freeholds, and that was farewell to the open space which belonged to the people of the borough. This purloining of land may well have begun in the 16th century or earlier, but the borough records give several such cases dating from 1632, and if the bailiffs of the borough were doing this, it must have been taken for granted that it was a respectable operation, which it was not.

As permanent buildings increased, there was less open space, and the congestion of the Fair by the end of the last

Social Life

century was too much for the increasing awareness which people had of sanitary considerations. There were protests from several quarters, and in February 1870 the church authorities complained that the gypsy encampments 'were very prejudicial to the Town in a sanitary point of view'. Eventually the Home Secretary was asked to make an order in 1874 limiting the Fair to one day, and a further order in 1886 removed the Fair from the Carfax altogether, and it then was set up on the Jews Meadow, where Merryfield Drive now is. In 1877 the Duke of Norfolk presented the Fair, and the land in the Carfax on which it was held for centuries, to the town, but it was never his to give!

There were other fairs, and also markets, but the latter will be considered in Chapter Six. Horsham was important and being the only settlement of any size for miles around, Henry VI gave charters for two fairs in 1449 at Whitsun and 16 November, both to be of three days. The November Fair was mainly concerned with horses and with cattle, some of which had been driven all the way from Wales. Both the Whitsun and November Fairs were held in the Bishopric at first, but the November one was split into a fair on the Common, east of St. Leonard's Road and known as the St. Leonard's Fair, until the Common was enclosed in 1813. There seems to have been an even earlier fair, as the Chief Ranger's accounts for St. Leonard's Forest mention money received from tolls and dues held on St. Leonard's Feast Day (6 November). The 1449 charters were granted to the Archbishop of Canterbury, who owned land through the Manor of Tarring-cum-Marlpost in what is now called the Bishopric, a corruption of Archbishopric.

Public Hangings

The public have always had a ghoulish interest in crime and punishment, and public hangings attracted large crowds who were encouraged in their fairground behaviour by sellers of various trifles including ballads about the criminals to be executed. By the time of the last execution in Horsham in 1844 there had grown up a considerable revulsion against these spectacles, and the Rev. Jarvis Kenrick preached a sermon beforehand which resulted in school children being taken by their teachers up Denne Hill to get away from it. Holding this execution at the time of the April Fair was a callous move on the part of the authorities. Henry Michell, who bought the gaol the following year when it became disused, said this in his diary:

> I obtained possession of the Gaol the beginning of November and the St. Leonard's Fair was held near the Queen's head on the 17th of November and as I allowed any one to go over it (in fact I threw it quite open to public view) and thousands of people flocked to see it, (there were very few, even in the town of Horsham who had ever gone over it) and I was called upon to give my personal attendance to so many of my own friends and also to reiterate an explanation of the different parts of the building and the purpose to which each was applied from the 'condemned cell' to the murderers' grave, that I got quite tired of it and was enabled to form some idea of the life of a showman.

Activities in the Carfax

Carfax has seen many sides of public life, but it is a far cry from the gentle guitars of the evangelists on Saturday mornings today, or the patient bus queues, to the raw life of a July Fair. Wives were sold, for as little as 3s. 6d. in 1820, and the last in 1844 for £1 10s. 0d. The usual bloody sports were enjoyed by some, doubtless because of the added zest of betting on the result, and the bull-ring (now in the Museum) was last used in 1813, the resulting meat being sold afterwards in Butchers Row, now Middle Street. Public feeling has shown some curious twists. In 1572 a preacher, the town clerk, a beer brewer, and a winer of Rye, were indicted as they 'assembled riotously and illicitly to play an illegal game called bowles', and John Champion of Horsham, before he could get his alehouse licence at the Quarter Sessions of July 1794, had to undertake that he would not only sell 'good and whollsome Drinke and victuell at reasonable rates, but also he must not permit anye Unlawfull playe at the tables, cardes, dyce, bowles etc.'. But tearing bulls to pieces with dogs, who also suffered from the bull's horns, there was nothing wrong in that.

Social Life

Another, but shorter-lived, occasion for a public outing was horse-racing in St. Leonard's Forest, which started in 1835 and brought tremendous crowds with all the sharpers and tricksters one would expect, not to mention the sellers of strong drink, so the Rev. Jarvis Kenrick persuaded the landowner to call the whole thing off after seven years of fun and sin. The little church in the forest at Coolhurst was built partly from funds raised by a bazaar held at the races in 1836.

Other occasions for fun included May Day, when children went round the town with garlands and nosegays visiting the houses of the gentry, where they were given gingerbread and money, while the chimney sweeps adorned with evergreens danced to a fiddler. Students of folklore will recognise very ancient customs, which also included the hanging of effigies of unpopular persons on trees, and burning the effigies on 5 November.

In 1772 we were much criticised for the material nature of our life, when interest in public affairs was said to be low, and our amusements trifling. The critic was John Baker, a lawyer who moved into Horsham and lived at Park House. He recounts walking down to the town mill and finding some men and boys wagering on whether the cat from the *Anchor* hotel would or would not swim in the millstream with a pound weight tied round its neck. The cat survived, but Baker does not say that he interfered, although he was of a very kindly disposition. He much enjoyed watching the children run races at the *Dog and Bacon* one day for the prize of a smock.

Public Houses

The inns of Horsham have always been centres of social life. When the cattle market was located in the Bishopric, almost every cottage was a beershop, and at a higher level the larger inns such as the *King's Head* and the *Black Horse* (on the corner of the Worthing Road and West Street, and now demolished) were the chief venues for balls, dinners and suchlike social gatherings. The *Anchor* inn (Market Square) and the *Crown* were the main centres of political meetings and celebratory dinners, the former particularly as it overlooked the hustings which were set up in Market Square.

Keeping an alehouse, beershop, inn, or whatever name it went by was subject to licensing from very early times, and there have been Acts from 1495 attempting to control the sale of 'the authenticall drinke of Englande'. Quarter Sessions in 1645 dealt with four Horsham citizens for keeping unlicensed alehouses and for 'sufferinge drinkinge, and disorder in their houses on the Lords Daye', and 21 men and two women were also presented for the unlicensed offence only. Until Horsham developed more contacts with the outside world because of better roads, the inns and alehouses obtained custom from local people and traders in the markets, but the coming of the coaching era in the 18th century consequent upon turnpike roads being extended, meant that the *King's Head* (*Ye Olde* is a modern accretion) in particular assumed a considerable importance as a coaching stop with accommodation and refreshment for humans and horses alike. Seeing that the railway was coming to Horsham, one optimistic developer anticipated the demand for hotel accommodation and built the *Pioneer* hotel, which he thought would be next the station to be constructed in the Brighton Road, but land prices being too high the railway company decided the line should run where it does today, and the hotel was a white elephant which has had a mixed history as school, doss house, offices, and is today private accommodation.

Notwithstanding the long hours worked, there were opportunities besides fair day for celebration. The church wardens' accounts tell of payment for ringing the church bells at the Restoration of Charles II, while most coronations and similar royal occasions were also celebrated. The coronation of Queen Victoria in 1838 was marked by fun and games on Swan Meadow, now submerged under Albion Way. It is recorded that two small boys walked all the way to Crawley to wave to Queen Victoria when she passed in a carriage on the way to Brighton, and all the way back without having anything to eat. Pleasures were simple, or else they also

served the double purpose of being useful, like the libraries and industrial societies of the early 19th century. For the first Jubilee of Queen Victoria in 1887, an industrial exhibition was held with prizes for original handicrafts, and no doubt one was awarded for the canoe made out of discarded meat tins.
Funerals were social occasions and drew larger crowds than ever knew the deceased, and some were held at the dead of night with many torches accompanying, which had the air of novelty. With the rise in medical research in the 18th century, there was an increasing demand for bodies for dissection, and the revolting practice of body-snatching led to watch being kept from the belfry or the cottages near the church, but the Anatomy Act of 1832 brought the practice to an end when the obtaining of bodies was legalised.

Cricket in Horsham

Many would say that the greatest sport in Sussex is cricket. An early record of the game is 1662 at Worth, but the first at Horsham seems to have been in 1768. Cricket caught on rapidly and we have references to games by John Baker in the 1770s. His diary can be drawn on for several aspects of daily life, and once he rode from Shoreham to Horsham in a gale of wind to see the match versus Dorking, who were beaten by six wickets. He also watched games on the green, and was delighted when the Horsham team beat the Warnham boys 'out of sight'. Sometimes to the ladies, however, the game was a bit of a bore. Lady Sussex, whose husband, the Earl, was a cricket fanatic, complained that the only prevailing amusements were hunting, hawking, ninepins and cricket, and one of the early aspects of the game which did not improve it was the betting, which played a large part at one time.

The original Horsham cricket ground was in Denne Park, north-east of the present house, as the Tredcrofts who lived there had a lot of interest in the game, but people got tired of wending their way up Denne Hill, so Edward Tredcroft gave the present ground to the town in 1850. It is on the site of the old barracks, and John Baker's diary refers to cricket matches on the Artillery Ground, although in fact mainly infantry were quartered there. Poor Tredcroft became financially embarrassed after this and had to leave Horsham.

For a time in the 1830s there was a cricket ground in the northern part of Horsham Park. The first time a Sussex team came here was in 1853, but the tradition of a County Cricket Week started in 1908 when A. C. Oddie, captain of the Horsham Cricket Club and a County Committee member, worked hard to get a County Cricket Week organised, and this continued with war-time intervals to 1956 when the County Committee decided to end it, to the great regret of many. In the same year the Urban District Council decided to withdraw financial support. The Cricket Weeks were always great occasions; additional to the actual game there were plays, dances, concerts, garden parties and a colourfully decorated town.

The Growth of Societies

In the early years of the 19th century for many organisations and societies the economic aspect had to be emphasised more than any other because of the hardness of the times. One of the oldest societies still going in the present century was the Horsham Maternal Society, founded in 1815 'to provide poor married women of good character with assistance at the time of their confinement', the assistance taking the form of clothes, groceries and coal, but wives of beershop keepers were excluded. Next comes the Book Society of 1830, which also ran a library, and in 1831 the Horsham Friendly Society. 'In the fear of God, it is declared that this Society is established . . . for the purpose of relieving and maintaining those of its Members, as by Sickness, Lameness, Blindness, or other infirmity (not occasioned by his or their own fault or misconduct) shall be rendered unable to work and gain a livelihood, and of defraying the funeral expenses of deceased Members'. There was a monthly club night, at which one shilling had to be paid, and threepence for

Social Life

liquor. This last was presumably the reason for Rule V, 'That if any member of this Society shall break down any fences, or do any kind of mischief, coming or going, on club nights, he shall, on the evidence of two or more credible witnesses, be immediately excluded this Society'. The age limits being 18 to 30 years, the Society would include the liveliest of the drinking population.

The original Archery Society of 1833 was shortlived, but a revived one, of course, flourishes today. The Labourers' Friendly Society went some way in 1837 to meet the loss of the free commoners' rights when Horsham Common was enclosed in 1813, and even in this time of acute food shortage there was still time to pursue learning and a new Library Society started, an earlier one having closed in 1820. The Literary and Scientific Society began in 1847 and provided lectures which were much esteemed by working men who sought to improve themselves, and it also had a reading room for newspapers, and a chess room.

A Horsham Football Club was started by the church in 1870 and the rules were largely those of Rugby football, invented nearly 50 years earlier. 'Rule 18. No hacking allowed . . . Rule 20. No one wearing projecting nails, iron plates, or gutta-percha on the soles or heels of his boots shall be allowed to play'.

Horsham has been proud of its bands for over 100 years. Some time around 1865 there was a town band and in 1892 the bandstand in the Carfax was built for it. The Horsham Recreation Band started life in December 1900 and its first public performance was for the inmates of the Workhouse in Crawley Road on Good Friday 1902. It first performed on Carfax bandstand in 1903 and was renamed the Borough Silver Band in 1919 by William Albery, who did so much to build it up. Albery always regretted the loss of borough status by Horsham, and used this occasion to underline his contention that we still were a borough. The band won the Southern Counties Championship 13 times between the wars, and came second at the Great Crystal Palace Festival in 1936.

Social Welfare

The principle of self-help, much preached in Victorian times, was behind the formation of organisations like the Industrial Society, founded under church auspices in 1866 to give plain needlework to poor respectable women. In all similar organisations, more was given to those who helped themselves, yet curiously enough the systems of poor relief which had been tried since the time of Henry VIII had never really coped properly with the problem of the able-bodied without work. An Act of 1782 enabled parishes to get together to organise workhouses on a 'union' principle, but Shoberl in his history of Sussex talks of the 'union of a certain number of parishes to form houses of industry . . . but there is little prospect that this practice will ever become by any means general, notwithstanding the evident good effects of the system'. The trouble was that no one knew how to organise the labour properly, and the employment in this area of men and women in agriculture at poor relief rates merely amounted to a subsidy of agriculture at the ratepayers' expense. In spite of much public-spirited effort to alleviate the lot of the pauper, morale of workhouse inmates was very bad.

Our Union was formed with neighbouring parishes in 1835, and the workhouse built in the Crawley Road in 1838-39. (Previously the parish almshouses had been in the Normandy.) The accounts of 1868 show that the staff consisted of a master, matron, schoolmaster, schoolmistress, two nurses, and an assistant, a book and a porter. There were 122 in the workhouse, 16 died, and 241 had been admitted in the last six months, 40 of whom were children. Altogether 1,201 paupers had been relieved in the half year, including vagrants, a decrease of 679 compared with the year previous. Outside relief was given to 1,602 persons each week on average. The centralisation of local government proceeded rapidly in the early years of this century, and it took on responsibility for poor relief, so few regretted the passing of the Poor Law Guardians in 1929. The workhouse building continued its function until 1939, and during World War II it was used as a hospital for the Canadian forces, and now forms part of the Forest Hospital.

Parish of Horsham.

A Meeting of the Town Committee
FOR
PROVIDING EMPLOYMENT
FOR THE
UNEMPLOYED POOR OF THIS PARISH,
Held at the LAMB INN December 18th, 1833.

PRESENT.

Mr. WILLIAM FEIST in the Chair.

Messrs. S. MITCHELL,	Messrs. W. ALDRIDGE,
E. LEE,	C. SMALLWOOD,
W. FOREMAN,	C. FEIST,
W. LAKER,	J. TOLHURST,
T. R. WARNER	S. ROWLAND.

IT WAS RESOLVED---

1st---That it is extremely desirable that the able-bodied Poor of this Parish should be provided with Employment to enable them to earn sufficient wages to support themselves without resorting to Parochial Relief.

2nd---That this Meeting view with much regret that a very considerable Number of the Labouring Poor are at the present time dependent upon the Parish Officers for Employment or Relief.

3rd---That, at a General Meeting of the Inhabitants held on the 29th day of November last, it was Resolved "to be expedient that the System (*viz. of apportioning the unemployed Poor between the Farmers' Committee and the Town Committee*) "pursued last "Winter should *be continued until Lady Day next,*" and that Town and Country Committees were then formed to carry such Resolution into effect.

4th---That in compliance therewith, this Committee provided Employment for their apportioned Number of the unemployed Poor, and have continued until the present period so to do; but they regret to learn *that the Number apportioned to the Farmers' Committee have not been Employed by them; but on the contrary have fallen upon the Parish Officers for Employment.*

5th---That this Committee are therefore with great reluctance compelled to discontinue to provide Employment for the Labourers apportioned to them---but at the same time they willingly express their readiness to renew their Engagement with the Farmers' Committee; upon having a full understanding with them, that the Terms agreed upon at the several Meetings held for that purpose be mutually complied with.

6th---That this Committee do adjourn until again called upon by the Secretary.

7th---That Three Hundred Copies of the above Resolutions be immediately printed and circulated.

(Signed,)

WM. FEIST, Chairman.

Hunt, Printer, West Street, Horsham.

Fig. 9. An attempt to cope with the relief of the numerous unemployed poor in 1833.

Without getting involved in any arguments about private versus State charity, it must be said that a great deal of good was done by private organisations. The band concert of 1903 mentioned above was in aid of unemployed relief at a time of much distress, and on a similar occasion in 1870 the following notice appeared in the Parish magazine:

> Great distress in Horsham—Distribution of bread, coals &c.—In consequence of the inclement weather in the month of February, and the want of work, great distress was believed to exist in the Parish of Horsham; a Meeting was called and a Committee formed to enquire into it. At first there was only an extra distribution of soup; but finding that the frost continued, the Committee set to work in earnest, and invited all who were out of employ and in distress to come to the Town Hall, at nine o'clock, on Monday, February 21st. Mr. Bostock, the chairman of the Committee, assisted by the Churchwardens, the clergy, and several of the really benevolent gentlemen of the Parish, distributed tickets for bread, soup and coal to 194 families, according to the necessities of each case. Much care was taken in enquiring into the wants and characters of the applicants, and some well-known individuals were a little disappointed at their reception; but the Committee have generally received much encouragement and thanks for their work, while funds have been abundantly supplied by the charitable. On the 21st, 250 quarts of soup, 200 loaves and 17 cwt. of coals were distributed.

There have been many such occasions in our history, and today such relief may be more efficient, but is it more human with its complicated rules and computerised workings? The problems arising from wayward human nature are always with us. The alcoholism of today used to be called intemperance, which was much more serious for the family when the breadwinner spent such a comparatively large proportion of his wages on liquor. The Temperance Association formed in 1868 made great efforts to improve the situation, and was later aided by the Salvation Army. We may not have scenes nowadays in the Carfax such as those at election times in the last century, when scores of incapable persons were lying about, but we still have our social troubles of one kind or another. The following is an extract from the *Sussex County Magazine* of 1949:

Social Life

> Some daring souls at Horsham have decided to set up a marriage guidance council. The local Rotary Club is credited with the original move in the matter. They consider that such a council is an 'absolute necessity' in Horsham.

The Growth of Leisure

Leisure as the 19th century wore on became practical reality for more and more people, and purely leisurely societies developed. The Horticultural Society began in the 1870s, and so did the Working Men's Club. The building in East Street, now part of the *King's Head* hotel, was built as a music hall in 1869, and *Albery's Horsham Journal* of September that year has this to say:

> Velocipedes, bicycles and tricycles, are very popular in this neighbourhood just now . . . A large number of boys and young men are constantly practising in the neighbourhood of North Street and Carfax on these new-fangled riding-machines, which are let out to them by the hour by an enterprising tradesman. The movements of these would-be velocipedists are watched by many spectators, who, as is natural, find amusement in the accidents and over-turnings which, it seems, are the penalty all beginners have to pay for their experiences.

A roller-skating rink was opened in November 1864 in the Brighton Road, and no doubt added to the casualties from 'over-turnings'. Swimming was customarily done in Mill Bay, the stretch of the River Arun which runs past the cricket ground, and until recent years this was wider and deeper and unencumbered with trees and undergrowth. At last in 1934 the Council opened the swimming pool in the park, after Mrs. Laughton, J.P., had spent 10 years agitating for one. Most golf courses in Sussex were constructed at the end of last century, and the first Horsham golf club opened at Warnham in 1906.

Even before the days of King John, who used Knepp Castle as a hunting lodge, hunting must have played an important part in our economy both as a necessity for food and as recreation, and as training for war. Among the horses sent to France in the Great War were many hunters from this neighbourhood. The Crawley and Horsham Hunt started some time around 1847, over country some 20 miles from east to west and 25 miles from north to south. The Boxing Day meet in the Carfax is still watched by a large crowd.

Horsham Theatres

There have been theatres of various sorts in Horsham since time out of mind, and the following notice once appeared on public notice boards:

> Gentlemen,
>
> Take Notice that We intend making Application to the Magistrates to be assembled at the next General Quarter Sessions of the Peace to be holden at Midhurst in and for the County of Sussex on Tuesday the Fifth day of April next for a licence to Exhibit Plays Farces Interludes and other Dramatical Representations at Horsham in the County aforesaid according to the Tenor of the late Act of Parliament Authorizing and Empowering Justices of the Peace to Licence such performances.
>
> Dated this 10th day of March 1796.
>
> To Mr John Wickens)
> and   ) Bailiffs of Horsham
> Mr. John Attree   )
>
> John Jonas
> Sampson Pinley
> Managers of the Theatres
> Lewes Eastbourne &c.

The *Capitol* theatre started in 1923 as an idea to employ ex-servicemen who formed the nucleus of the band of the 4th Battalion of the Royal Sussex Regiment. It was owned and managed by Captain Middleton who formed the Blue Flash Cinema Company for the purpose. It was always intended as a theatre and cinema, first accommodating an orchestra of 15 under Mr. Yarnold, and later obtaining an organ by Willis and Beard. The cinema was operated by back-projection, which was thought to give a clearer picture as the beam did not have to struggle through a smoky atmosphere to the screen. The style of the building was Italian throughout, with Lombardic roof tiles and a fountain in the forecourt copied from the Villa Albani in Rome (where is it now?). The soaring cost of land meant that when the town was recently redeveloped there was a battle to save the *Capitol* from demolition, but the battle was only won at the cost of nearly drowning the building in acres of red brick walling and losing its original landscaping entirely.

Throughout much of Horsham's history the quality of life has been conditioned by communications. Just as the price of poultry was affected in the 18th century by the opening of turnpike roads, so our entertainment has been acquired over a wider area since the advent of the railway and the motor car. The dilution of the community spirit in Horsham by the very rapid growth in its population and its mobility has militated ever increasingly against adequate support for leisure organisations, which have to suffer undue anxiety about their financial situations. Often the smaller and more localised ventures are more successful, which perhaps bears out the view of the National Council for Social Service that a community centre should cater for only about 5,000 people. This would have been the total population of Horsham a century ago.

Chapter Eight

EDUCATION

CONSIDERING the number of children involved, and the importance of the matter, it is surprising that there is so little information to be had on schooling in Horsham before 1800, with the exception of Collyer's. Such ignorance is not peculiar to Horsham, but has been remarked upon by educational historians for the country as a whole. The great mass of the people in medieval times were still servile, and it entered no one's head that they needed education, even King Alfred with his very advanced ideas of education only envisaging a freeman's son being taught English, and as late as 1391 the House of Commons petitioned the king that no one of servile status should be educated.

Adult education began with the clergy, who in the 13th century numbered one in a hundred of the population. The many religious upheavals meant that often the standard of the clergy was very low, but nevertheless the association of the Church with education was close, and until the late 17th century every schoolmaster had to be licensed by the bishop. Both Church and secular development of education took place side by side—the Church always needed education as a handmaid to evangelism, and as no community could manage without clerks who had Latin,

Education

these being taught by the priests for a fee, and then the civil authorities, in our case the borough, would appoint a teacher to be paid by themselves. As the civil organisation developed, so would the need for those able to cope with Latin in the courts, or with accounting in the expanding economy.

Chantry priests were expected to teach in addition to their usual duties, but no organised chantry school is known in Horsham, so the dissolution of the chantries under Edward VI would not have set education back so much here as it did elsewhere.

The parish clerk was supposed to be an educated man, although the standard of his entries in the registers might sometimes belie this, and both before and after the Reformation he was expected to give lessons in reading. Teaching was very badly paid, so schoolmasters had to have another occupation.

The Foundation of Collyer's

The apprenticing of youths certainly helped their general education as well as teaching their craft, and it is to such an apprenticeship that we owe the foundation of Collyer's school, as Richard Collyer was born in Horsham but apprenticed to the Mercers' Company, and becoming a wealthy man he left in his will provision for the founding of a free school for 60 Horsham boys, together with endowment for its upkeep and for salaries. The school opened in 1541 on a site which today is the playground of St. Mary's church school, the Mercers making the necessary payments and the vicar and churchwardens with other parishioners choosing the staff, which only amounted to a headmaster and an usher until 1889. The schooling was the usual Tudor kind, everything being based on Latin grammar which gave the name 'grammar school', and Latin being spoken in and out of class by compulsion. University entrance was then at 15, and this required a high standard of proficiency in the language of culture and of the professions of the Church, law and medicine. The school was from the first closely associated with the Church, in daily services, feast day celebrations and catechism, and the master saw to it that his own position of importance and esteem was not lowered by unruly behaviour by his pupils during divine service. After the Reformation the Church was well aware that she must keep education under her wing if Roman influence was to be kept at bay. Yet Collyer's was not affected by the dissolution of the chantries under Edward VI, even though built on chantry land, as its foundation was secular and the income came from a city company. The education it provided continued during the period of Elizabeth, but to modern eyes it must read strangely that the Master acted as parish clerk, raised a troop of irregulars in case of Spanish invasion, gave services as a doctor, and was also a part-time lawyer. It was at this time that pressure for a curriculum not entirely composed of Latin grew up, and in 1595 the three Rs were taught by the usher to the lower half of the school, as there were still no elementary schools in Horsham. This had the effect roughly speaking that the advanced pupils had a good chance to proceed to university, while those who were entering their fathers' trades would at least be able to read and write and keep accounts.

The churchwardens' accounts show that in 1618, when the pressure on space in the church was acute, a special gallery was built for the school near the north door, at a time when several such galleries were erected much to the detriment of the fabric. Education was advancing with several other grammar schools being founded in this area, and it was the usual practice for children of the gentry to spend a lot of time away from home where they would benefit from the upbringing of strangers rather than their own family: the daughters would perhaps be sent to London. Anthony Stapley of Hickstead in 1657 sent his two sons to Horsham for schooling and paid £10 for board, and only £2 for schooling—the boarding being with an uncle.

The Seventeenth Century

The great rebuilding of 1570–1640, brought about by a rising prosperity and standard of living, does not seem to

Education

have brought any schools of note to Horsham, although in 1635 an elementary school was opened in West Chiltington through private charity. Already in 1629 the coming struggle between king and parliament was casting its shadow, as in that year a faction tried to secure the appointment of a master who opposed the policy of Archbishop Laud, and a later master, John Sefton, was dispossessed of his parish of South Stoke and lost his headship of Collyer's because of his professed Royalist sympathies. During the Interregnum much attention was paid to schooling by the authorities, who issued a stream of instructions about its conduct, and it is safe to conjecture that standards of schooling suffered thereby, as they did when the periodic outbreaks of smallpox visited the school at the same time.

In 1660 there was much repairing of Collyer's buildings, with additions, but the Restoration brought general disfavour on the part of the Royalists against country grammar schools, and it was fortunate that the then Master maintained a high reputation for the school. Schoolmasters still had to be licensed by the bishop before they could practise their profession, and the interest of the established Church in education remained strong in the face of the growth of Dissenting schools.

Decline in the Eighteenth Century

Education in the 18th century suffered a considerable decline, from universities downwards. As far as the grammar schools were concerned, they ignored the new sciences and interest in literature and language, but continued to study the dead languages for their own sake. Collyer's was no exception, and also suffered from not teaching what the industrial revolution was wanting. Another cause of Collyer's eclipse was the appointment of masters who were parsons with parish interests elsewhere. These appointments were bound up with the political infighting described in Chapter Two, and the appointees had several interests outside both Church and school. Small wonder that as the century wore on the numbers of scholars at Collyer's dwindled, so that in 1807 there were none at all, the master and usher drawing their pay nonetheless.

The Thornton Academy

The 18th century saw the rise of many private schools, of all kinds and sizes. Probably the most famous at this time was one established in 1765 in the old gaol buildings in the Carfax by Richard Thornton, a man who was not afraid of the law when it came to enclosing part of Horsham Common, for which he was fined, and also when he invited trouble for depositing filth on the highway. He took boys from four years upwards in astronomy, fencing, and the Italian method of book-keeping, besides the more usual subjects, and quite clearly his numerous advertisements in the newspapers were aimed at the burgeoning middle-class in Horsham. Although his premises had been ridden with all the things that gaols of that period usually had, nevertheless they were used to board the pupils for which he charged 12 guineas inclusive. In 1782 he sold the premises to Lady Irwin who wanted them for the accompanying burgage vote. His son, James Thornton, managed to get himself appointed usher of Collyer's, but as there were no pupils there he continued to assist his father in running the Academy.

It is extraordinary that so little was done about the virtual extinction of Collyer's. That the situation was generally known is evidence by an entry in the *Universal British Directory* for 1791 which stated that Horsham had 'a free school, and other charitable gifts, which are most shamefully abused'. The Mercers' Company did wake up eventually in 1807 and a fresh impetus was given to the school by filling it with the 60 pupils stipulated in the founder's will, but trouble with the usher, James Thornton, for several years prevented the school from progressing as it should have done. Eventually a new constitution was approved after a Chancery case, but this downgraded Collyer's to nothing more than an elementary school, which it remained until 1889.

Education

Rapid Expansion after 1820

The beginning of the 19th century marks an explosion in educational history. Besides the numerous academies and private schools already referred to, many dame schools sprang up, and the standard of many of these was sometimes so bad that a Royal Commission in 1858 said that 'none are too old, too poor, too ignorant' that they cannot be found running such establishments, 'unqualified in every way'. If other occupation failed, a private school could always be opened, unlicensed and uninspected. Henry Burstow, the Horsham bellringer, went to one of these, which he much appreciated. It was kept by Miss Jane Sayers and was said to have been the first infant school in Horsham when it opened in 1831 in the Bishopric. There was no systematic education in England at this time: any person or organisation could set up an establishment to teach, and the great interest in science, particularly applied science for the industrial revolution, demanded schools, although there was always the reactionary element which considered that the poor working classes might get dangerous if they were educated. Lord John Russell when Home Secretary in 1834 said he would not encourage abominations such as popular education.

British and National Schools

The theory of education was beginning to attract interest, and two teachers, Lancaster and Bell, started experimenting with the monitorial system, whereby older children taught younger, which reduced the need for teachers. Lancaster was a Quaker and the undenominational Lancasterian Society founded in 1808 'to make arrangements for the education of every poor child in the kingdom at a trifling expense' (becoming the British Society in 1814) spread their schools over the country, Horsham having a British School from 1814 in the London Road, with 200 boys and 100 girls, both sexes being taught reading, writing and grammar, the boys linear and perspective drawing, and the girls needlework and domestic arts. The premises were rebuilt in 1826 and later used by the Salvation Army until their recent demolition.

No. 3.   *THE*

HORSHAM

BRITISH SCHOOL,

MAGAZINE,

PUBLISHED, May 30th. 1833.

Printed, by J. Philpott,
HORSHAM.

LECTURE on MINERALOGY.

On Monday April 15th. a Lecture on the above subject was delivered at our School, a full report of which was promised in this Magazine.

The Lecturer commenced by producing several beautiful specimens of hard substances such as Crystal, Jasper, Emerald, Agate, Amethyst, Quartz, Beryl &c.

The hardness of all this class of minerals was shown by the facility with which they scratched glass.

He also exhibited a great variety of other Minerals, such as Carbonates, Fluates, Sulphates, & Phosphates of Lime; specimens of the different sorts of Granite; Ores of the various Metals, as Copper, Antimony, Iron, Lead &c.

The Lecture was very instructive, and gave great satisfaction to the Scholars who heard it.

Reporter.

Fig. 10. The magazine of the British School, 1833.

Education

The rules for the British School in Horsham state that it was for the education of poor children of all religious denominations from seven to 13 years. Reading lessons must come only from Holy Scripture. The hours were from nine to twelve, and two to five in summer, shorter in winter, and the staff consisted of one master and one mistress. The tuition was not free—a subscriber of ten shillings per year could nominate one child, or a child whose parents could afford it would have to pay 2½d. per week.

By contrast the National Schools were free, and very much associated with the Church of England which fiercely opposed non-denominational schools. The first National School was started by the National Society for the Promotion of the Education of the Poor in the Principles of the Established Church in 1811 (itself an offshoot of the Society for the Promotion of Christian Knowledge), and within a year Horsham had its first National School established in the parish church porch, which was then part of Trinity Chantry, by the curate the Rev. George Marshall. About 100 children were crammed into a not very large space, so within a short time a proposal was made to build a school for the girls at the north entrance to Denne Park. However, a petition was got up to oppose the idea because of the 'lowlands of the riverside it cannot be regarded as salubrious', but nonetheless the school was built and the building is still there today. In 1840 another curate, the Rev. Jarvis Kenrick, paid for the erection of a school next to St. Mark's school, and the girls moved to the other side of the church as St. Mary's school in 1862, on land bought originally for a Sunday school and school for adults. Later, an infants' school was added. In the 1830s a school for infants was established by the Church of England in Denne Road.

There were therefore two free schools early in the century, Collyer's and the National School, and a fee-paying British School, the last two being opposed to each other on religious denominational grounds, although both were of Christian foundation. The iron Broadbridge Mission Room, forerunner of St. John's church, was built in 1853 and included a school. The Roman Catholic church in Springfield Road had a mixed school attached, and also opened an infant school in Trafalgar Road.

Other Church Schools

The hold of the Established Church on education was maintained when Sunday schools spread rapidly at the end of the 18th century. Horsham had one from 1787, and the idea was to keep the children in Sunday school throughout the whole day, ending with evensong. Everyone seemed to think this was an excellent way of keeping the children out of mischief, except perhaps the children themselves. The Free Christian church was not backward in education, a day school being started by the minister, Thomas Sadler, in the 1820s in a room adjoining the church, later moving to North Parade, and his daughters, Ann and Elizabeth, ran a private boarding school in Oxford Road. Thomas Sadler was assisted by Robert Ashdowne, who later became minister and built a small school next his house in Albion Terrace, his wife also running a school for infants. The Albion Terrace Academy had a great name because of its lively *Gazette*, not printed, but copied in manuscript from 1839 to 1842. The contributions by the boys were wide-ranging and included subjects like capital punishment, national education, natural science, local geography, and kindness to animals, in contrast to the stereotyped formal education of the later State schools. In 1838 the Union workhouse was built at Roffey and about 40 children on average attended the school there, but it must be remembered that workhouse teaching was purely vocational to fit the children for manual labour.

Adult Education

Arising out of the industrial revolution, concern had been growing about the question of giving an opportunity to the adult manual worker to improve himself through education, and in 1829 the Mechanics Institute was founded in the British School in London Road, as an offshoot of the Society for the Diffusion of Useful Knowledge which provided cheap books. It had a lending library of 352 volumes, and the subjects taught included reading, drawing and music, although the original intention of Lord Brougham who founded the Society was to enable workers to understand the new manufacturing processes, but, of course, in Horsham at that time there were not many of these. As a contemporary observer wrote, the Institute 'afforded to the Members a rational occupation of their leisure and fostered a taste for the cultivation of their faculties'. There was some hesitation about allowing a newspaper room, as newspapers introduced the dangerous subject of party politics, but the argument also ran that if denied the newspaper in the Institute, the worker would seek it in the alehouse instead. There were originally 62 members, and half a dozen lectures were given each year, but the average attendance was not good, according to the official report. The Horsham Literary and Scientific Institute, on the other hand, was on a higher plane, and in 1851 it had 52 members and 200 volumes in its library. It seems to have a patchy existence as there are accounts of its formation or reformation in 1840, 1847 and 1851. The 1847 foundation provided a library, rooms for reading, music and classes, lectures on literature, science and art, and a museum of natural and artificial curiosities. The introduction of political and religious controversy was prohibited. A contemporary journal said in 1869 that it was only used by 108 persons out of a population of 7,000 to 8,000, there being a prejudice due to distinction in subscriptions between rich and poor, the mechanic and workingman paying 1s. 6d. per quarter. In the reading room, poor working-men were not as a rule treated sociably by other members. This may have accounted for its fragmented history.

The criticism of this type of adult education was that it over-estimated the standard of education of the workers so that the lectures provided were simply incomprehensible, the science lecture, for example, needed quite a knowledge of the subject if it was not to be over the head of the listener, and later the formal technical education made these institutes superfluous. Schooling was for such a short

HORSHAM
Mechanics' Institution

A LECTURE ON
GEOLOGY

WILL BE DELIVERED

At the British School Room,

On Thursday, September 23, 1830, at 8 o'Clock in the Evening,

BY MR. HINDMAN.

☞ Tickets of Admission, One Shilling each, to be had of Mr. T. Honywood, Mr. John Browne, or Mr. R. Sheppard.

HUNT, PRINTER, HORSHAM.

Education

period in a child's life by today's standards, and this was recognised. In 1858 the diocesan inspector of education wrote to the bishop, 'In this Rural Deanery, as almost everywhere else, the Complaint is—the tender Age at which the Child of the poor Man is removed from School, and is supposed to have had its Education. No very abiding effects on the population can be expected, while this continues'. At this time church schools taught from the ages of five to eleven. The State did not begin to concern itself with elementary education until 1833, when it became evident that voluntary schools could not hope to solve the problem alone as they only catered for about half the children, but it was not until 1870 that board schools were established, the delay being largely because of Anglican versus non-conformist arguments in parliament. Education became compulsory in 1876, and wholly free by 1891.

Library Societies

Various other organisations sprang up in the 19th century to cope with the ever-growing thirst for knowledge. In 1830 a Book Society with library was started by the Free Christian church, which lasted until 1940, and another Library Society began in 1842, replacing one which had foundered in 1820. These library societies were of the lending kind, and great care was taken to ensure that no explosive literature of a religious or political nature was admitted. Private schools continued to flourish, including the Causeway Academy, Oxford Road boarding school, run by Mary and Ann Evershed, and Phoebe Puntis's day school in South Street. Gone were the days when overwhelming poverty sent children out to work, thus denying them schooling, and every chance was now seized of education for betterment.

Collyer's Revival

Collyer's School was in a bad way still, in 1867 being reported on as a rather inferior kind of National School, with Mercers' Company and Parish still tolerating a poor standard of teaching owing to the preoccupation of the Master and Usher with other means of livelihood. The premises had been rebuilt in 1840 which at least provided an adequate base for a much superior master, William Pirie (1822–1868), but the teaching remained at primary level in spite of some criticism by those who wished it to return to full grammar status. Numbers were raised to 80 in 1855 from the old maximum of 60, but the leaving age was still fourteen. Religious controversy arose when the high church vicar, John Hodgson, introduced his own doctrine, but this was settled amicably; however, a more serious matter was the formation of the Horsham Free School Defence Organisation, formed in 1833 to combat the proposal to make Collyer's partly fee-paying.

The town was plastered with handbills and the newspaper columns filled with letters on the subject, the chief point made by the opposition being the loss of Collyer's places to the working-man's children. Many sections of the community were utterly divided, some of the clergy giving their support and also some of the business people of the town who had themselves been educated at the school. After years of discussion with R. H. Hurst and the vicar, the Rev. H. B. Ottley taking leading parts, a new scheme was adopted in 1889 which meant that all except 20 boys had to pay fees, the age limits would be seven to 17, and the numbers increased from 80 to 100, with boarding facilities.

State Schools Arrive

In the meantime the State school boards set up in 1870 had reached Horsham in 1873, but the Elementary Education Act merely supplemented voluntary schools, and in 1878 the first Horsham board school in what was then called East Parade (later moving to Clarence Road) was quickly followed by the second in Trafalgar Road to cope with the growing population.

The Free Church was continuing its tradition of providing good schooling, the minister in 1879, Thomas Scott, running a private school so successfully that he gave up his church post to devote full time to the school.

Education

Collyer's Removal

In 1890 the decision was taken to move Collyer's from its rather cramped site near the parish church. R. H. Hurst gave the land in Hurst Road and the school re-opened on its present site in 1893; in the previous three years there were no pupils while the issue of either improving the old site or moving was settled. The new school started off with 48 boys, but the academic standard rose rapidly with several scholarships to universities, and during this century Collyer's gained a fine reputation not only for academic excellence but for games and other out-of-school activities, only to succumb to the comprehensive tide of egalitarianism which the Governors did not have the spirit to resist, and Collyer's Grammar School has become a two-year finishing school under the name of Sixth Form College. Also submerged at the same time was the Horsham High School for Girls, which started life in 1909 as a pupil teacher centre, becoming the High School in 1922 and also having a very good academic record. Its sojourn in Tanbridge House dated from 1927.

Technology for Adults

Adult education continued to develop during the 19th century, encouragement being given to enter for examinations run by the Society of Arts from 1856 in basic sciences, and in technological subjects by the City and Guilds Institute from 1879. From 1882 the Society of Arts concentrated on commercial subjects, and in Horsham there were private establishments teaching these, such as the Causeway Academy (1860) in East Street. Technical evening classes were started by the County Council at Collyer's in 1895, but they were not supported and ended three years later. The grant of £200 for the classes came from the County Council to Horsham as an educational centre, and £300 more for the Art School and University Extension lectures. The infant school in Denne Road was adapted to take practical classes in carpentry and wood carving, and the Parish Room for classes in mathematics, modern languages, book-keeping and shorthand. Libraries, which are dealt with in the next chapter, grew apace with the cheap presses pouring out books from the '90s onwards, and museums were developing, over half of them in 1900 being privately originated. Our own Museum dates from 1893.

University Extension and the W.E.A.

The University Extension Scheme of the 1870s was intended to supply lecturers to the Literary, Scientific and Mechanics Institutes, and Horsham was chosen in 1887 as the South Eastern Centre, to include Sussex, Surrey, Kent and Hampshire, with support from the County Council. Eight courses were run in science, seven in literature ahd history, and by 1892 these had expanded to 11 in science and 33 in literature and history, but the Workers Educational Association (founded 1903) took over the scheme with the formation of a branch in Horsham in 1918. The University Extension Scheme had done marvellous work, and helped a lot in the cause of women's education. Hilaire Belloc was among the lecturers in our area.

Horsham Art School

The Art School had humble beginnings, originally in a private house belonging to Alexander Wood, the first chairman. The actual founder was W. E. Hubbard, who built the Volunteers Headquarters in Park Street. A small room was then taken in Springfield Road, but this, too, was inadequate, and a two-day bazaar in Horsham Park in 1890 raised over £400 towards the new school in Hurst Road, for which R. H. Hurst gave the land. The school opened in 1891 in purpose-built premises now occupied by the W.R.V.S., and moved after the war a short way along the road.

Springfield

Springfield has more than once been an educational establishment. In 1887 the following notice appeared in the Parish magazine:

Education

> To meet the requirements of the professional and commercial classes of the town and neighbourhood is an event of sufficient interest and importance to justify a passing notice in our Parish Magazine.
>
> The fine old property of Springfield Park, with its mansion—after being thoroughly renovated and adapted for the purpose—was thrown open for the reception of pupils on Jan. 24th, and the College is now in active progress.
>
> Since entering into residence, the pupils appear to have become thoroughly at home in their new quarters, and to be greatly charmed with everything about them. the objects of special interest to them, so far, have been the fine open country, the antique structure and arrangements of the picturesque old town, and magnificent edifice of St. Mary's, with its earnest stirring and impressive Sunday Services.
>
> Principal—Mr. & Mrs. Lydgate.

One may be forgiven for wondering whether this puff was written by the vicar or the Lydgates. The college in 1890 had 50 boarders and 30 day scholars, but it was replaced by a preparatory school in 1904 run by Gerald Blunt, whose ancestor had built this fine house two centuries before, and today it is a girls' school.

Christ's Hospital

Although strictly speaking not within the scope of this book, Christ's Hospital has had such an effect on the cultural life of the town in particular that it must not be omitted. There is no ancient connection between Horsham and the school; it was merely fortuitous that when it was decided to move out of London, the land at Stammerham was on the market at a knockdown price because of the bankruptcy of the Aylesbury Dairy Company, as related in the chapter on industries and trades. Christ's Hospital opened on its new site in 1902, and has contributed in many ways to the community.

In the same year the 1870 Education Act was superseded by another which converted the board schools into council schools, the Trafalgar Road schools dating from this year and those in the Oxford Road from 1914.

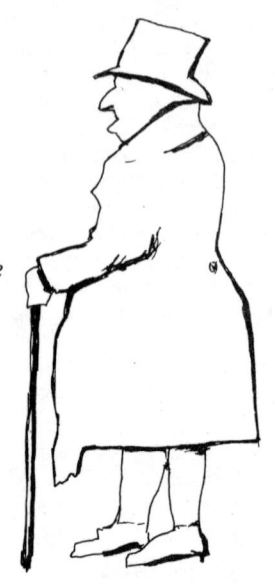

Dan Roberts,
Town Crier and Beadle
of Horsham.
Died 1825

Chapter Nine

INFORMATION

THE EARLIEST public dissemination of information must have been by word of mouth, before any other than the very few could read. In addition to doctrine, a lot of news was given out from church pulpits, and as a large proportion of the population attended church, this was an effective way of keeping everybody in the know. The Court Leet in Horsham appointed two permanent officers from medieval times, the Steward and the Crier; all others such as constables, ale conners and so forth being annual appointments. From the time when Horsham was identifiable as a town, there would have been a town crier. Later on there are records of election proclamations and other public announcements being made by the crier, for which he was paid a fee for the occasion; for example, the election accounts in 1790 have the entry, 'By Town crier's fee as usual . . . two guineas'. He was also the caretaker at the town hall and would have been able to pick up quite a lot of largesse from the numerous lawyers and others attending sessions and assizes, but when the assizes went to Lewes and the Court Leet ceased to function in the 1830s, the crier was pretty well out of a job, although he still existed until this century when William Law issued a challenge to all other town criers in the country for a contest, which he won, against 37 others at Devizes in 1912. He was the last of a long line, but long before this time public notices were being increasingly used to keep the town informed. The earliest record we have is the election of 1701, the first one ever to be contested in Horsham. A poster of 1792 announcing that the Bailiffs have procured a standard bushel measure which the farmers and corn dealers were to use was printed in Dorking. It must have upset local printers that official town notices were not being given to them to print. Here is an example of one handwritten:

> Shavings Dun here for a penny each person. Likewise children carefully Eddicated in Reading, Righting and account at this House by me James Moorfoot.

With improvement in printing and cheap paper production, posters became more elaborate and more colourful, and there is a large collection in the Museum. Those produced during the First World War are particularly striking.

The First Newspapers

Before the large-scale dissemination of news by the press, many people depended on correspondents in London keeping them informed of what was happening in the big city, and very valuable these letters are to the historian. The rigid censorship and licensing of news-sheets kept these small and scarce, but a handful of early London newspapers would have found their way down to Horsham when they began in the 17th century, especially during the Civil War when there was a great thirst for news, but the first Sussex newspaper was the *Sussex Weekly Advertiser* of 1749, published in Lewes. Local newspapers did not trouble overmuch about local news at first, because this was better known in the

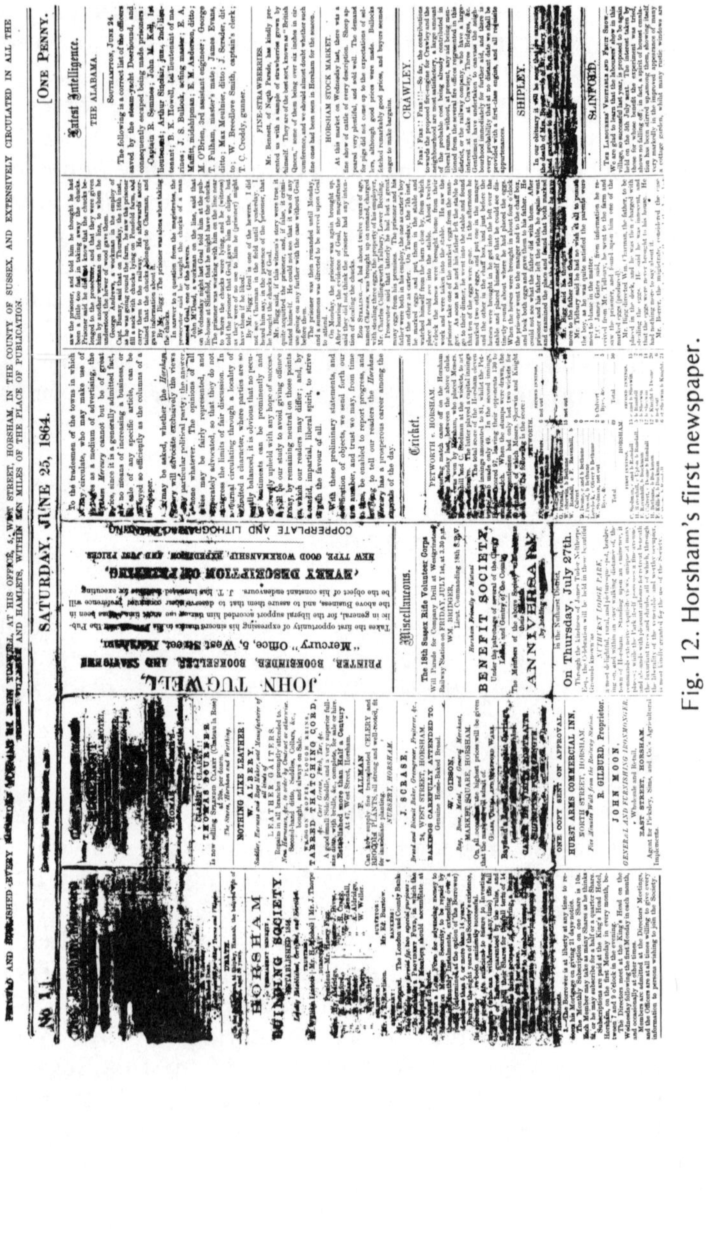
THE Horsham Mercury, AND MID SUSSEX AND SOUTH SURREY ADVERTISER.

PRINTED AND PUBLISHED EVERY SATURDAY MORNING BY JOHN TUGWELL, AT HIS OFFICE, 5, WEST STREET, HORSHAM, IN THE COUNTY OF SUSSEX, AND EXTENSIVELY CIRCULATED IN ALL THE TOWNS, VILLAGES AND HAMLETS, WITHIN TEN MILES OF THE PLACE OF PUBLICATION.

No. 1.] SATURDAY, JUNE 25, 1864. [ONE PENNY.

HORSHAM PERMANENT BENEFIT BUILDING SOCIETY. ESTABLISHED 1856.

NOTHING LIKE LEATHER!

JOHN TUGWELL, PRINTER, BOOKBINDER, BOOKSELLER, AND STATIONER. "Mercury" Office, 5, West Street, Horsham.

EVERY DESCRIPTION OF PRINTING, NEW TYPE, GOOD WORKMANSHIP, EXPEDITION, AND JUST PRICES.

COPPERPLATE AND LITHOGRAPHIC PRINTING.

Miscellaneous.

The 18th Sussex Rifle Volunteer Corps

BENEFIT SOCIETY.

ANNIVERSARY

On Thursday, July 27th.

ONE COPY SENT ON APPROVAL.

HURST ARMS COMMERCIAL INN, NORTH STREET, HORSHAM.

Cricket.

PETWORTH v. HORSHAM.

Latest Intelligence.

THE ALABAMA.

FINE STRAWBERRIES.

HORSHAM STOCK MARKET.

CRAWLEY.

SHIPLEY.

SLINFOLD.

Fig. 12. Horsham's first newspaper.

alehouses, of which Horsham as a market town had plenty. Producing a newspaper was a most expensive business owing to the duty on paper, stamp duty on the newspaper itself and a tax on advertisements as well. This prevented any expansion of the press until the middle of last century, when the imposts were removed. First the advertisement tax went in 1853, then the tax on the newspaper itself in 1855, and finally the paper duty in 1861, but in the face of strong opposition from people like Lord John Russell, who said he would not encourage abominations like popular newspapers.

The first Horsham publication identified was not strictly speaking a newspaper, although news did creep into later numbers in spite of the editorial statement that the stamp duty prohibited the publication of news. The full title *Horsham Record, Gratuitous Advertiser, and Miscellany of Literature, Science and the Arts* describes it well, with emphasis on the miscellany. It came out on 13 February 1840 'to furnish a cheap Miscellany of what is new in science, useful in art, instructive in education, sublime and pathetic in poetry, interesting in literature, and amusing in anecdotes, narratives and miscellaneous subjects', and was published by William Laker in West Street. There were to be no politics, for which the national press was adequate. The *Record* was to be a tradesman's journal and cheap advertising medium. The first article dealt with the assassination of Henry IV of France in 1610! The second number came out a month later, the latest number known being October 1840. As no charge could be made for advertising, an ingenious scheme was devised for advertisers to purchase copies in bulk at a favourable rate, thus bringing in revenue and also ensuring a wide distribution without distribution costs.

The *Horsham Express*, published weekly at 1d. by Thomas Jull of Market Square from 13 January 1863 was a Horsham edition of the *Sussex Express*, which had started in 1861, and was printed by Baxter of Lewes. Its full title was *Horsham, Petworth and Steyning Express*, alternative title *West Sussex Journal*, reflecting the custom of such papers

HORSHAM
CORN MARKET.

THE successful establishment of a Market for Fat Stock on Wednesdays, in the Town of Horsham, has materially interfered with the business of the Corn Market held on Saturdays.

There is no doubt that when the several Railways are completed, of which Horsham will be the centre, that a great increase in the Markets will take place, and a general extension of trade in the Town.

We, the undersigned, Buyers and Sellers at the said Markets, are decidedly of opinion that it would be more convenient and beneficial to all parties attending the Markets, that the *Corn Market* should be held on Wednesdays instead of Saturdays, as heretofore, commencing at 2 o'clock; and we pledge ourselves to use our best exertions and influence to carry out this object.

Thomas Sanctuary, *Roughey Park, Horsham.*
Edwd. J. Bonny, *Slinfold.*
James Braby, *Rudgwick, Farmer.*
Thos. Child, *Slinfold, Farmer.*
Henry Allberry, jun., *Horsham, Miller.*
John Ray, *Lower Beeding, Land Steward.*
C. W. Farhall, *Newbridge, Farmer.*
John Briggs, *Slinfold, Farmer.*
W. Allberry, *Rudgwick, Miller.*
Jos. Robinson, *Crawley, Miller.*
Edwd. Holden, *Slinfold, Farmer.*
Chas. Saunders, *Horsham, Manure Merchant.*
Jas. Vincent, *Shipley, Farmer.*
Wm. Nash, *Warnham, Farmer.*
Geo. Napper, *Pulborough, Farmer.*
Robt. Knight, *Itchingfield, Farmer.*
Thos. Knight, *Slinfold, Farmer.*
Wm. Linstett, *Horsham, Farmer.*
P. Chasemore, *Horsham, Farmer.*
Wm. Wood, *Ifield Court, Farmer.*
John Agate, *Warnham, Farmer.*
Robt. Mills, *Slinfold, Farmer.*
Robt. Rowland, *Horsham, Maltster.*
R. Potter, *Horsham, Miller.*
J. B. Killick, *Nuthurst, Miller.*
Wm. Botting, *Rowner, Miller.*
Harry S. Sturt, *Slinfold, Farmer.*
John Lee, *Horsham, Salesman.*
Peter Caffin, *Warth, Miller.*
Wm. Botting, jun., *Rudgwick, Miller.*
Allen Bristow, *West Grinstead, Farmer.*
M. H. Bristow, *Shipley, Farmer.*
Edwd. Botting, *Shipley,* „
Hy. Botting, *Rudgwick,* „
Geo. Golds, *Warminghurst, Farmer.*
H. P. Thorpe, *Horsham, Miller.*
W. Linstett, jun., *Horsham, Provision Merchant.*

J. Redford, *Ifield, Farmer.*
Jas. Pronger, *Lower Beeding, Farmer.*
Jas. Waller, *Horsham, Farmer.*
E. Churchman, *Rudgwick, Farmer.*
B. Challen, *Petworth, Corn Merchant.*
Edwin Golds, *West Chiltington, Farmer.*
H. Comper, *Pulborough, Farmer.*
Thos. Elliott, *Rudgwick, Corn Dealer.*
Geo. Hammond, *Wisbro' Green, Farmer.*
A. Mighell, *Cowfold, Farmer.*
A. Baker, *Wisbro' Green, Farmer.*
Jas. Woods, *Loxwood, Farmer.*
H. Hide, *Pulborough,* „
H. Ireland, *Rudgwick,* „
Thos. Jupp, *Pulborough, Farmer.*
Wm. Churchman, *Warnham, Farmer.*
R. Botting, *Horsham, Farmer.*
J. Botting, jun., *Rudgwick, Farmer.*
W. F. Chitty, *Itchingfield,* „
E. Bristow, *Itchingfield, Farmer.*
W. Evershed, *Wisbro' Green, Farmer.*
W. Grinsted, *Billingshurst,* „
Caleb Shaw, *Warnham, Farmer.*
S. Agate, jun., *Warnham, Farmer.*
T. M. Moon, *Horsham, Farmer and Tanner.*
E. Vickress, *Slinfold, Farmer.*
Jas. Grinsted, *Slinfold, Farmer.*
Jas. Puttock, jun., *Slinfold, Farmer.*
J. Jenkins, *Rudgwick, Farmer.*
H. Challen, *Horsham,* „
Jos. Nash, *Capel, Farmer.*
W. Leopard, *Hurst, Corn Merchant.*
W. Challen, *Wisbro' Green, Farmer.*
W. Tobitt, *Wisbro' Green,* „
Chas. Churchman, *Rudgwick* „
H. Michell, *Horsham, Brewer.*
H. Tuppen, *Wisbro' Green, Farmer.*

W. M. Stanford, *Broadbridge, Farmer and Miller.*
R. Halloway, *Shipley, Farmer.*
R. Wood, *Ashurst, Farmer.*
Jas. Faire, *Shipley, Land Steward.*
Wm. Smart, *Ashfold, Land Steward.*
F. Botting, *Billingshurst, Farmer.*
Jas. Stanford, *Horsham,* „
Wm. Wood, *Broadbridge,* „
Thos. Elliott, *Wisbro' Green, Farmer.*
John Churchman, *Loxwood,* „
J. Mellersh, *Wisbro' Green,* „
J. Turner, *Billingshurst,* „
J. D. Evershed, *Billingshurst,* „
Jas. Botting, *Billingshurst,* „
Geo. Ireland, *Billingshurst* „
Albt. Agate, *Warnham,* „
Jas. Jackson, *Brighton, Machinist.*
Walter Sanders, *Pulborough, Manure Merchant.*
O. Hawes, *Slinfold, Farmer.*
H. Ireland, *Slindon and Billingshurst, Farmer.*
Jas. Haynes, *Ifield, Farmer.*
Jas. Puttock, *Slinfold, Farmer.*
Thos. Plouts, *Washington, Farmer.*
D. Cheale, *Lewes, Machinist.*
Chas. Sharp, *Horsham, Farmer.*
R. S. Rubie, *Willingdon, Corn Merchant.*
W. J. Williams, *Horsham.*
W. Atlas, *Dorking, Miller.*
W. Holden, *Horsham, Wine Merchant.*
Jas. King, *Horsham, Maltster.*
E. Stanford, *Eatons, Farmer.*
M. Mason, *Brighton, Merchant.*
P. Puttock, *Slinfold, Farmer.*
J. Butcher, *Billingshurst, Farmer.*
F. Chasemore, *Nuthurst,* „

In pursuance of the above Resolution,

NOTICE IS HEREBY GIVEN,

That the HORSHAM CORN MARKET will, from and after Wednesday the 23rd day of July, inst., be held on **Wednesday** in each week **instead of Saturday**, as heretofore.

HORSHAM, *9th July,* 1862.

S. PRICE, Printer, Bookbinder, and Stationer, West Street, Horsham.

Fig. 13. Posters were used more widely than today for general information. This one of 1862 was of great importance to a market town like Horsham.

to claim as wide a circulating area as possible. There was only half a column of Horsham news in its four pages, of which three contained news from outside Sussex. There must have been at this time a considerable interest in foreign affairs if the amount of news coverage is anything to go by, and the expressed intention of the editor seems wide of the actual mark: 'Whatever is calculated to advance (Horsham's) trade, to raise its political position, or to add to the social comforts of its inhabitants, shall have our hearty assistance'.

A rival paper started in the following year, the *Horsham Mercury and Mid-Sussex and South Surrey Advertiser*, being a genuine local paper printed and published by John Tugwell at 5 West Street, and intended to cover only Horsham and the surrounding 10 miles. The only issue known is No. 1 of 25 June 1864, published at 1d., and on the front page is an advertisement for the rival *Horsham Express*. Local news occupies half the front page, advertisements the other half, and the remaining three pages consist entirely of news and articles from the rest of the country and abroad.

There was no local newspaper in 1869, as in March of that year *Albery's Monthly Illustrated Journal* gave this as the reason for its own appearance. It was printed for the proprietors, M. and R. J. Albery, by William H. Albery, and edited by R. J. Albery, first in West Street, then North Street, and finally Market Square next to the *Anchor* hotel. The *Journal* proclaimed itself 'a local magazine of useful information and instruction', containing 24 pages in quarto size. The middle eight pages contained local and county news, and the remainder, consisting of news and articles from everywhere, including one on Herod the Great and another on the Battle of Balaclava, was a syndicated magazine.

By the June number there were 26 pages, but the last number known is October 1869. Perhaps the political tensions of the day were too much for it, as in August it announced that two or three Liberals had cancelled their subscriptions over the account of the Liberal dinner, to which the *Journal* replied, 'If we had to report the same dinner again we should report it exactly as we did last month'. A journal of similar format appeared in 1881 as *Albery and Thompson's Monthly Illustrated Journal,* containing three pages of local news out of 24 pages of largely syndicated material, although there was a useful train timetable.

The *Horsham Advertiser,* direct ancestor of the present-day *West Sussex County Times,* started life on 21 October 1871 with the additional title *Crawley, Cuckfield, East Grinstead, Petworth, Cowfold and Pulborough News,* and was published by P. and P. Cheverton at 10 East Street, later North Street and finally Market Square. It was only four pages to begin with, and evidently was worried by the *West Sussex Gazette,* published at Arundel, as on 10 May 1876 it made the mistake of advertising its rival in a leading article by saying, 'The fact of the matter is the influence of the *West Sussex Gazette* has passed away from this town for ever'. In 1888 the title was changed to *West Sussex Times, Horsham Advertiser, Mid Sussex News, Crawley Gazette, Pulborough Star, Petworth Herald, Arundel Express, Chichester Standard, Bognor and Littlehampton News and County Record,* but even that imposing title does not seem to have demolished the rival paper. The title in 1891 was *West Sussex Times and Sussex Standard,* becoming the present *West Sussex County Times* in 1893.

The Egregious William Worth

Next on the scene comes the incredible William Worth, a gentleman of small scruple who has been mentioned elsewhere in the political and other life of the town. There is no doubt about his energy, and his objectives seem to have been sincere, but he was not particular about the means he adopted. On 23 October 1875 he published the *Sussex Herald, Horsham Crawley and Pulborough News,* four pages for 1d., of which the two inside were news from elsewhere. From the first, Worth plugged his scheme of a poultry show, and some of the correspondents' letters about it were probably written by the editor. He took frequent swipes at Fitzgerald, the late member of parliament, the Local

Board, Major Aldridge, the opponent of R. H. Hurst at the 1875 election, and at anyone else he felt inclined. The first leading article said, 'we mean to Make the *Sussex Herald* a newspaper which shall maintain "Truth" . . . we do expect to row together as brethren on the road to a better country, where sorrows and trials are unknown', but he never explained how this difficult feat would be performed. He kept on announcing that in the New Year his paper would be printed by machinery and would be doubled in size, but January 1876 came without any sign of the improvement. In order to keep going Worth had several other jobs such as insurance agent and debt collector.

One of Worth's brazen habits was to obtain support for his ventures by writing to important people saying that unless they replied in the negative he would assume their support, so his poultry show committee starts off with Lord Leconfield, the Duke of Norfolk, Disraeli and Gladstone at the head of the list, presumably because they had failed to notice the letters he sent them. Another habit was to put local names at the bottom of notices summoning public meetings, but at the meetings the owners of the names disclaimed all knowledge of their names being so used, and eventually Worth had to fold up his tents and steal away, the newspaper lasting only a year.

The Horsham Times and West Sussex Courier was really a Crawley paper, starting on 29 January 1882 and covering a large area from Horley to Ardingly and from Petworth to Crowborough, and similarly the *Horsham and Crawley News* (for Crawley, Horsham, Handcross, Three Bridges, Worth and Rusper) of 1898 was published at Crawley, and lasted until 1900. Later *The Horsham Times* moved to Lewes where it expired in 1941. Up to 1941, when legislation abolished advertising to cure disease, newspapers gained a great deal of revenue from patent medicine advertising, and without this in the early days of many papers it is difficult to see how they could have existed. One directory of Horsham produced by a local chemist consisted of practically nothing but his own advertisements for every nostrum under the sun, with only a small amount of local information, although it had the grand name of *Brassington's Directory*. The only proper index in it was to the innumerable products sold in the shop.

There have been other papers with 'Horsham' in the title, but they were not really local papers, just an attempt to obtain local readers by producing a syndicated paper with local editions. One was the *Horsham and Mid Sussex Guardian,* No. 1, which is dated 29 October 1921, but it was printed in Croydon and published at 11 Market Square and then 6 Market Square. This became the *West Sussex Guardian* in 1923 and died in 1925.

Some Specialist Organs

There have been a number of attempts this century to produce specialised weekly and monthly papers, but none have lasted long. The Liberals brought out the *Southern Standard* in July 1904 to put heart into their supporters within a 15-mile radius of Horsham, but there was little hope for it, and the same fate overtook *The Dawn*, the official monthly organ of the Horsham and Worthing Divisional Labour Party. By the tenth number the editor proclaimed that 'owing to the fact that Labour people in this Division will not support adequately this paper, the present number is probably the last', and it was, with a final snarl at 'the backward and reactionary south'.

A very successful quarterly trade journal was run by the Horsham Chamber of Trade from 1923, and was only killed by the Second World War. Local traders supported it well and it contained lively and controversial articles about issues in the town. In August 1937 Albery and Apedaile used it for their campaign against the Urban District Council's closure of the reading room in Park House, when the two of them got themselves elected to the Council on this issue by the largest number of votes ever recorded at a local election. The name of this journal started as *The Sign Post* and became *The Horsham Journal* in the early 'thirties.

The Red Light was a valiant monthly which started in 1904 with temperance and non-smoking as its main planks.

Information

The sub-title, *Magazine of Fact,* must be accepted alongside its claim to have 'a larger circulation than any other local publication'. The shopping guide omitted all public houses and hotels except the *Temperance* hotel at 10 Market Square, kept by the prominent temperance man, Jury Cramp.

Mention must be made of an excellent regimental magazine during the First World War. The 22nd Battalion of the Royal Fusiliers arrived at Roffey Camp in October 1914 and ran a fortnightly gazette from February to June 1915, when they left for Nottinghamshire. The commanding officer was Lieutènant-Colonel Innes of Roffey Park, and the troops had much local involvement which made a very lively and well-produced magazine.

Libraries, Private and Public

Although libraries may be considered to be part of our social life, besides being educational and informative, they are chiefly considered in this present chapter. One might expect the earliest library in Horsham to be connected with the church, as the clergy were once virtually the only people who could read and write, but in our case there is only the occasional early record of bibles, service books and books of sermons. Perhaps, as elsewhere, they were disposed of in the various religious upheavals around the time of the Reformation, when one parson wrote in another parish 'Memorandum i burned all ye boockes'. The headmaster of Collyer's school reported in 1673 that there were no libraries in or near Horsham, and he should certainly have known. The first reference to a library in Horsham would seem to be of the Free Church minister, Robert Ashdowne, in the 1840s introducing the Book and Tract Society into his church, and this later turned into a library of over 4,000 volumes, which lasted until 1940. The Horsham Library Society opened in the Chantry next the church in 1842 with subscription of 2s. per quarter and 850 books. In the first quarter there were 85 members, and only 57 in the third quarter, but it struggled on for at least two more years. Next, a small library was started by the parish in Trafalgar Road in 1875 with 400 volumes, the subscription being 1d. per month for small volumes, and 2d. for large. There have been several such parish libraries, one of which was presented by Miss Ewart in 1885 which operated in St. Mark's school with children being charged 2d. per month and adults 5s. per annum. Books could be exchanged twice a week. The Parish Room was opened in 1888 and the library was transferred into a small room there.

When the Horsham Literary and Scientific Institution was re-founded in 1847 'for the diffusion of useful and entertaining knowledge' it included a library for reference and for lending. One volume at a time might be borrowed, and two weeks were allowed to read a small volume, three for a large.

The public library as we know it today, run by the County Council, is really a child of this century, as it did not appear in the town until 1926, when it began to function in the Workers Educational Association Hall (later the W.I. Hall) on the corner of Albion Road and the Carfax. In 1934 it moved to St. Mark's Boys School and has only been in its present building for 25 years; it is already too small, but lack of funds preclude any move at present. The day of the circulating library such as Boots seems to be over, but the public library gets more and more used.

Chapter Ten

COMMUNICATIONS

THE EXTENT to which communications facilities have been available to Horsham people has not always been related to their needs, nor yet to their political energy or finances. Today, some unknown official in Whitehall has a major influence on road patterns in the South-east, or some nationalised transport industry amends budgeted proposals for new rolling stock or vehicles, both of these having a profound effect on some of Horsham's travelling public. Equally, in the 14th century wars in France meant that Horsham industry was ordered to transport arrows, horse-shoes and scaling ladders down to the Channel ports, chiefly Shoreham. Thus in spite of the fact that the 18th-century turnpike roads and the 19th-century railways opened up Horsham to the outside world, the general need until then was for local communications only.

Except for pathways forced through the thick Weald forest, the first means of communication was the river. Geological evidence suggests that the Arun was much wider and deeper than it is today, when it does not fill the available valleys as it once did, but instead meanders within those valleys. Even the One Inch map shows this, and so does looking into the Arun valley from a hilltop. The first settlers in the Horsham area may have arrived by raft or dug-out canoe (examples of which have been found in the mud of the lower reaches), or they may have arrived along forest paths. The Saxon invaders used the rivers to penetrate inland from the coast, and there are plenty of rivers in Sussex. If Horse-ham was indeed a settlement where horses were bred, then tracks would be developed by the horse traders, and it is known that the Saxons used horses for riding rather than for draught purposes, for which oxen would be used. Many writers have stated that the Weald was quite impenetrable in these remote times, but this must be an exaggeration as at least three major Roman roads crossed it, from London to Chichester, Lewes and Hove, and Saxon settlements often occurred near Roman roads. Stane Street, one of the best Roman roads in the south of England, passes on its way from Chichester to London only three miles from Horsham, and crosses the Arun at Dedisham. There would probably be communication between this highway and the Roman iron works at Broadfield, and a look at the map does suggest that a stretch of the modern A264 towards Horsham from Broadfield does have the straight Roman look, but on the whole the direct route between Broadfield and Stane Street would seem far too wet for Roman engineers, unlike the Roman route from Rowhook north-west to Farley Heath. Was the Arun deep enough in Roman times? If so, the iron would only have to be pack-transported to somewhere in St. Leonard's Forest and thence by raft or boat along the Arun to Dedisham. Whatever the hypotheses may be, over 30 furnace hearths at Broadfield must have disposed of their iron somehow.

The cattle droveways which are still evident across the North and South Downs were important to Horsham's markets, but they cannot be shown by archaeological evidence to be as early as Saxon times.

Medieval Roads

Further evidence that the Weald was not so trackless as later authors have suggested is given by the accounts of the

Communications 179

journeys of the Bishop of Chichester at the end of the 13th century, when he managed more than a dozen miles a day, and between his scattered manors there was undoubtedly a lot of traffic, which must surely postulate some sort of road system. It is to the south that we should look for evidence of early roads, as opposed to tracks, between Horsham and neighbouring villages. From the south came Saxon penetration of the Weald, shown conclusively by the marvellous work done on place-name development, from the south came the Norman invaders, and the castles they set up to defend each of the Sussex rapes together with other Norman settlements clearly indicate that communications were mainly north and south. When William invaded he had to secure his links between southern England and the channel ports to France, and with a Norman baron at Chesworth, Horsham would have been a staging post between Shoreham port and London. King John was famous for his rapid journeys. To take up the crown of England in 1199 he landed at Shoreham on 25 May from Normandy, and was crowned at Westminster on 27 May. He may have spent a night at Knepp castle, which he was to use on many occasions as a hunting lodge. The roads must have been good enough for a man in a hurry.

The French wars which went on for so much of the 14th century would call for similar routes. Shoreham was then the fourth port in England. Our earliest road without much doubt is Denne Road and its continuation up Denne Hill, although how old is not known. Certainly it seems likely that it was in use before the parish church was built, as it by-passes the church and may therefore originate from the junction with East Street. Indeed this junction is thought by some to be the actual origin of the Horsham settlement, with the Carfax not the centre but a market place to the side of the main north/south and east/west roads. How agreeable it would be to excavate this junction and settle the matter, and a chance may come one day if there is ever enough money to carry out updating of Horsham's road pattern in this area.

The Iron-working Period

Certainly a case can be made for constant use of Denne Road and its southward extension from medieval times to mid-17th century, and S. E. Winbolt, who did the first research on this route in the 1930s thinks it may be even older. One of the best pieces of evidence given by roads in use during the iron-working period is slag, and this has been found all along the lower part of the road in Denne Park, and also nearer the river. On the town side slag is to be found about two feet below the modern road surface, and the old route was a few yards west of the present bridge before the railway came, crossing a ford or a timber bridge. It is safe to say that if a suspected road in wet areas does not yield slag traces, then it cannot have been in use in the iron-working period, as the laws about this were strict. From medieval times each locality was responsible for maintaining the roads, the actual organising being done by the church, the manorial court, and the borough corporation, but in 1555 the parish was made responsible, and the labour required by statute was supervised by the justices. Towards the end of the 17th century the labour was replaced by a rate levied on the parish.

The 1534 'Acte for Amendynge of Highe Wayes in Sussex' was not really for repair of roads, but for providing a new road when one was required. On the other hand the 1584 'Act for the preservacion of Tymber' specifically enjoined 'the occupiers of all mannor of yron workes' to provide one load of road material—'sinder, gravell and stone' —for every six loads of coal they transported or for every ton of iron. Again this was supervised by the justices, and slag having no value as a waste product, it was easiest to use this excellent material which is so helpful in identifying roads of about 1550–1650, when in our area the furnaces at Warnham, Dedisham, Roffey, Southwater and St. Leonard's Forest were active. There is little gravel in our area, and the stone is comparatively soft.

Difficulties of Administration

With such stress on local autonomy at this time, when it came to such things as road provision and maintenance it was very difficult to get a co-ordinated scheme for any distance. A landowner might provide quite a good road for use on his estate, but he would not put out more than his share when it came to making a good road to the market town, and if the parish was lax in presenting at the assizes those who did not contribute their fair share, in the event the road would have a very patchy quality, and one would see alternate stretches of good and bad. It is easy to imagine what a continuous bother this was to the authorities, and the assize and quarter session records abound with presentments for allowing the roads and bridges to decay. No doubt all sorts of excuses would be thought up, including shortage of labour if the harvest was good, and hard times would be blamed if the harvest was bad. To meet this, the Act of 1597 made the iron manufacturers pay a highway rate. Every three cartloads of coal or iron ore, or every ton of iron, would cost them one shilling for every mile traversed, and this provided funds for road maintenance additional to the parish effort.

The streams and valleys of Sussex required adequate fords or bridges for the roads to be of any use. A simple bridge across marshy ground or shallow stream could be provided by planks on posts, called 'clappers', and these were commonly provided for pedestrians and can still be encountered today. Pack animals and carts might be able to make do with a ford, but if not, a bridge was essential and someone not only had to pay for it but also pay for its upkeep. Cox's 1720 edition of Camden's *Magna Britannia* has this to say:

> This County . . . is extremely Dirty, insomuch that it is better measured by Days Journies than by Miles . . . The Gentry contented themselves with their bad Roads, and are not very soliticious to make them better, because it keeps down the Prizes of Provisions, which could be carry'd to London in greater Abundance, if Higglers found the Ways to their turn.

So that was another reason for Horsham to be unenthusiastic about opening up to the outside world—keeping down the cost of living for the landowners, as well as reluctance to see rates increased to pay for roads and bridges. In his will Richard Collyer not only founded our grammar school but also left £50 to be spent on the road between Horsham and Crawley, but not many were so public-spirited.

An indictment at quarter sessions in 1628 states that the king's highway in the parishes of Warnham and Horsham, called Broadbridge, and at the bridge called Farthing Bridge, is greatly in need of repair. Such indictments, which were always endorsed 'true bill', number scores until the 19th century saw proper road administration outside the turnpike system. Not surprisingly, 17th-century maps do not show main roads running through Horsham, indicative of its decline in importance at this time, although by 1693 one town carrier was known to be operating. Ogilby's road map of 1675 shows one main road through Sussex from London passing through Dorking to Arundel, the other through Croydon and East Grinstead to Newhaven, but none through Horsham. There are no other principal roads in the county, but he does say of the London–Arundel route, 'The Road we exhibit is by Darking, yet some will pass by Horsham 3 or 4 miles to the Left'. Sussex was said at the beginning of the 18th century to be against road improvement because the benefits were outweighed by the cost, but gradually criticism from outside forced the authorities to think again. Much of the pressure came from the legal world, and the Spring assizes were held at Horsham or East Grinstead in order to avoid as much as possible having to travel the roads of Sussex. It is ironic that one of these reasons why the assizes were eventually lost to Horsham was that Lewes was more accessible when the roads improved. A barrister attending the 1690 assizes in Horsham wrote about 'the Sussexways which are bad and ruinous beyond imagination. I vow 'tis a melancholy consideration that mankind will inhabit such a heap of dirt for a poor livelihood'. Lord Irwin, living at Hills Place in 1735, said that the road into Horsham was 'so bad that there is no passing with a coach and pair'. The trouble was that increased traffic was too much for what were after all crude roads, usually consisting of nothing more than rolled stones without much base material which is so necessary on clay subsoil.

Communications

Tolls and Turnpikes

Late in the 17th century the idea was adopted of collecting tolls so that parishes would not have to pay so much for the roads, and the first Act for Sussex was passed in 1696. The preamble states that the road 'between Ryegate in the county of Surrey and Crawley in the county of Sussex . . . being the road from Stenning, Horsham, and other parts of great trade and commerce in the county of Sussex, to London, are very ruinous and almost impassable for above three miles in length', and it is laid down that the justices shall appoint a collector of tolls at turnpikes located where the justices determine. It is obvious that just as London was anxious to get produce from Sussex, so were traders anxious for the London market, but they did not like paying the tolls, and every device was used to avoid doing so, including the use of by-paths, and on occasion breaking the toll gates and assaulting the keepers.

Road engineering made no improvement until the early 19th century, and although there had been surveyors of the highways since an Act of 1555, these were appointed by the parish and had neither technical skill nor payment for their services, so it was a most unpopular post. The surveyors were by the Turnpike Acts empowered to borrow money against future tolls to repair the highways, but the situation was getting worse all the time, not only because of increased traffic but also because of its nature. The old broad-wheeled wagons of the past did not do so much damage to the roads as the new-fangled carriages with their narrower wheels, which cut the surface up, so tolls were adjusted so that broad wheels which helped to consolidate the surface by rolling were charged less, or nothing at all. The tolls were shown on boards at the gates, and to get through the toll gate on the road to Dorking (approximately at the junction with Wimblehurst Road, but see below) it cost 1s. 6d. for a six-horse coach, 1s. for one with four horses, and only 6d. if drawn by two. A cart or wagon was 6d., and a single horse or ass 2d.

For every drove of cattle 10d. per score had to be paid, and half that rate for calves, sheep or swine.

The well-to-do would not be unduly worried by this kind of toll for their carriages, but the purveyors strongly objected to the tolls cutting into their profits, and the townspeople grumbled at the price of meat being put up because of them.

To London via Canterbury

Horsham's interest in roads was turning to London and the north, whereas as we have seen until the 17th century, apart from trade with neighbouring villages, Horsham's chief concern was southward to the feudal links with Bramber, Steyning, and the port of Shoreham. Now that the government was taking more interest in local affairs in the aftermath of the Civil War, there needed to be better communications with London, and the numbers of local residents having links with trade, commerce and government in London were increasing, so were the numbers of top people working in London who liked a house in the country—indeed the age of the commuter was beginning. As the Rev. Arthur Young put it in 1771 'the numbers who have seen London are increased tenfold, and of course ten times the boasts are sounded in the ears of country fools to induce them to quit their healthy clean fields for a region of dirt, stink and noise'. In 1755 a petition was sent to the House of Commons from 'the Justices of the Peace, Clergy, Gentlemen, Freeholders and others of the inhabitants of the Borough of Horsham' claiming that the road to London via Dorking 'by reason of the soil thereof and of the many heavy carriages frequently passing the same, some parts thereof are become so ruinous and bad that in the winter season are almost impassable for any manner of carriages and very dangerous for loaded horses and travellers and in many parts so narrow as to render them dangerous to passengers'. Such was the speed of process of the House of Commons, incredible today, that the ensuing Bill became law by March 20 that same year! The usual procedure for appointing trustees and erecting gates followed, with the unpleasant result for some that farm rents rose from 7s. to 11s. an acre. However, the traders were pleased with the increase of business, particularly in corn, as shown in Chapter Six. A legend has arisen about the time of this petition for a better road to London that the inhabitants of Horsham were claiming to be unable to go to London at all in the winter months because of the state of the going, unless they went round by Canterbury. Dudley's *History of Horsham* (1836) says that 'Horsham, though at present remarkable for the excellent state of its turnpike roads, was, before the year 1750, one of the most extraordinary instances of non communication in the kingdom: previously to the abovementioned period, the London road was so execrably bad, that whoever went there on wheels, was compelled to go round by Canterbury!'. This is obviously quoting the Rev. Arthur Young's *General View of the Agriculture of the County of Sussex* (1793) which has very similar wording, and the story is repeated in Miss Hurst's *History*, but the origin of this story is unknown. A glance at the map will show the absurdity of the claim, which formed no part of the petition of 1755. There were several alternative roads, including one to Guildford, where travellers could join the London-Portsmouth highway, and another to East Grinstead, which would enable traffic to go to London via Croydon. Also, there was a road to Petworth going on to Haslemere which would have sufficed, so presumably Canterbury was a figure of speech.

One good road out of Horsham was not good enough, in spite of a contemporary record that the lanes were sufficiently numerous, although barely passable in winter to the natives! Timber was a valuable commodity but difficult to move, and Daniel Defoe, writing in 1726, says that it was in some places only still growing because water transport was too far off for it to be economical to cut the trees down. 'I have seen one tree on a carriage drawn by two and twenty oxen, and even then it is carried so little a way, that it is sometimes two or three years before it gets to Chatham, for if once the rains come on it stirs no more that year, and sometimes a whole summer is not enough to make the roads passable'. The emparking of

Denne in the 17th century ruled out the old road south up Denne Hill, but there was a road of sorts out of the town over Tan Bridge to Southwater and Shipley. In 1764 this was turned into an excellent turnpike road, one of the best in the country, and the first good coach road from Shoreham to London went by this route. The cutting was made on Picts Hill in 1809 to ease the gradient. Winbolt has established by excavation that only horseshoes and no iron slag are to be found in the foundations of this road, so it cannot date back to the iron-working period of 1550-1650.

Other turnpikes followed rapidly, to Cuckfield in 1771, Guildford in 1809. The old name of Guildford Road in Horsham was Oxford Road, as it does eventually lead to that city, which contained the headquarters of the king in the Civil War. In 1811 the road to Five Oaks was made up, and in 1823 the turnpike to Crawley was made by Macadam, and largely paid for by Thomas Broadwood, who came into our history as the builder of 'Holmbush' and as parliamentary candidate in one of our famous elections.

Traffic Increases

By the 1820s Macadam's roads were common in England, connecting most important places with fast stage-coach services. His method of road construction was to put angular stones on a road and roll them in so that they aligned with each other to form a hard surface, about 10 inches thickness on the natural subsoil, and cambered for drainage. Tar did not come in until 1848. Because of its economy, Macadam's system was used extensively.

Before the coming of the turnpike road to London in 1756 only wagons, carts, hired and private carriages, were accustomed to use the road, but in 1763 a regular passenger coach service was started twice a week, increased to three times two years later, and in 1775 there were six each week, taking about five hours and costing 6s. or 7s. a passenger. Until the coming of the railway in the 1830s coach services continued to improve, and the craftsmanship that went into the building of the coaches and making of harness was of the highest standard. Horsham Museum has a large collection, including a complete saddler's shop and probably the world's largest collection of horse bits.

As might be expected the trouble with the turnpikes was not the basic idea, but its administration. At least the cost of the road was transferred to the user from the unfortunate parish, but the system engendered all sorts of abuses and bureaucratic costs. (By an Act of 1820 the trusts had to render each year an account under 10 headings of the workings of each turnpike.) The turnpike trustees appointed a clerk, surveyor, treasurer, and the necessary collectors, and naturally the object was to make as much money as possible out of the operation. Enthusiasm for constructing toll gates sometimes outran discretion, as on the occasion in 1856 when complaint was made to the Secretary of State that a toll gate had been erected 'within half a mile of the Town Hall shutting out the residents of North Parade at Springfield'. It was ordered to be removed, in spite of the trustees' protests that without it they would not be able to catch the traffic going out on the London road. Still, turnpikes undoubtedly did improve the road until the trusts lost so much money with the coming of the railways that they were wound up, and responsibility for the main roads devolved upon the County Council in 1888, and the town streets upon the Urban District Council when it was formed in 1894.

The Motor Vehicle Arrives

When the motor car arrived in this area about 1895, followed by motor buses in 1905, the tyres created much more of a dust nuisance than had ever the coaches and carriages, so there was pressure for a larger programme of tarring the roads, but the actual road pattern until recent motorway development has remained substantially the same since coaching days. By 1913 there were already over 200,000 motor cars and cycles privately owned in Britain.

Horsham's situation amidst a network of streams meant that bridges were essential. The early bridges on the highways out of Horsham were Tan Bridge on the Worthing Road, Farthings Bridge on the Guildford Road, Bean Bridge at Springfield, and Cobbett's Bridge at the bottom of Denne Road. Since before the Norman Conquest the neighbouring community had the task of the upkeep of bridges, and since Henry VIII's Statute of Bridges in 1531 there have been disputes between county, parish and borough about responsibility, and in recent times when Cobbett's Bridge was rebuilt the County Council persuaded the Urban District Council to pay half the cost, although this had been deemed a county bridge for a long time. Tan Bridge became a county bridge under the Act of 1870 which said that when tolls ceased on a turnpike road the county was then responsible. Quarter Sessions lost the powers of administering bridges to the County Council in 1889.

Town Streets

The highways and turnpikes considered above at some length may lie outside the strict scope of this book about Horsham, but they were vital to its prosperity. The town streets also were of much concern, and many have been the complaints unto the present day about some aspect or other of them. It would be natural for the parish authorities to ensure that the approaches to the church were kept in good order, so in the Churchwardens' Accounts for 1620-21 we find 'Item payd for 5 loads of causie stones for the Church Casey . . .10s.'. These would have been flat stones still to be seen in the churchyard. In 1638-39 again is 'Paid for 13 load of stone to repair the Church causy . . .£2 12s.'. There is marked inflation of costs here, besides three spellings of 'causeway'. Although Horsham's local government was slow to catch up with the rest of the country (see Chapter Two) it did adopt the General Highways Act of 1835 which abolished many restrictions on wheel sizes and so forth, and enabled the town to have a Highway Board which greatly improved matters. The Board had no sooner begun operations than the gas lighting of the streets was instituted in 1836 and Dudley says, 'the good people of Horsham have lately been much annoyed by the dirty conditions of their streets, occasioned by the insertion of the gas pipes'. The habit had begun, continued today, of laying a road or pavement preparatory to its being torn up again for underground services of some sort. Electricity succeeded gas for street lighting in 1901.

Transport by River and Canal

In this area there was a brief return to water transport. Success in building a canal system in the Midlands in the 18th century led to its development in the South-east, but as elsewhere the chief trouble was the smallness of the rivers and hence the scarcity of water in summer. In 1726 Defoe had noticed that a great quantity of timber was brought along the River Wey to London from Sussex, but first it would have to be brought to somewhere like Godalming in Surrey over those dreadful roads. On the return journey from Chatham the barges brought back seasoned ships' timbers for house-building. Mineral traffic—lime, coal, bricks and stone—was carried a great deal by river and canal to save transport costs, so it seemed that Horsham would benefit a good deal if a waterway could be made to connect with the Arun at Newbridge near Wisborough Green. Accordingly, a well-attended public meeting was held in the Town Hall in 1792 when it was resolved that the scheme would go forward at a cost of £18,000, of which £15,000 was promised in subscriptions. The Horsham terminus would have been at Farthing's Bridge, and the famous engineer, John Rennie, produced a plan which can be seen in Horsham Museum. However, projects like these were fiercely commercial ventures, with no public money or public authorities involved, and it was found impossible to come to satisfactory terms with the proprietors of the Arun Navigation Company, whose chairman, Sir Harry Goring, owned land in Wisborough Green through which the canal would have to pass.

Other schemes were suggested: one in 1798 would have involved widening the Arun, another cutting a canal to the River Mole and thence to Dorking, but these schemes came to nothing. The Napoleonic Wars gave impetus to proposals for linking London and Portsmouth to avoid French warships in the Channel, and Rennie suggested in 1802 a canal through Croydon, Horsham and Pulborough, and although a Bill was presented to Parliament not enough money was forthcoming. Undaunted, Rennie tried again in 1810 with a scheme to join the Medway to Portsmouth via Tonbridge, Crawley, Horsham and Pulborough, which would have required large reservoirs of water in St. Leonard's Forest, but again it failed through lack of support. Land carriage costs were still high, so efforts were persisted in to link Horsham with London somehow, and another meeting in 1812 supported the idea for a canal to Newbridge in one direction and another via Crawley to the railway which had been opened at Merstham. Engineering objections killed this idea, and further schemes in 1812, 1817 and 1839 were likewise not pursued. Objections had come naturally enough not only from landowners, but also from the turnpike trustees, who stood to lose their tolls, and in any case the end of the Napoleonic threat and the demonstration elsewhere that the newfangled railways would surely kill the canals took most of the steam out of enthusiasm for risking money on such ventures, so the nearest Horsham ever got again to actual use of water transport was the Adur Navigation at Bay Bridge wharf, near Knepp castle, five miles away. This ceased operation in 1861. Nevertheless, Horsham's economy was affected to some extent by the road carriage of goods to and from Newbridge and thence north by canal to Guildford and the Thames, and southward to the sea.

Invasion of the Railway

Early in the last century a new enemy had come to confront both the canals and the turnpikes. After opening in the north of England of the first regular railway service in 1830 the 'railway mania' as it was soon called took hold in our area as much as anywhere. The London-Brighton line was opened in 1841, passing through Three Bridges, and carriers and buses took the traffic to it from Horsham.

But already in 1838 there was a meeting in the Town Hall to get up a petition for a railway which would join the Brighton line when it came. Railways did not progress without opposition of several kinds, and one master of hounds said, 'we cannot but wonder at the blindness which has countenanced the growth of a monster, which will rend the vitals of those by whom it has been fostered'. However, the monster could not be denied, and in anticipation that it would have a station in the Brighton Road, one enthusiast opened a hotel called the *Pioneer* opposite Elm Grove, but land was too dear, and the station was opened in 1848 where it is today.

We owe our first railway line as much to commercial jockeying as to real need. The various railway companies all over Britain were vigorously trying to cut each others' throats by getting their lines in first, and to anticipate the railway from London to Portsmouth via Brighton, the branch from Three Bridges to Horsham was started as a London–Horsham–Portsmouth line, short-circuiting Brighton, and preventing the London and South Western Railway from entering Sussex. Horsham was the terminus from 1848 until 1859 when the next section to Petworth was opened, then came the line to Guildford in 1865 and that to Dorking in 1867.

The Effect on Horsham

Even when the only railway out of Horsham was to Three Bridges, for nine years, the effect on the town was considerable. There were still many people who would never dream of having anything to do with the newfangled monster, but both passenger and freight increased rapidly after that dramatic day when the first train pulled out of Horsham.

Before 1848, in spite of turnpike roads, we were comparatively isolated as the Brighton trains rushed by less than eight miles away, but when Horsham became a junction in the 1860s, we became an important railway town of the new era, and Horsham's isolation was ended. In 1845 Lord

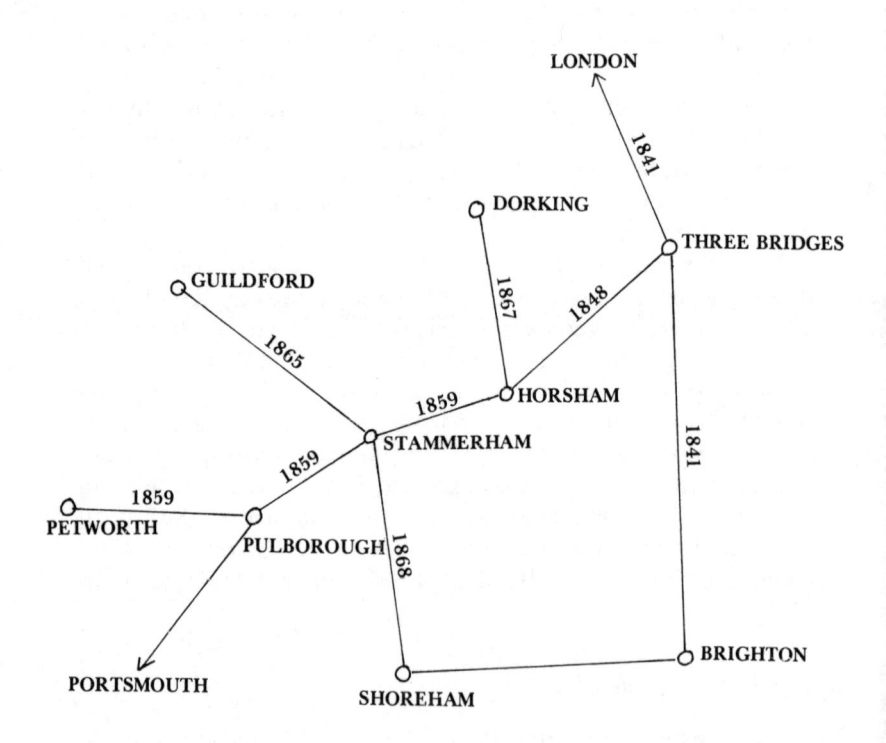

Fig. 14. Railway development.

Communications

Campbell wrote from Abinger that it was a common expression that those who lived on the south side of Leith Hill were 'in the dirt'. From 1867 the railway passenger could sweep by Leith Hill on his iron road not even aware that the hill was there. One of the first casualties of the new railway was the road carrier to London, the daily service ceasing at once, although a twice-weekly wagon struggled on until 1860, becoming then once weekly and finally giving up in 1868. After 1862 there were no coach services from Horsham. Eight miles an hour and a bumpy ride in a coach and four were replaced by 25 miles an hour in a noisy and dirty railway carriage, but to most people this mode of locomotion seemed marvellous, and particularly was it advantageous for freight, being cheaper as well as quicker. The passenger fare to London from the first day was 4s. 6d. compared with the coach's six shillings. Safety was improved, for there had always been tales of coaching accidents, usually through overturning in a rut. An incident in the early railway days cannot have reassured timorous people, however. At Petworth an engine had its boiler lit, and while the engineer was having his breakfast the locomotive began to move as the regulator had been left open. It was not noticed until it had gathered speed, and by the time it was secured passing through Horsham station it had collected a number of level crossing gates on the way.

In early railway days, return of money invested was more important than providing a public service, and finances were very closely watched. There came an opportunity to save on materials for embankments when the old Horsham gaol was pulled down in 1845, and practically all the railworks between Horsham and Three Bridges were made from rubble from this source. Railway engineering naturally advanced with experience, although in 1875 a gentleman who signed himself 'Prevention' wrote to the *Horsham Advertiser* about the bridge over the Arun at the bottom of Denne Road. 'Only the other day, when two trains happened to meet on the spot, the bridge creaked and swayed in a manner frightful to contemplate'.

More Railway Development

The line to Petworth started as a single track, but development of lines into Sussex continued when the link with Shoreham was made in 1861, thus connecting Horsham with the south coast route. The junction with the Petworth line was at Itchingfield, about a mile south of the present Christ's Hospital station, and a further junction (Stammerham) became necessary when the Horsham-Guildford line was opened in 1865, or as the *West Sussex Gazette* put it in the issue of 10 October that year, 'Puffing Billy threaded the even tenor of his way through the charming rural district between Horsham and Guildford'. Six years previously there had been mooted a scheme to convert the Wey-Arun canal into a railway from Guildford to Pulborough, but engineering difficulties were considerable and it was abandoned. Had it been constructed, of course, the Guildford-Horsham link would not have come about. This latter railway was never outstandingly successful, and was another of the lines opened largely to forestall a rival company. The running of it was odd—only four trains a day, and none of them went anywhere else, but terminated at Horsham and Guildford so that unless connections were worked out properly, the line lost a lot of its usefulness, and during the 100 years of its existence connecting times were always a weak point. From the freight point of view it completely killed the Wey-Arun canal, which could not hope to compete against the railways with the constant difficulties of water levels, quite apart from the speed of railway travel. Farsighted shareholders in the canal companies had transferred their interest to the railway companies once it was seen that the latter had come to stay.

The chief value of the line to Guildford was for freight, chiefly cattle feed, agricultural equipment and coal. Fuller's earth was carried from Baynards. In the First World War it was of great use in transporting troops and war material from the Midlands to the channel ports of Newhaven and Littlehampton, and in the Second World War it had a similar value for Portsmouth and Southampton. With the advent of motor bus services between the two towns, passenger

Communications

traffic fell, and the railway was no longer competitive except for heavy freight, especially as the question of making proper connecting times at both ends had never been solved. By 1961 there were only eight trains a day, the same number as in the 1880s, and three years later only six. It became a victim of the Beeching axe and was closed in 1965, in spite of many protests from those commuters who used it to reach the main lines. The lines were lifted and part of it was turned into nature walks. When Christ's Hospital was in building at the end of last century, it was envisaged that the area would develop a good deal, and the station opened in 1902 was an elaborate affair suited to be the future major junction. It was at one time called West Horsham, but its potential was not developed in the event, and losing both the Guildford and Shoreham lines under the Beeching plan, it is no longer even a junction, and some of the station has recently been demolished.

Electrification

In 1938 the Southern Railway electrification scheme reached Horsham, necessitating rebuilding of the station and lengthening the platforms. The increase in passenger traffic was 13 per cent. in the first year, and there is no doubt that the railway has been responsible more than any other factor for the rapidity with which Horsham has developed. The census in 1861 acknowledged this, and said that 'Villa residences have been erected and continue to be in great demand'. Trading patterns were completely altered throughout the middle of Sussex; instead of the towns being markets for local produce, as Horsham has been for nearly 1,000 years, they imported food and cheap Midland manufactures for local distribution, thus seriously affecting local industries. Being halfway between London and the sea, Horsham became one of the dormitory suburbs long before the motor car took over. British Rail, formed in 1948, has been proud of the development in this area, and the first exhibition ever staged by B.R. was in Horsham Town Hall in 1948.

Postal Communications

The postal services have naturally followed the fastest routes. Posting was largely a royal prerogative until the 17th century, and there were no post roads in Elizabethan Sussex, but gradually the privilege of using the post spread downwards from the officers of State until in 1635 rates were fixed for the public and a letter office established. A map by Ogilby shows two principal roads in Sussex in 1675, those from London-Croydon-East Grinstead-Newhaven, and London-Dorking-Arundel. These were the post roads which Horsham's mail had to use, and in the early days messengers had to be sent to letter offices on those roads to collect and deliver mail. By 1756 there was a daily post from London to East Grinstead via Dorking, resulting from road improvement, and by 1828 Horsham was a post town, that is a terminal for the national service which had been established, and Horsham distributed to nine sub-offices. We may be keen on better and better communications, and without entering into any controversy about the present-day postal service, it is not without interest that from 1855 until the 1950s the Post Office in Horsham was open on Sunday mornings as well as the rest of the week. The Head Post Office has moved about quite a lot. At one time in Market Square, it was then in West Street, at two locations, and finally in the Carfax from 1896. In the middle of the last century there were no postman's uniforms and smock frocks were worn.

One of the means by which mail was carried in Horsham was unique: Edward Burstow, a local architect, invented a strange development of the penny-farthing bicycle which had four small wheels as outriders. This was the pentacycle, or more colloquially the 'hen and chickens', and was adopted in some numbers by the Post Office. William Albery describes it as 'slow to move, hard to propel, difficult to steer, and dangerous to ride' and that it had a short and freakish life! Henry Burstow tells of dog carts being commonly used by rural postmen and fish hawkers from Worthing and Brighton. Three dogs were harnessed abreast, and there were instances of them being cruelly treated. On one occasion a man was made to apologise to his dogs or be fined by the magistrates, but the law abolished this mode of transport in 1854.

To travel fast in pre-mechanical times all a man needed was a good horse, and a royal messenger in 1574 made exceptional time through Sussex at 25 miles per day, something to reflect upon while speeding smoothly along the motorway to London at 70 miles per hour.

BIBLIOGRAPHY

Albery, W., *A Parliamentary History of the Ancient Borough of Horsham*, 1927.
Albery, W., *A Millenium of Facts in the History of Horsham*, 1947.
Armstrong, J. R., *A History of Sussex*, 1974.
Brandon, P. F., *The Sussex Landscape*, 1974.
Brent, C. E., Fletcher, A. J., and McCann, T. J., *Sussex in the 16th and 17th Centuries: A Bibliography*, 1974.
Briault, E., *Sussex*, 1942.
British Library, Dept. of Manuscripts:
    Hayley's *Notitiae Sussexiae*. Add. MSS. 6343.
    Dunkin Collection. Add. MSS. 39, 326.
    Burrell Collection. Add. MSS. 5670.
British Rail (pub.), *How the Railway came to Horsham*, 1948.
Burstow, H., *Reminiscences of Horsham*, 1911. Repr. 1975.
Churchwardens' Accounts.
Comber, J., *Sussex Genealogies (Horsham Centre)*, 1931.
Copley, G. J., *An Archaeology of South East England*, 1958.
Cowley, G. O., 'Sussex Market Towns 1550–1750'. Unpublished M.A. thesis, London University, 1965.
Cunnington, L. W., *The Parish Church of St. Mary the Virgin, Horsham*, 1967.
Curwen, E. C., *Prehistoric Sussex*, 1954.
Dallaway, J., *History of the Western Division of Sussex*, 1815–1832.
Dudley, H., *The History and Antiquities of Horsham*, 1836. Repr. 1973.
Ellis, W. S., *The Parks and Forests of Sussex*, 1885.
Elphick, G. P., *Sussex Bells and Belfries*, 1970.
Elwes, D. G. C., *A History of the Castles, Mansions and Manors of Western Sussex*, 1876.

Bibliography

Farrant, J. H., *Sussex in the 18th and 19th Centuries: A Bibliography*, 1973.
Fletcher, A. J., *A County Community in Peace and War: Sussex 1600–1660*, 1975.
Gray, A., *The Railways of Mid-Sussex*, 1975.
Hamblin, F. A., 'Horsham: A Geographical Study'. Unpublished M.A. thesis, London University, 1962.
Harmer, H. R. H. (ed.), *A Picture of Horsham*, 1976.
House of Commons *Journal*.
Hurst, D. E., *Horsham, Its History and Antiquities*, 1889.
Jessup, R. E., *South East England*, 1970.
Kensett, E., *History of the Free Christian Church, Horsham*, 1921.
Kuhliche F. W., and Emmison, F. G., *English Local History Handlist*, 1969.
Leslie, K. C., and McCann, T. J., *Local History in West Sussex*, 1975.
Manning, R. G., *Religion and Society in Elizabethan Sussex*, 1969.
Margary, H. (ed.), *Two Hundred and Fifty Years of Mapmaking in the County of Sussex*, 1970.
Mawer, A., and Stenton, F. M., *The Place-names of Sussex*, 1969.
Neale, K., *Victorian Horsham*, 1975.
Parish magazine.
Parish registers.
Pearmain, H. F., 'Horsham and its Functions, Local and Regional, Past, Present and Future'. Unpublished M.A. thesis, London University, 1944.
Quarter Sessions records.
Straker, E., *Wealden Iron*, 1969.
Sussex Archaeological Collections.
Sussex County Magazine.
Sussex Notes and Queries.
Sussex Record Society volumes.
Tate, W. E., *The Parish Chest*, 1974.
Victoria County History: Sussex, 1907.
Vine, P. A. L., *London's Lost Route to the Sea*, 1965.
Willson, A. N., *A History of Collyer's School*, 1963.

Winbolt, S. E., *History of the Parish Church of St. Mary the Virgin, Horsham*, 1941.
Wooldridge, S. W., and Goldring, F., *The Weald*, 1953.
Yorke, P. (ed.), *The Diary of John Baker*, 1931.

INDEX

References to illustrations are in italics

Adur Navigation 190
Agate's Timber Yard 131
agriculture 10, 117, 122, 144
Albery, M. and R. J., printers 171
ALBERY, William 1, 48, 106, 126, 143, 174, 196, *pl. 13*
   papers 126
Albery and Thompson's Monthly Illustrated Journal 172
Albery's Monthly Illustrated Journal 171
Albion Road 176
   Way 39, 128, 140
Albion Terrace Academy 38, 158
ALDRIDGE, John 56, 57, 58
alehouse licences 67, 138, 140
Alfoldean 7
ALLEN, Rev. Henry 88
Allman's Nursery Garden 134
almshouses 31, 34, 144, *pl. 2*
Anatomy Act (1832) 141
Anchor inn 53, 77; 79, 139
Anglo-Saxon law 41
apathy 66, 89
APEDAILE, Ernest G. 174
apprentices 119, 122, 123, 151
April Fair 138
archers 101
Archery Society 143
Armada 101
arms, coat of 8, 63, 65
arms of war 66, 70, 101, 104, 106, 108, 112, 129, 194
arrows 101
Art School 163, 164
Artillery Ground 142
Arun Navigation Company 189
Arun river 13, 93, 131, 147, 177-178, 189
ASHDOWNE, Rev. Robert 38, 158, 175
assizes 9, 63, 64, 66, 71-89 pass. 120
   established 71
   lost to Horsham 182
   sermon 72, *73*
   superseded 67
athletics 111
ATKINS, Rev. Francis 27
ATTREE, John 148
AUBREY, Sir John 63
axes, stone 5, 6
Aylesbury Dairy Company 116, 164

Back Lane, *see* Denne Road
BACON, Francis 43
badge of poverty 92
bailiffs 43, 47, 53, 58, 70, 116, 136
BAKER, John 61, 72, 78, 94, 139, 141, 142
BAKER, William 105
bakers fined 117
ballads about condemned 74, 137
Ballot Act (1872) 57
bands 51, 126, 143, *pl. 13*
bandstand 143
banknotes 132
banks 132
Baptist Church 39
Baptist Union 39
Baptists—Calvinist 38, 39
   General 25, 37, 38
   Particular 37, 38
   Strict 39
BARNARD, Richard 132
Barracks 95, 106-108, 142
   demolished 108
   regiments in 107
Barttelot Road 40
Bay Bridge 190
beacons 101, 109
Bean Bridge 188
beer 94
beershops 57, 126, 139, 142
bell, market 115
bell foundry 21
BENNETT, Mrs. 28
Bewbush 11, 129
bicycles 147
Birchenbridge 129
Bishopric 112, 116, 126, 127, 134, 137, 139, 155
Black Horse hotel 118, 139
blackout 130
BLOUNT, Edward 51
Blue Flash Cinema Company 111, 148
BLUNT, Gerald 165
BLUNT, Samuel 127
bodies of criminals 76
body-snatching 141
Book Society 142, 161
Book and Tract Society 38, 175
Borough of Horsham 9, 42-66 pass.
   boundaries 42, 61
   control by Duke of Norfolk 50

201

Borough of Horsham—*continued*
  death of 60
  independence lost 47, 143
  political control 44-60 pass.
  possible revival 62, 65, 66
  records 47, 136
  reformed (1832) 51
  survey (1611) 44, 85
  survey (1723) 47
Borough Band 126, 143, *pl. 13*
BOROUGHE Sir John 59
boroughs 113
  rotten 51
BOSTOCK, E. I. 146
BOTELER, Henry 16
bounties for enlistment 108
Boxall's Foundry 131
branding 78
brass foundries 131
Brassington's Directory 174
breweries 126
bribery 44, 45, 46, 53, 54, 56, 57
bricks 126, 130, *pl. 10*
  Warnham 90
BRIDGES, Rev. A. H. 35
bridges 180-182, 187-188
  upkeep 188
BRIGGS, Widow 94
BRIGHT, Thomas 134
Brighton Road 125, 140, 191
British Legion 111
British Rail 195
British Schools 155-158
British Society 155
BROADBENT, Edward 77
Broadbridge 182
  Heath 77
  isolation hospital 98
  Mission 36, 157
  sewage works 98
Broadfield 7, 129, 178
BROADWOOD, Thomas 51, 53, 186
Bronze Age 7
broom-making 125
Brotherhood of St. John and St. Anne 16, 17, 34
BROWN, James Clifton 58
bull baiting 138
  ring 138, *pl. 4*
burgages 42-64 pass. 87
Burgess Roll 45, 49
burgesses 44, 45, 49, 51, 60
  disappearance 59
BURGEYS, Walter 14, 44
BURSTOW, Edward 118, 196
BURSTOW, Henry 134, 155, 196
bus depot 118
  terminus 66
Butchers' Row 138

bypass 3, 4, 6
BUTLER, John 19

C.I.B.A. 128
CAFFYN, Matthew 36
CAFFYN, Thomas 38
CAMDEN, William 10
Canadian soldiers 112, 144
canals 131, 189-190, 194
candles 132
capital punishment, *see* death penalty
Capitol 111, 148-149
Carfax 64, 85, 97, 136, 137, 138, 143, 146, 179, 196
carriers 182, 190, 193
CARYLL, Sir John 129
cattle 115, 116
  breeding 116
  market 126, 139
  plague 117
  Welsh 102, 115, 137
Causeway 17, 188
  Academy 161, 163
  House 46
cemetery 20
census, religious 25, 36
Chamber of Trade 66, 124, 174
CHAMPION, Charles 34
CHAMPION, John 138
Champion's Mill 118
chantry priests 151
chantries 151
  see also St. Mary's Parish Church
'Chantry' house 16, 175
charters 8, 41
  by prescription 42, 43
  for fairs 137
  of incorporation 44, 65
CHATFIELD, John 24
Chesworth 8, 9, 13, 15, 41, 114, 125, 127, 179
Cheverton, P. and P., printers 172
CHICHESTER, Lucy de 72
chimney sweeps 139
CHITTY, Mary 123
cholera 95
Christ's Hospital 116, 165, 195
  Station 194, 195
Christian Scientists 40
  Church 40
church 12-40
  ales 135
  and education 150, 151
  benefactions 32, 33, 34
  community activities 33, 40, 135
  decline in 18th century 26
  fairs 135
  in history 40
  library 33

Index

church—*continued*
  markets 135
  origins in Horsham 12
  revival in 19th century 28, 35
  schools 33, 161
church, parish, *see* St. Mary's
churchwardens' accounts 15, 152, 188
cider 127
Civil War 101-105, 129, 167, 184, 186
clappers 181
Clarence Road 35, 162
CLARKE, John 132
CLARKE, Robert 77
CLARKE, Thomas 134
clay pipes 134
clergy 18, 26, 28
  and education 150
  privilege or benefit of 78-79
  visiting gaol 88
CLERKE, Thomas 15
cloth-making 114
coach-building 125, 187, *pl. 15*
coaching 140, 186-187
  ceased 193
coal 126, 131
COBBETT, William, v, 115, 119
Cobbett's (or Copper's) Bridge 188
COE, Dr. Robert 45
COLBORNE, W. R. N. 50
COLLIS, William 134
COLLYER, Richard 151, 182
Collyer's School 23-33 pass. 98, 150-163 pass. 175, *pl. 14*
  church gallery 152
  foundation 151
  no longer a grammar school 163
  religious controversy 162
  removal 163
  revival 162
  smallpox at 153
  virtual extinction 154
Collyer's Sixth Form College 163
Comewell 93, 127
commercial importance 9
Commonwealth County Committee 66
communications 114, 149, 177-197
community spirit 66, 149
commuters 132
Compton's Lane 118
  Mill 118
Congregationalists 39
Conservative Party 56, 57
constable 54, 69-70, 75, 101, 120, 122
constituency boundaries 51, 58
Constitutional Association 56
CONYERS, vicar 23, 24
Coolhurst 139
COPLEY, Roger 16
COPPARD, Thomas 35

corn 117
  markets 117, 118, 170
  prices 118-121
  shortage 121
Corn Exchange 118
Corn Law 122
Corporation 43, 44, 53, 58, 60, 61, 64
Cottage Hospital 98
County Cricket Week 142
Court Baron 41, 42, 44, 45, 47, 49, 63
Court Leet 42, 47, 48, 49, 53, 60, 63, 70, 71, 93, 117, 166, 167
courts, crown 67, 71
COVERT, Sir John 59
COWPER, Henry 45, 46
CRAMP, Jury 57, 175
Crawley and Horsham Hunt 147
Crawley Road 119, 144
cricket 141-142
  betting at 141
  ground 108, 141, 142, *pls. 11, 12*
Cricket Club 142
crime 69-90
crown courts 67, 71
Crown inn 140
CRUTTENDEN, Ann 77
CUMBE, Hugo de 100
customs, ancient 139

Dawn, The 174
DE BRAOSE family 14, 15, 63
DE BRAOSE, John 14, 118
DE BRAOSE, Thomas 14, 16
DE BRAOSE, William 8, 13, 41, 114, 136
DE MOWBRAY, John 8
DE MOWBRAY, Margaret 8
DE MOWBRAY, Thomas 8
death penalty 72, 74, 78, 89
  by burning 75, 77
  last execution 76, 137-138
  see also hanging
debtors 80, 81, 88
Declaration of Indulgence (1672) 37
Dedisham 178
  furnace 180
deer 117
DENDY, John 38
DENDY, Richard 19
denne or dene 8, 41
Denne estate 9, 62, 107, 108, 125, 129, 141, 157, 180, 186, *pl. 11*
Denne Road 13, 20, 40, 105, 118, 157, 163, 178, 180, 188, 193
Depot 106, 108, *pl. 7*
  Road 130
DINNAGE family 130
directories 125

disease 62
    mental 94
    see also health
Dissenters 25, 27, 36, 37
Dog and Bacon inn 139
dog carts 196
    whipping 24
Domesday Book 8
double return 49
Dr. Williams' Worm Cakes 94
dragon in the forest 2
drainage 62, 95-98
    absent 93
Drill Hall (Denne Road) 111
    (Park Street) 111
droveways 178
DUDLEY, Howard 87, 185
duffers 82

EADRIC 41
East Parade 162
East Street 39, 105, 147, 163, 172, 179
education 150-165
    adult 150, 158-159, 163, 164
    decline in 18th century 153
    expansion in 19th century 155
Education Act (1870) 165
effigies burnt 139
ELDRIDGE, Brian 22
ELDRIDGE, Richard 22
elections 45-68 pass.
electricity supply 128
Elementary Education Act 162
ELIZABETH, Queen 16
ELWES, D. G. C. 1
Enclosure Act (1813) 50
engineering 130
evening classes 163
EVERS, Samuel 133
EVERSFIELD family 9, 62, 63, 102, 105, 129, *pl*. 15
EVERSFIELD, Anthony 62
EVERSFIELD, Sir Charles 125
EVERSFIELD, Sir Charles (M.P.) 39, 45, 46, 47, 62, 63, 67
EVERSFIELD, John 62, 129
EVERSFIELD, Sir Thomas 62, 103
EVERSHED, Ann 161
EVERSHED, Mary 161
executions, *see* death penalty
Eyre Court 43

fairs 114, 115, 135-138
    cattle 115, 137
    horse 114, 115, 137
    sheep 115
famine 115, 119
farming 6

farming—rents 184
Farthing(s) Bridge 7, 182, 188, 189
feasts 60
FEIST, William 145
felony 78
feudal levy 100
fever 97
FILDER, Edward 105
fire engine 61, 120
FITZGERALD, Sir Seymour 53, 54, 56, 57
flax 114
FLETCHER, Sir Henry 54, 58
flints 3, 5, 6, 113
Football Club, 33, 143
Forest Hospital 144
forestallers 116
FOSTER, John 78
fountain 127
Fountain Brewery 126
FOYS, Elizabeth 25
FOYS, Richard 25
franchise 51, 56, 60
Free Christian Church 38
    library 38, 161, 175
    school 158, 162
Free School Defence Association 162
freemen 41
French wars 100, 179
Friendly Society 142
Friends Meeting House 37
fuller's earth 114, 194
funerals 34, 141
furze 130

gallows 76, 118
GANDER, Agnes 71
GANDER, Richard 71
gaol, 27, 37, 66, 67, 76, 80, 81, 84, 86, 122
    bricks from 130, 193
    chaplain 27, 88
    disuse 88-90, 137
    employment in 87-88
    enlargement 88
    first mentioned 83
    infirmary 98
    medical care in 88, 94
    sites 85
    sold 89
    water supply 127
gaolers 37, 84
    fees 80, 84, 87, 88
Garden of Remembrance 35
gas lighting 61, 188-189
    works 128
General Highways Act (1835) 188
General View of the Agriculture of Sussex 185

Index

GEORGE III 48
George Inn 84
gibbets 76
Gibbings, Harrison & Company 125
GIFFARD, Sir Hardinge 58
ginger-beer 127
gingerbread 134, 139
glass industry 10, 130
GODMAN, Lt.-Col. C. R. B. 111
golf 147
GORING, Sir Harry 46, 189
GORRING, John 34
Gospel Hall 40
Grandford House 126
GRAUNTFORDE, Henry de 126
Greedie's Cafe 44
GREENFIELD, Daniel 81
GREENFIELD, Zephaniah 80-81
GREEVE, John 38
GRINSTED, Richard 132
Guild of St. John and St. Anne, *see* Brotherhood
Guildford Road 40, 186
Gymnastic Society 38
gypsies 97, 137

Habeas Corpus Act (1679) 37
-ham names 7
HAMPER, William 132
hanging 74-77, 122
    in chains 76
    in public 77, 137
Hanging Plat 76
hard labour machine 88
harness-making 126, *pl. 8*
HARRINGTON, John 134
HARRISON, Edith 99
HATKINS, Abraham 71
HATKINS, Jana 71
Hawkins Pond 82
headboroughs 70
health 61, 91-99
Heath's Carriage Manufactory 125
hemp 114
Hernbrook Drive 76
Henbrook Hill 6
HERTFORD, Marquis of 50, 63
higglers 115
High School for Girls 163
highway 61
    rates 181
    robbery 76
    surveyors 183
Highways Board 96, 128, 188
Hills Farm 62
Hills Place 46, 50, 59, 182
Historical Manuscripts Commission 43
History of Horsham 185
HODGSON, Rev. J. F. 20, 28, 32, 35, 95, 162

Holbrook estate 53
Holmbush 186
Holy Trinity Church 36
Home Guard, 3rd Sussex (Horsham) Battalion 112
HOO, Thomas 16
Hope Baptist Chapel 39
hops 126-127
Horsam 8
Horse-ham 178
horse racing 139
    shoes 100, 129
    trading 178
horses for war 147
HORSHAM, Nicholas de 91
Horsham Advertiser 172
Horsham Building Society 65
Horsham Common 50, 76, 77, 104, 106, 108, 115, 137
    enclosure 50, 130, 143, 154
Horsham and Crawley News 173
Horsham culture 113
Horsham Engineering Works 130
Horsham Express 169, 171
Horsham Hospital 33, 98-99, *pl. 5*
    maternity unit 99
Horsham Journal, The 174
Horsham Mercury, 132, *168*, 171
Horsham and Mid-Sussex Guardian, 174
Horsham Museum 38, 164
Horsham Park 142
    see also Park House
Horsham, Petworth and Steyning Express 169
Horsham Record 169
Horsham stone 2
Horsham Times 173
Horsham's habit of losing things v, 42
horticulture 134
Horticultural Society 147
'hotbed of sedition' 120
House of Correction 83-84
house-building 10, 130
HOWARD, Henry Charles, Earl of Surrey 50
HOWARD, John (D. of Norfolk) 8
HOWARD, John (prison reformer) 84, 85, 87
HOWARD, Lord Edward 55, 56
HOWARD, Sir Robert 8
HOWARD, Thomas 9
HUBBARD, Capt. W. E. 109, 164
'hungry 'forties' 10, 75-76, 119
HUNT, Charles 132
hunting 147
HUNTINGDON, William 27
HURST family 20, 59

HURST, Dorothea 185
HURST, Robert (M.P.) 48, 50, 59, 63, 120
HURST, Robert of Hurst Hill 59
HURST, Robert Henry 51, 53, 59
HURST, Robert Henry jun. 56, 57, 58, 59, 61, 62, 65, 95, 99, 162, 163, 164
Hurst Hill 59
Hurst Road 163, 164
hustings 57, 140
HUSSE, Henry 59

Ifield 129
iguanodon 2
Independents 39
industrial revolution 153, 155
Industrial Society 144
industrial exhibition 141
  societies 141
industry 3, 113-134, 177
  affected by railways 195
  development 131
inflation 121
information 166-176
INGRAM family 46, 47, 48, 59, 60
INGRAM Charles 48
INGRAM, Henry, Lord Irwin 47, 48, 71, 182
INGRAM, Richard 46
Inland Revenue 132
INNES, Lt.-Col. J. A. 175
inns 139-140
Iron Age 7
iron ore 129, 181
  slag 129, 180
  working 7, 10, 100, 119, 125, 128-129, 130, 178, 180
  destruction 105
IRWIN, Lady Frances 48, 49, 50, 87, 154
IRWIN, Lord, see INGRAM, Henry
Itchingfield 113, 194

Jack o' the clock 29
JAMES, Edwin 54
JAMESON, Rev. William 27
javelin men 72
JENDEN, Edward 34
JERVIS, John 53, 54, 56
Jews Meadow 137
jobbery 58
JOHNSON, Robert 75
Journey from Bassora to Baghdad 132, 133
Jubilee of Queen Victoria 141
JULL, Thomas 169
July Fair 136, 138
justice, Anglo-Saxon 69

justices of the peace 67, 71, 76, 83, 84, 106, 115, 121, 122
  see also quarter sessions

KELLY, Dr. C. 97
KENNETT, Zechariah 132
KENRICK, Rev. Jarvis 28, 34, 77, 138, 139, 157
King's Arms inn 132
King's Head inn 53, 106, 132, 139, 140, 147
King's Road 76, 118
Knepp Castle 104, 125, 147, 179
knighthood 67

labour in agriculture 117
Labour Party 174
Labourers Friendly Society 143
LAKER, Richard 96
LAKER, William 132, 169
Lamb inn 94
Lambsbottom 130
Lancasterian Society 155
Lanham's Bank 132
Latin 151
LAUD, Archbishop 24, 153
LAUGHTON, Mrs. N. V. 35, 147
lavatories, public 66
LAVENDAR, Edith 75
LAW, William 167
lecturers 23
lectures 159
LEE, Arthur 132
leisure, growth of 147
  organisations 149
letter office 196
letters from London 167
Letters Patent 43
LEWIS, Roger 115
Liberal Party 56, 57, 58, 171, 174
libraries 33, 38, 141, 159, 161, 164, 175-176
library societies 161
Library Society 143, 161, 175
Lighting and Watching Acts 61
Linden Road 85
LINFIELD, John 45, 46
Lintott, H. & E. 130, 131
LINTOTT, John 68
Literary and Scientific Institution 33, 95, 159, 164, 176
Literary and Scientific Society 143
LIVESAY, Sir Michael 104
Local Board 65
local defence 101
local government 41-68
Local Government Acts 57, 61, 65, 95
Local Government Board 61, 62
lock-up 89

Index

Lollards 18, 39
London Road 39, 155, 158
London and South Western Railway 191
LOWER, Mark Anthony 1
Loyal Volunteers 106
LUCAS, C. J. 99
LUCKENS, Richard 84
lych gate 20
LYDGATE, Mr. and Mrs. 165

MACADAM, John 186
MACHELL, John 46
machine-smashing 119
Maglemosian culture 3, 5
magistrates *see* justices of the peace
malt 126
MANN, Thomas 94
MANNING, Cardinal 35
manor of—
    Chesworth 42
    Hawkesbourne 100
    Hewells 42
    Horsham 41
    Roffey 42
    Tarring-cum-Marlpost 42, 137
    Washington 41
manor courts 13, 41, 42
manor, lord of 41
Manor House 61
MANSFIELD, Lord Chief Justice 87
MANTELL, Dr. Gideon 2, 95
manufacturing 10
Margetson's Leather Dressers 125
Market House 46, 62, 63, 66, 74, 104
Market Square 109, 139, 140, 169, 171, 172, 174, 175, 196
markets 9, 113-118 pass. 131, 170
    for London 115, 116
Marriage Guidance Council 147
marriages 25
MARSHALL, Rev. George 157
MARSHALL, Thomas 105
Maternal Society 33, 142
May Day 139
MARTEN family 38
Mechanics Institute 122, 158, 159-160
Medical Officer of Health 97
MEDWIN, Pilfold 55, 58, 60
MEDWIN, Thomas C. 48, 49, 55, 60, 108, 133
Members of Parliament 9, 14, 16, 43-59 pass.
Mercers Company 151, 154, 161
merchants 9, 114
Merryfield Drive 137
Mesolithic culture 3-6, 113
Methodist Church 39
Methodists 39

Methodists—Primitive 39
MICHELL family 18
MICHELL, Henry (Brewer) v, 56, 58, 59, 89, 126-127, 128, 130, 137
MICHELL, Henry (constable) 70
MICHELL, John (ob. 1648) 104
MICHELL, John (ob. 1520) 18
microliths 4-6
Middle Street 138
MIDDLETON family 102
MIDDLETON, John 59
MIDDLETON, Capt. R. C. G. 111, 148
MIDDLETON, Thomas 59, 103-105
military 100-112
militia 102, 105, 106
Militia Act (1662) 101, 102, (1757) 101
Mill Bay 147
Millennium of Facts in the History of Horsham 1, 126
mills 118
    steam 118, 119, *pl. 14*
    wind 118
Millthorpe Road 118, 119
mineral water 127
Moated House 59
MOORFOOT, James 167
mortality 97
MORTH, John 39
Morth's Gardens 39
motor transport 10, 187, 194
motorway 187, 197
Municipal Corporations Act (1835) 60, 61
municipal reform 61
music hall 147

Napoleonic wars 10, 82, 88, 105-109, 119, 189
NAPPER, Matthew 23
National Schools 28, 40, 155, 157
National Society 157
Neolithic culture 6
New Street 39, 98
Newbridge 131, 189, 190
newspapers 167-174
    duty on 169
NIGHTINGALE family 130
Nonconformists 25, 37
NORDEN, John 10
NORFOLK, Duchess of 36
NORFOLK, Dukes of 8, 9, 39, 47, 48, 49, 50, 52, 53, 58, 60, 63, 64, 65, 71, 74, 108, 137, *pl. 3*
Normandy 31, 34, 144, *pl. 2*
Normans 8, 13, 41, 100, 179
North Parade 158, 187
North Street 17, 85, 93, 127, 171, 172

Northchapel 16, 17
November Fair 137
nuisances 93

Oakhill Road 39
ODDIE, A. C. 142
Ogilby's road map 182, 196
Order of the Royal Oak 105
OSBOURN, Peter 59
OSGOOD, Rev. Francis 26, 27
OTTLEY, Rev. H. B. 162
overseers 119
owlers 82
Owlscastle 82
Oxford Movement 27
Oxford Road, 98, 158, 165
    Boarding School 161

PADWICK, Henry 31, 54
Palaeolithic man 3
Paludina snail 2
parish clerk 151
    library 175-176
    origin of 13
Parish Highway Board 61
parish registers 19, 76, 83, 92, 93, 105, 107, 115, 130
Parish Room 163, 176
Park House 61, 126, 139, 174
Park Square 89
Park Street 109, 111
Park Terrace 128.
Parliamentary government 41-68
Parliamentary History of Horsham 126
Parliamentary seats, buying of 50
Parochial Clothing Club 33
Patriot Engineers, Horsham Scheme of 112
paupers 78
paving 61
peine forte et dure 79
pentacycle 196
Pentecostal Church 39
pest houses 98
petit *or* petty treason 75, 77
petitions 116, 121, 184, 191
PETTER, James 134
petty sessions 67, 71, 93
Picts Hill 186
PILFOLD, Henry 33, 34
Pilfolds Farm 3
pillory 70, 78
Pioneer hotel 140, 191
PIRIE, William 162
plague, 92
    in cattle 117
PLEDGE, Sarah 77
Plymouth Brethren 39
police, county 70

poor book 92
Poor Law Guardians 61, 144
Poor Laws 119, 122
poor rates 121
poor relief 33, 144
Poor Relief Act (1601) 119
poorhouse 34
population 9, 102, 149
post town 196
    office 196
postal services 196
posters 167, 170
poultry 117
prehistory 2-7
pressing to death 79
Prewitt's Mill 118
PRICE, Sydney 170
printing 132
prisoners' clothing 84-85
Public Health Act (1848), 65, 95
    (1872) 97
public houses 139
PUGH, Capt. J. E. 112
punishment 69-90
PUNTIS, Phoebe 161
Puritans 15, 23, 24, 25, 126

quack remedies 94, 173
Quakers 25, 36, 37
quarantine 95
quarter sessions 63, 66, 67, 71-72, 80, 85, 87, 93, 106, 117, 138, 140, 148, 182, 188
Queen Street 76, 85, 87, 89
Queen's Head inn 138
Quo Warranto 43

rabbits 117
railway 10, 11, 90, 115, 131, 140, 149, 177, 186-195 pass.
    closures 195
    development *192*, 194
    electrification 195
    engine *pl. 17*
    junction 191
    mania 190
    petition for 191
    station 140, 191, 195
Railway Mission Hall 39
RANDOLF, Walter 44
ratepayers 61
rates, church 32
    poor 121
RAVENSCROFT, Hall 67
Recreation Band 143
recusancy 24, 25
Red Light, The 174
Reform Bill (1832) 51, 60
refugees from France 93

Index

Rehoboth Chapel 39
RENNIE, John 189, 190
rents 121, 184
Representation of the Peoples Act (1867) 56
revenue officers 82
REYNELL, Canon John 26
RIBLEY, Thomas 18
RICHARDSON, Thomas 57
RICHMOND, Duke of 87
rick-burning 75, 119-122
rifle range 111
RIGGE, Ambrose 36, 37
Riley Scott's Nursery Garden 134
riots 119-122
roads 114, 115, 116, 118, 129, 140, 177-197 pass.
  engineering 183
  estate 181
  improvement 182
  maintenance 180-181
  medieval 178
  post 196
  to Oxford 186
ROBERTS, Dan *166*
ROBINSON, Rev. Charles 33, 98
Roffey forge 100, 180
  Manor 16
  Park 175
roller-skating 147
Roman Catholics 25, 36, 47
  Chapel 36
  Church 36, 157
Romans 7, 113, 129, 178
ROMILLY, Sir Samuel 50
ROSE, Rev. H. J. 28
Rotary Club 147
Roundheads 17, 102, 104, 105
Royal Fusiliers 111, 175
Royal Sussex Regiment 107, 109, 111-112
  4th Battalion 34, 110, 111-112, 148
Royalists 59, 66, 129, 153
Rushams Road 76
Rusper Priory 14, 20, 118
RUSSELL, Hannah 95

SADLER, Ann 158
SADLER, Elisabeth 158
SADLER, Rev. Thomas 38, 158
St. John the Evangelist R.C. Church 36, 157
St. John's Church, Broadbridge Heath, 36, 157
St. Leonard's Church 35
St. Leonard's Fair 115, 137, 138
St. Leonard's Forest, 2, 11, 82, 95, 109, 129, 137, 139, 178, 180, 190

St. Mark's Church 28, 35
  re-opening 35
St. Mark's School 33, 157, 176
St. Mary's Church School 151, 157
St. Mary's hospital 34
St. Mary's Parish Church 9, 11, 12-40, *pl. 1*
  All Saints Chapel 18
  aumbry 11
  bells 21-23, 140
    ringers 22
  brasses 25
  chantries 14, 16, 17, 18, 29
    Boteler's 18
    Roughey 18
  charnel house 20
  churchyard 19, 20, 26
  clerestory 14
  clock 22, 29
  communion rails 32
  east window 31
  Easter Sepulchre 16, 17
  font 25
  galleries 19, 23, 29, 152
  inscriptions 25
  invaded by mob 120
  Jesus Chapel 18
  Lollards Tower 18, 32
  Memorial Chapel 14, 21, 34
  monuments 18
    Delves 25
    desecrated 120
    Michel 18
    Shelley 18
  Norman door 32
    masonry 14
  organ 31
  paintings 14, 16, 31
  plate 25
  porch 32
  Puritan despoliation 15, 25
  rebuilding 13
  restoration (1864-65) 29
  St. John the Baptist altar 17
  St. Nicholas altar 16, 18
  school in 31, 157
  seating 23
  Shelley Chapel 18
  stained glass 25, 31
  threatened collapse 29
  tiles 32
  tombs 14, 16, 17, 25, 82
  tower 13, 19, 21, 22, 29, 31
  Trinity Chapel 21, 31, 32, 34
Salvation Army 40, 155
  Citadel 40
  and temperance 146
SANCTUARY, Thomas 51
Sandeman Way 76

sanitation 98, 137
Savings Bank 132
Saxon settlement 7, 12-13, 178, 179
SAYERS, Jane 155
scarlet fever 61, 95
SCARLETT, Robert, Lord Abinger 53
schoolmasters 151
schools, art 163, 164
   board 161, 162, 165
   boarding 161
   British 155-158
   church 158, 161
   council 165
   dame 155
   elementary 152, 153, 154, 161
   girls 157
   infant 155, 157, 158, 163
   National 155 *57
   private 154, 155, 158, 161, 162
   pupil teacher centre 163
   state 162
   Sunday 158
   workhouse 158
science 155, 164
SCOTT, Rev. Thomas 162
SEFTON, John 153
sequestrations 103
servants, household 123
sewage works 62, 98
sewers 61, 97, 128
sheep-rot 119
SHELLEY family 18
SHELLEY, Percy Bysshe 134
SHELLEY, Theobald 34
SHELLEY, Sir Timothy 106
sheriff 53, 67, 72, 83
Shire Hall 66
shire town 66
Shoe Club 33
shoe-making 126
shop assistants 123-124
   hours 124
   keepers 124
   trade 131
SHORTT, William 132
Sign Post, The 174
smallpox 92, 94, 153
SMITH, Edmund 106
smuggling 81-83
snatch papers 45
social life 135-149
societies 142
Society for the Diffusion of Useful Knowledge 158
Society of Independents 39
Society for Prosecuting Thieves 70
SOMERSET, Lord Protector 9, 11
soup kitchens 33, 146
South Street 161

Southern Counties Band Championship 143
Southern Railway 195
Southern Standard 174
Southwater 2
   furnace 180
SOWTON, Richard 82
Splitting Act (1696) 45
sports 138
Springfield 164-165, 187
   Road 39, 157, 164
Stammerham Farm 116, 165
   Junction 194
Stane Street 7, 178
STAPLEY, Anthony 152
Star Mill 119
Statute of Bridges (1531) 188
STEADMAN, R. 63
Steele & Dodson 130
steward 41, 47, 60, 70, 166
stocks 70
street lighting 128, 188-189
STURT, Nicholas 105
SUMMERS, Thomas 34
SURREY, Earl of, *see* HOWARD, Henry Charles
SURREY, Thomas, Earl of 8
Sussex Agricultural Society 122
Sussex Express 169
Sussex Herald 57, 172-173
Sussex Rifle Volunteers 109
Sussex Territorial Force Association 111
Sussex Volunteer Regiment 109, 111
Sussex Volunteers, 2nd Administrative Battalion 109
Sussex Weekly Advertiser 167
Swan inn 54
Swan Meadow 39, 140
Swedenborgian Church 39
swimming 147
SWINYARD, James 134
SWINYARD, William 134
SYMONDS, Elizabeth 79

Tanbridge 126, 186, 188
   House 163
   School 163
tanning 125-126
Tardenoisian culture 5
Tasters 117
taxation 121
temperance 57, 146, 174
Temperance Association 146
Temperance hotel 175
territorial forces 109, 111
TEULON, S. S. 29
theatres 148
THORNTON, James 154

Index

THORNTON, Richard 154
Thornton Academy 154
Three bridges 190, 191
THRIFT, W. 132
Tilgate Forest 2
timber 124-125, 131, 185, 189
tithes 20, 32, 120
tokens 132
Toleration Act (1689) 37, 38
tolls 115, 183-184, 187
  market 118
Tories 46, 53
TORNE, J. 63
Town Band 143
town crier 166, 167
  streets 188
Town Hall 46, 62-65, 71, 74
  bells 64
  clock 63
  enlargement 63
Town Mill 118, 139, *pl. 9*
trade 11, 113-134
  links with London 184
  patterns 195
  route 92
Trafalgar Road 158, 162, 175
trained bands 100
transportation 75, 79, 122
treadmill 87-88
TREDCROFT family 141
TREDCROFT, Edward 108, 141
TUGWELL, John 132, 171
tumbril 70
Turnpike Acts 183
turnpikes 27, 118, 140, 148, 177, 183, 186, 187
  trusts 187, 190
tythingmen 70

unemployment 144-146
Unitarian Church 38
University Extension Lectures 163, 164
Urban District 1
Urban District Council 65, 66, 142, 174, 187, 188
  first elections 98

vaccination 94
vagrants 70, 78
Vestry 61, 120
vicarage 20, 24
  sequestrated 103
Victoria Street 128
Volunteer Corps, 7th Sussex 109, *pl. 6*
Volunteers Associated Company 105, 109
votes, buying of 45, 51

votes—splitting of 47, 48

wages 119-123
  riots 75-76, 119-122
WAGGETT, Dr. 94
WAKEHURST, Richard 16
WALTER, Thomas 82
war memorials 112
WARBURTON, John 85
Warnham Mill 129
  furnace 180
watchmen 61
water, from sea 128
  reservoir 128
  supply 93, 96-97, 127
  wheel 93, 127
  wooden pipes 127
Water Works 62, 89, 96-97, 128
Weald 178
WEEKES, John 79, 80
weights and measures 78, 117, 167
  false 117
welfare 144
wells 62, 93, 97
  artesian 128
West Horsham Station 195
West Street 118, 126, 127, 169, 171, 196, *pl. 16*
West Sussex County Council 65, 66, 187, 188
West Sussex County Times 172
West Sussex Gazette 172
West Sussex Guardian 174
West Sussex Journal 169
West Sussex Times 172
Wey-Arun Canal 194
WHALE, Anne 77
Whigs 46
whipping 78, 119, 123
  post 70, *pl. 4*
WHITE, Richard 67
Whitsun Fair 137
WICKENS, Henry 34
WICKENS, John 148
WICKER, John 45, 46, 115, 127
WILFRID, Bishop 12
Wimblehurst 118
  Road 183
WINBOLT, S. E. 2, 7, 13, 180, 186
witches 83
wives sold 138
Women's Institute Market 117
WOOD, Alexander 164
Workers' Educational Association 164, 176
workhouse 81, 94, 122, 143
  infirmary 98
  school 158
  Union 144

Working Men's Club 147
World War, First 34, 111, 147, 194
   Second 34, 112, 194
WORTH, William Henry 57, 172-173
Worthing Road 112

Y.M.C.A. 112
YARNOLD, A. S. 148
YATES, Henry 45
YOUNG, Rev. Arthur 184, 185